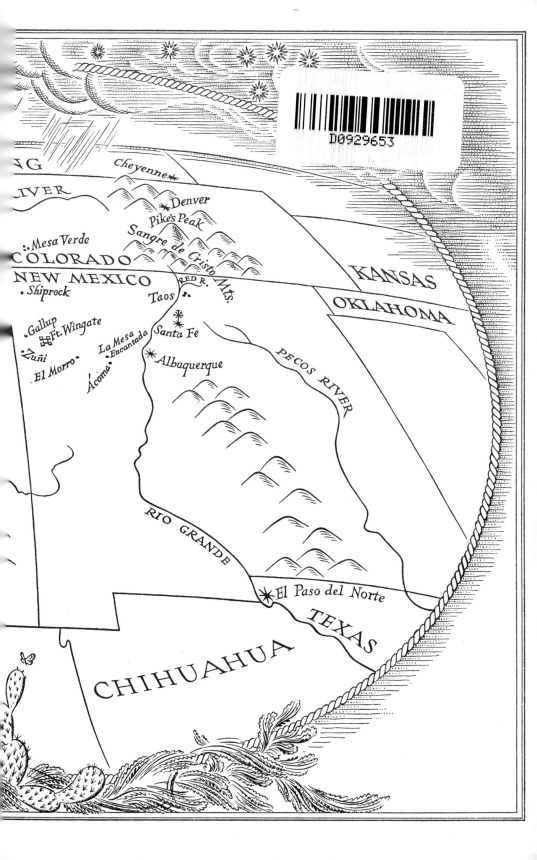

D0929653

ROBERT MANNING
STROZIER LIBRARY

Tallahassee

Southwest Classics

Southwest Classics

The Creative Literature of the Arid Lands
Essays on the Books and Their Writers
by Lawrence Clark Powell

Ward Ritchie Press
Pasadena

Robert Manning Strozier Library

DEC 18 1975

Tallahassee, Florida

Second printing, 1975
Copyright © 1974 by Lawrence Clark Powell
Library of Congress Catalog Number 73-89437
Casebound ISBN 0378-07751-1
Paperback ISBN 0378-07752-x
Printed in the United States of America
Designed by Ward Ritchie
End-papers by William W. Bellin

To Richard A. Harvill

Contents

Southwest Classics

The greatest part of a writer's time is spent in reading, in order to write. A man will turn over half a library to make a book.

DR. JOHNSON TO BOSWELL

But here are the books. I list them not so much to give knowledge as to direct people with intellectual curiosity and with interest in their own land to the sources of knowledge; not to create life directly, but to point out where it has been created or copied.

I am at home here, and I want not only to know about my home land, I want to live intelligently on it. I want certain data that will enable me to accommodate myself to it. Knowledge helps sympathy to achieve harmony.

J. FRANK DOBIE

The Southwest of the Travelling Reader

Although much of this book was written under the sheltering roof of the University of Arizona, a large part of the research was pursued under the Southwestern sky. All of my life I have been a travelling reader, a reading traveller, and the field work began long years ago.

As I explain what I mean by the Southwest and why I have chosen to write about only a few of the books that form the literature of the region, I ask what are the forces that have shaped these literary classics of the region? I see the greatest as the Southwest itself, the land and its climate and configurations of desert, mountains, rivers and skies, as well as its history and culture as they have influenced writers of sensitivity and responsiveness, of stamina and genius. If there is a central theme, this is it. In essays on the works and lives of these writers, my effort has been to show how their environment has helped create their books.

These works of vital men and women are the fruits of strength and imagination and craft, bearing on a beautiful land of reciprocal power and fertility. If land has determined books, then have books also exalted land. Unions forceful and tender have been consummated between writers and a region as magnificent as any on earth.

Its heartland is Arizona and New Mexico, an area distin-

3

guished by a tri-cultural fusion of Indian, Hispano, Anglo, and by an unmistakable landscape, from dark-robed northern mountains and incarnadined mesas to the dove-colored desert which merges with Mexico.

I once half-jokingly located the heart of hearts—the *cor cordium*—in Albuquerque at The Alvarado, that mellow old turquoise and silver Harvey House beside the Santa Fe tracks. Alas, it suffered a fatal heart-attack and was bulldozed into rubble to make a parking lot. Before that happened I paid it a fond farewell, lunching first in the cool buffet to the tinkle of the patio fountain and the sigh of relaxing air-brakes on the eastbound *Superchief*, stopped for passengers and servicing; then going out to stand in the shade of a tree-shaped oleander. There a golden-skinned boy shined my shoes as the engineer revved up his deep-throated diesels and the long train rolled on upriver. Where were my Pullmans of long ago—Blue Lake, Red River, Coconino Princess? Probably sold off to some railroad in a distant land.

The passing of The Alvarado made it necessary to relocate the heart of hearts. No problem. West southwest a half-day's journey stands El Morro, that buff-colored sandstone battlement called by the Anglos Inscription Rock and preserved since 1906 as a National Monument by act of President Theodore Roosevelt against all enemies save two—the wind and the rain. "Here I shall haunt," prophesied Mary Austin, and I just might join her. When all the rest of the Southwest has fallen to Progress, I pray that El Morro will stand inviolate as a sanctuary for those who seek peace and quiet on a clean earth.

My choice and definition of classics is as personal as my delimitation of the Southwest. A basic criterion is the presence of an extra quality, of an inner fire that lights the prose and which appears to come from a mystical union between writer and region. These writers experienced that union in varying intensity and with differing results, so that their works are not of uniform excellence. Willa Cather is a greater writer than Zane Grey

4

because she saw deeper into life and grew as an artist as he never did. Although Mary Austin was more learned and wrote better than Ross Calvin and Will Comfort was a more skilled novelist than Gene Rhodes, in the intensity of their response to the Southwest all four are coequals.

I will be criticized for omitting favorite works of other readers, as well as for ignoring the ethnic-politico-economic Southwest. Another book could be written about the books I have not written about. Living writers have been excluded, painful though it has been not to write about Paul Horgan and Frank Waters. Some may accuse me of espousing a mystique of the creative act. I plead guilty. Even though he tries, one cannot escape the limitations of his own nature. As James Thorpe, director of the Huntington Library, said of a similar book, "I suppose that every such collection is an exercise in taste and in that sense a kind of autobiography."

My taste, though not my essential nature, (another way of saying prejudices) will inevitably change in the future as it has in the past. Now in the 1970's I do not respond to some of the books as I did in the 1950's. It is I, not they, who has changed. *Tempora mutantur* . . . times change and we change with them. Or should. In the end I leave it to the reader to bring his own judgment of the data gathered here, himself to question, reject, or embrace.

Again I say, if this book has a dominant theme it is the Southwest itself, this stark and colorful region which has enthralled its writers. The length of their stay was not paramount. Intensity transcended duration. Lawrence was a transient, Rhodes gone for twenty years; Krutch came late and Comfort at the end. Van Dyke, Powell, Summerhayes, Browne, Gregg, Garrard, Magoffin, all were passers through, and yet this intensity of response exalted their works.

The Southwest is more than landscape and climate, more than history, anthropology, archaeology, ecology, economics or literature. It is the combination of these elements and more, unified

5

by the passage of time and the presence of man. In books, and memorably in these of my choice, we see one Southwest refracted through many prisms. During my travels in the heartland these lines of Shelley have often come to mind:

> *The One remains, the many change and pass;*
> *Heaven's light forever shines. Earth's shadows fly;*
> *Life, like a dome of many-coloured glass,*
> *Stains the white radiance of Eternity.*

II

Twenty years ago while dining with Haniel Long in Santa Fe, that wise man warned me against trying to be two things at once, an administrator and a writer. In the optimism of middle-age I thought to prove him wrong. As a result I did neither as well as I should have.

Time passed. Long died. Eight years ago at sixty I left administrative work to devote nearly full time to writing, sharing it only with occasional teaching, an activity more compatible than administration. The reading, research, and travelling which led to the writing of *California Classics* took three years. *Southwest Classics* has taken even longer. As I turned to the writing, fortune brought us to live in Arizona, near the University and its resources of Southwestern materials. It proved an ideal location in which to demonstrate my belief that writers about a region should spend as much time outdoors with nature as indoors with archives.

In the rocky soil of the *bajada* at the base of the Santa Catalinas above Tucson, we put down roots. On quiet roads around I resumed work-habits lost in Southern California where the automobile has driven pedestrians off the streets and determined the way of life of the inhabitants. In this new life I rise before dawn to read and make notes, and then on sunrise walks reflect on my material.

Here on the alluvial slope whose dominant vegetation is the

6

palo verde and the saguaro, I am monarch of a far kingdom, ringed by ranges with ringing names—Catalinas, Tucsons and Tortolitas, the Tanque Verdes and the Rincons, Whetstones, Baboquívaris, and Santa Ritas, beyond to the far Dragoons. The view is essentially that of Kino, Garcés and Anza, of Ross Browne, Martha Summerhayes and Dr. Krutch, over an ancient landscape only superficially changed by man; and if the water table keeps dropping, a landscape that will some day return to its pristine state minus modern man and his works.

If the city seems too near, I travel over Redington Pass to the valley of the San Pedro and meet the river-course followed by Coronado on his first *entrada* in 1540. Or go west across the Papaguería and climb Kitt Peak to the cool zone of oaks where "men with long eyes" scan the skies. Or trail Will Comfort to Tombstone on its "high mesquite mesa." Is my goal there the O.K. Corral? No, it is the Lady Banksia rose, now proliferated incredibly from the Scottish rootstock of the 1880's. My return is via Patagonia and Nogales and down the valley of the Santa Cruz to rest at Tumacácori in the herb-garden patio where Arizona cardinals sip and splash in the fountain. Then Tubac. It was there in 1776 that Captain Juan Bautista de Anza marshalled his colonists and their animals for their trek to Alta California.

The road to Tucson follows the river, thicketed with mesquite, its flow of water long since gone underground. As I near town the bittersweetness of mesquite smoke recalls my first reading of *Dark Madonna*, Richard Summers' ill-fated novel of the *barrio viejo* in the Depression—ill-fated because a warehouse fire destroyed most of the edition and it has never been reprinted. This simple story saves a vanished Tucson from utter oblivion. Here at the "base of the dark mountain" was the Papago village which gave the city its name. Here in a clump of sprawling mesquite was the hidden shack of the *bruja* to whom the little madonna crept at midnight for a love potion. These images, not the massive civic center, enthrall me when I regain Tucson from the south.

I have now sensed the change of seasons in the arid lands and taken journeys at different times of the year. Once in the blaze of summer at a diversion point on the Imperial Dam above Yuma, where the roar of river-water smothered all other sounds, I cast a charm into the turbulence to appease the river-gods; and the surrounding shades were captained by Anza and by Palma, the Yuman chief, who sought to save Garcés from martyrdom.

One winter morning at Los Alamos the forest lay under snow, the people under covers, while steam from the laboratories indicated that the Atom was still monarch. At the turn-off to the National Monument in Frijoles Canyon, I recalled Bandelier's *The Delight Makers*, the first novel of the Pueblo Indians who once inhabited the Pajarito Plateau.

Later I took the Santa Fe Trail between the capital and Las Vegas, over the route of Gregg, Kearny, and the Magoffins, and at Ribera I paused at the midpoint of their run to watch the meeting of the *Superchiefs*. If sanctuary in Santa Fe lies in Lamy's cathedral, in Las Vegas it is gained in La Galeria de los Artesanos.

On these Southwest journeys I am guarded from evil by the Sacred Mountains—Baboquívari deep in the Papaguería, Sierra Blanca beloved of Gene Rhodes, and Mt. Taylor and the San Francisco Peaks at either end of Navajo-land. West from Gallup the eyes seek first sight of the Flagstaff mountains when suddenly they appear on the horizon (like white sheep in a pasture, Haniel Long said) and the heart quickens. Only a hundred miles to go. What was it like in the time of the first white travellers when these volcanic cones did not afford the security of familiar landmarks?

Mozart harmonized once with geography as the westward magnet. It was out of Albuquerque on old U.S. 66 that I heard on the radio of a performance that afternoon of *Cosi fan Tutte* at Northern Arizona University. I reached Flagstaff in a thunder shower, parked on campus, and dashed into the auditorium as the overture sounded.

Flagstaff has always occupied a special place on my map of the Southwest. Each winter during my earliest years we came to California from Washington on the B. & O. and the A.T. & S.F., and my first memory of the West is of that town's pervasive incense of sawmill. Flagstaff is still a lumber and railroad center, ruled by long freights and silvery streamliners and the thundering diesels that draw them, and piney smoke still sweetens the air. Culture has come with the University, Paul Weaver's Northland Press, and the Museum of Northern Arizona.

III

What determines life in the Southwest? Sky, said Ross Calvin, and wrote his classic to prove it. By determining the flow of the prevailing winds, he showed, mountains are sky's agents in establishing where is wet and where is dry, where green, where brown. I have come to know some of the mountains and their high canyons, up where water begins its fall to river and ocean. Places of peace are to be found there—up the Hondo to Twining and the Red to the lee of Wheeler, New Mexico's highest peak; up the Pecos to Cowles or downstate to Cloudcroft above the Tularosa basin. There is found surcease from too much city, and also in southernmost Arizona where the saddle-back Santa Ritas are entered by Madera Canyon, and in autumn the butterflies blend with the colored leaves.

And there are rivers to ascend, such as the Gila from its junction with the Colorado to the wilderness domain of Mangas Coloradas, warlord of the Mimbreño Apaches. The greatest of all—Rio Grande, San Juan, and Colorado—also lend themselves to exploration and adventure. One brilliant morning on the Rio Grande above Alamosa, I stood on the bridge and watched the water come foaming out of the Rockies, dancing with sunlit sparkle. At junction with the South Fork I took Wolf Creek Pass to the Continental Divide; and on the bare summit, warned by Forest Service signs against electrical storms, I paused

9

at the snow-melt drip-and-run headwaters of the San Juan to gaze down on the meandering river-meadow and beyond to the rough town of Pagosa Springs. At a fork in the road I was tempted to turn west to Durango and the Mesa Verde where many years before, I once had a fleeting vision of a band of Spruce Tree House's drought-stricken dwellers as they came toiling down on their final exodus. Instead I turned east to Chama and the descent to the Rio Grande at Española. Why? Because that night the Santa Fe Opera was to play *Der Rosenkavalier*. Music also determines.

What's to be gained from such goings up and down river-courses? A therapeutic cleansing of the spirit, I say, up where the Sky Gods empty their *ollas* so that the lands below be not wholly arid. There are guides to some of the rivers of the Southwest, notably to the Colorado, Rio Grande, and Gila. The San Juan and the Pecos, the Verde, the San Pedro, and the Salt have yet to be written about in depth. As for mountain books, Ungnade's *Guide to the New Mexico Mountains* is unmatched by one to Arizona's ranges. Its author, a Los Alamos chemist, died in a mountain fall while his book was in press. What better memorial? Jaeger's *The North American Deserts* is an essential book for those who would know the arid lands.

And so throughout these years have I gone roundabout the heartland with books in my baggage, a reading traveller and a travelling reader, sustained by these testaments, ranging in time from Kino to Krutch. If job or health or family compel one to stay at home, the magic will still work. He need not surmount Acoma to appreciate *Death Comes for the Archbishop*, although if he has seen that rocky pueblo and heard a mass for the dead in the Archbishop's cathedral, then will the reading of Willa Cather be more meaningful.

Because of these creative writers we see the Southwest differently than we would if they had not written. By the power of their prose, their vision becomes our vision. We perceive the landscape of Arizona with added dimension through the books

10

of Joseph Wood Krutch. We see New Mexico as Calvin, Lawrence and Luhan, Rhodes and the Fergussons saw it. To be pitied is the non-reader who has only his view of it. How impoverished he is! For as Patricia Paylore, Arizona's arid lands specialist, wrote, "The impact of historical landscape can drive a man to books, to deepen his understanding and sharpen his insight, for to live on the surface, without concern for the roots that distinguish his little piece of history from any and all others, is to live shallowly, unknowingly, is to deny the sense of the past which sets us apart from less rational creatures."

How real they are! I close my eyes and there is Zane Grey—I mean Lassiter—straining to roll the rock. There is Miss Cather and her friend, lost in the cañons below Mesa Verde. At the Painted Rocks on the lower Gila I spy that blithe spirit, Ross Browne, sketching the mysterious configuration, his rifle across his knees. Among the saguaros above Tucson I encounter the sorrowful shade of Dr. Krutch, deploring the city's destruction of the desert fabric. Everywhere in Arizona I meet Martha Summerhayes, as in New Mexico I overtake that other brave young wife Susan Magoffin, each living the book destined to be her immortality. Across the wide Southwest I am ever aware of my heroic predecessors—the healer Cabeza de Vaca, indomitable Kino and sturdy Garcés, inquiring Gregg, and old paisano J. Frank Dobie, egocentric Lummis and lusty Garrard, all of whom came this way and left their books on the land as legacies to those who follow in the procession of the generations—legacies to us their grateful beneficiaries.

If I am too fanciful, too mystical, you have only to put me down and go to their books and read for yourself. But first, let me try further to persuade you to my viewpoint. Read a bit more before you leave me for them. Read now what I have to tell you about Josiah Gregg and his *Commerce of the Prairies* . . .

Commerce of the Prairies
JOSIAH GREGG

Unlike a public library, used by many readers, wherein the books are systematically arranged on the shelves, my private library, used only by me, is arranged according to an inner logic not obvious to my friends. Why, they ask, do the books of Josiah Gregg and Richard Henry Dana, Jr., one of the prairie, the other of the sea, stand side by side on my shelf? Here is the answer I give:

The bonds between Gregg and Dana are several. In the 1830's each was a young man suffering ill health. Each embarked on a great westering adventure for restorative purposes, Dana by sea from Boston to the coast of California, Gregg by wagon train from Independence, Missouri to Santa Fe, New Mexico. From each experience came a classic book, *Two Years Before the Mast* in 1840, *Commerce of the Prairies* four years later. Gregg's book is to the Santa Fe trade what Dana's is to the trade in hides. Yet as literature, Dana's book is of a greater magnitude than Gregg's.

"Josiah Gregg just missed the boat that Parkman caught with *The Oregon Trail* and Dana with *Two Years Before the Mast*," wrote R. L. Duffus, historian of the Santa Fe Trail. "*Commerce of the Prairies* is a neglected classic. One would have thought that its portrayal of that wild and romantic episode would have caught America's imagination and kept the book alive. For some reason this did not happen."

13

Josiah Gregg was the son of a Scottish-American wheelwright, born in Tennessee on the 19th of July, 1806. The family moved to Independence, starting point of the Santa Fe Trail, where a wheelwright would find plenty to do. There, in Josiah's words, he was "cradled and educated upon the Indian border."

Josiah was one of several children all of whom received the same upbringing in an identical environment. Why was he the one destined to study, enquire, travel, and write? From childhood he was different, independent even of his mother, intellectually aloof, prudish and austere. And he was a scribbler.

That word is his. "Of all my memoranda," he wrote, "nothing is written expressly for publication. I scribble down every incident that occurs and happens to strike my attention; but if I should hereafter conclude to publish anything, I will make such selections and then alterations as the case may seem to require. The memoranda are only intended to aid in making a map."

His was the compulsiveness of the born writer.

Gregg was slow in finding himself. When he proved to be an apt student of the sciences, particularly mathematics, he became a frontier schoolteacher. He was denied a medical education. A study of the law failed to hold him. He was intensely mechanical, with aptitudes inherited from his father. Even as a lad he made a wooden quadrant and amazed his playmates by being able to measure the height of trees with this homemade device.

Then his health failed. Severe hypochondria is apparent in this self-diagnosis in the lofty style of the time:

"For some months preceding the year 1831, my health had been gradually declining under a complication of chronic diseases, which defied every plan of treatment that the sagacity and science of my medical friends could devise. This marked condition of my system, which originated in the familiar miseries of dyspepsia and its kindred infirmities, had finally reduced me to such a state, that, for nearly a twelvemonth, I was not only disqualified from any systematic industry, but so debilitated as rarely to be able to extend my walks beyond the narrow precincts of my chamber. In this hopeless condition, my physicians advised me to take a trip across the Prairie, and, in the change of air and habits which such an adventure would involve, to seek that health which their science had failed to bestow. I accepted their suggestion, and, without hesitation, proceeded at once to make the necessary preparations for joining one of those spring caravans which were annually starting from the United States, for Santa Fe."

This regimen proved to be of the highest therapeutic value. Gregg recovered from what ailed him, and as long as he led a rough outdoor life, he remained well. Dana's tragedy was in failing to obey his deepest impulse and continue to follow the sea, which prescription had likewise restored his health. He returned to Boston and a life of social respectability, indifferent health, and inner discontent. "My life on shore has been a mistake," Dana admitted years later. "I was made for the sea."

Gregg was made for the prairies, and fortunately he knew it. He was a wiser and happier man. For the next nine years he lived the life of a Santa Fe trader. Not only did he maintain good health during the annual round-trips through the 800-mile wilderness between Missouri and New Mexico, the experience "begat a passion for Prairie life which I never expect to survive." He learned Spanish and his fluency in speaking and writing it helped him to prosper as a trader.

Gregg was a happy man as long as he remained away from civilization. It was not that he went native. He never married, nor as far as we know did he ever have any kind of romance on prairie or in city. He was a "loner," a linguist and cartographer, an amateur scientist with curiosity about everything around him. And he was a scribbler, from which compulsion came the *Commerce of the Prairies*.

Now for a look at Santa Fe, that ancient city of the Holy Faith and mecca of the trading caravans that in 1825 began their annual pilgrimage from the Missouri frontier. Dobie has said it better than any other. "Looked at in one way, Santa Fe was a mud village. In another way, it was the solitary oasis of human picturesqueness in a continent of vacancy. Like that of Athens, its fame was out of all proportion to its size."

Here is how Gregg, having ridden ahead of the caravan, described his first sight of Santa Fe: "Ascending a table ridge, we spied in an extended valley to the northwest, occasional groups of trees, skirted with verdant corn and wheat fields, with here and there a square block-like protuberance reared in the midst . . . 'Oh, we are approaching the suburbs!', thought I, on perceiving the cornfields, and what I supposed to be brick-kilns scattered in every direction. These and other observations of the same nature becoming audible, a friend at my elbow said, 'It is true those are heaps of unburnt bricks, nevertheless they are *houses*—this is the city of Santa Fe.' "

Today, a century and a half later, Santa Fe looks much the same, although there are more mud houses and many trees, and the trade is in tourist dollars rather than cotton goods, Mexican silver, and mules.

Gregg went on to describe the arrival of the caravan, wagon after wagon pouring down the last hill into the town, the mules, horses, and oxen increasingly obstreperous. "I doubt, in short, whether the first sight of the walls of Jerusalem were beheld by the crusaders with much more tumultuous and soul-enrapturing joy."

From 1831 to 1840 Gregg prospered as a trader, while diligently enlarging his memoranda books. From the wooden quadrant of boyhood he had proceeded to a mastery of surveying. He became a veteran prairie navigator with a fondness for measuring routes, distances, and heights, observing watercourses, and speculating about mirages. He drew the best of all maps of the Santa Fe Trail and adjoining lands.

His mechanical ingenuity was employed by the Vicar of Santa Fe who wanted a clock for the tower of his church. Gregg agreed to make one for a price of $1000. He promised to bring the necessary parts when the caravan returned in the following

16

summer. Back in Missouri, Gregg assembled what was needed, making much of the clock out of wood, aided perhaps by his wheelwright father.

When the caravan returned to Santa Fe, Gregg went to work and installed the clock. As a special feature he included a little negro figure who emerged on the hour and bowed to the delighted populace. Then the vicar renegged. Gregg, he declared, had not put in a thousand dollars worth of time. The job merited only $700. Gregg did not argue. He took the lesser sum and departed with the caravan for Missouri.

Whereupon the little negro failed to make his hourly appearances. Word had gotten around town that the Vicar had not kept his agreement with Gregg. The people concluded that the automaton's defection represented a rendering of justice in favor of the clockmaker.

And so when the caravan returned the following year, the Vicar lost no time in asking Gregg to re-activate the black man, promising to pay the $300. Thus matters were set right.

Gregg's clock disappeared years later when Archbishop Lamy had the vicarage torn down to make way for the present cathedral. Is the clock still ticking away in some old Santa Fe adobe?

The Santa Fe trade came to an end in 1843 because of the Texans' violent inroads into New Mexico. Santa Anna's decree was the final blow. Gregg concluded that the time had come to make a book from his memoranda, in order that people might know what the trade and the territory were really like. He began his book while making a survey of Van Buren, Arkansas. He then went to Philadelphia, drawn by a trading supplier who helped him establish publishing contacts. Gregg became ill with an onslaught of his old complaints. His hair fell out and he had to wear a toupée. He then went to Camden, where Walt Whitman was later to live and die. There he completed his narrative.

In New York Gregg approached Dana's publisher, Harper's, with his manuscript and was turned down. Appleton accepted it subject to editing by a self-styled Irish count named Louis Fitzgerald Tasistro. This exotic character wished to embellish Gregg's prose with flowery language, whereupon the prairie man baulked. He sought advice from William Cullen Bryant, the literary arbiter, who had edited Dana's manuscript for Harper's.

For a similar purpose with Gregg's, Bryant proposed John Bigelow, a rising young literary lawyer. In our time Henry R. Wagner in his bibliography, *The Plains and the Rockies*, reported a New Mexican historian's statement that it was John Bigelow who really wrote *Commerce of the Prairies* from Gregg's memoranda.

Such was not the case. Bigelow went on to a distinguished career as lawyer, diplomat, historian, and elder statesman. Writing fifty years after his collaboration with Gregg, Bigelow stated, "He had no notions of literary art and he knew it, but he was morbidly conscientious, and nothing would induce him to state anything that he did not positively know, or to overstate anything . . . I soon found that all I had to do was to put his notes into as plain and correct English as I knew how. Gregg had about as little imagination as any man I ever knew. He would not allow his version of a fact to be expanded or contracted a hair's-breadth, no matter what might be the artistic temptation . . . He always had the critics of the plains before his eyes . . . Whatever the value his book possesses—and as a history of the trans-Mississippi commerce before the invasion of the railway, it has, I think, great and enduring value—was due to him and him only."

Commerce of the Prairies appeared in 1844 in two neat little volumes, illustrated from engravings of prairie scenes and with Gregg's handsome map of the region. A corrected second edition followed a year later, with a new preface, an index, and a glossary of Spanish words. Other editions continued to appear in the United States and England, and the work was translated into German. Altogether the book went through fourteen printings, seven in Gregg's lifetime. It was not until 1954 that a definitive

18

edition was published by the University of Oklahoma Press, superbly edited and introduced by Professor Max L. Moorhead. Whereas most of the other reprints of Gregg slavishly reproduce the first edition, Professor Moorhead properly included the corrections and additions Gregg made in his second edition of 1845.

Gregg did not linger in the East. "I have striven in vain to reconcile myself to the even tenor of civilized life in the United States," he wrote, "and have sought in its amusements and its society a substitute for those high excitements which have attached me so strongly to Prairie life. Scarcely a day passes without my experiencing a pang of regret that I am not now roving at large upon those western plains."

Gregg never returned to the prairies. In the five years of life that remained to him, he lived for a time with his brother John near Shreveport. Then, astonishingly, he realized his youthful ambition and became a doctor of medicine through a course of study at the University of Louisville. Next he was in Mexico with the American army as a civilian consultant. People annoyed him, especially the troops. It must be said that he gave them cause for ridicule when he appeared on horseback carrying a red umbrella to shade him from the sun. "I have no desire to be considered an odd fish," he once declared—which he obviously was.

After the Mexican war he practiced medicine in Saltillo, earning a reputation for devotion to his patients and modest fees. In 1849 the Gold Rush lured him to California.

Here is the place to answer R. L. Duffus's question as to why Gregg's book never caught the popular imagination. The answer appears to lie in Bigelow's observation that Gregg was the least imaginative man he had ever known. Great as *Commerce of the Prairies* is as a primary account of the Santa Fe Trail and early New Mexico, it lacks that transcendent quality of imaginative perception that illuminates both *Two Years Before the Mast* and Parkman's *The Oregon Trail*. Gregg was content to be a man of fact. His book's strength comes from its down-to-earth sobriety.

It also lacks symmetry of form, a quality that gives Dana's

book the power of transfixing the reader by the way it rises to a peak with the arrival in California, levels off, then descends with the return voyage and the rounding of Cape Horn. Those wintry chapters, Melville declared, read as though they had been written with an icicle. This is the creative force that elevates prose to the highest. Gregg lacked this power, as well as a sense of form, and his austere vision of life would not allow either the Irishman Tasistro or the Yankee Bigelow to supply what he knew he did not have.

If then Gregg's book falls short of the supreme level of literature attained by few writers, it has nevertheless an abiding place in Southwestern literature. "Bedrock Americana," Dobie called it. Gregg's stone-ground prose evokes the life of the Santa Fe Trail as no other book does. His passion for the prairies was also a passion for knowing. He was a tireless observer and recorder. "Gregg was of the order of men who create literature out of their daily preoccupations," wrote Paul Horgan in his profile of the plainsman, "that is, without a transfiguring act of the imagination."

The composition and conduct of the wagon train, the modes of packing, camping, repairing, and of dealing with accidents; the buffalo herds and thieving Indians; the cotton goods that made up the bulk of merchandise; the corrupt Mexican customs practices; statistics and distances; the history and the natural history of the region—all were recorded by Gregg.

But it was the Prairie itself, the sea of grass which he likened to an ocean, that seduced the sober young man and held him in lifelong thrall. In navigating the uncharted grasslands, Gregg found the compass as important as the sextant was to sea-going Dana.

Gregg never failed to be moved by landscape. Entering eastern New Mexico and attaining the first rise of land, he reported, "Looking southward a varied country is seen, of hills, plains, mounds, and sandy undulations; but on the whole northern side, extensive plains spread out, studded occasionally with variegated peaks and ridges. Far beyond these, to the northwestward, and low in the horizon a silvery stripe appears upon an azure base, resembling a list of chalk-like clouds. This is the perennially snow-capped summit of the eastern spur of the Rocky Mountains."

He called Chapter X "The Geography of the Prairies." It stresses the importance of rivers, particularly the Arkansas. The absence of navigable streams, except for the Missouri to the north, in those years before the railroad had opened the West, led Gregg to conclude:

"These great steppes seem only fitted for the haunts of the mustang, the buffalo, the antelope, and their migratory lord, the prairie Indian. Unless with the progressive influence of time, some favorable mutation should be wrought in nature's operations, to revive the plains and upland prairies, the occasional fertile valleys are too isolated and remote to become the abodes of civilized men."

The Santa Fe was one of three great trails of the last century, the others being the Chisholm Trail over which the great cattle drives proceeded from Texas to Kansas, and the Oregon Trail, that route followed by the majority of emigrants to the Pacific coast. By 1834, Gregg reported, the wagon ruts were worn so deep as to make the Santa Fe Trail easy to follow without need of compass or guide. Today those ruts are still discernible in some places, particularly when the route is seen from the air.

Gregg kept on the move, working his way by wagon through Mexico to Mazatlan from where he planned to embark for California. En route he collected hundreds of botanical specimens for Dr. George Engelmann of St. Louis, whose name is borne by that noble western conifer, the Engelmann spruce. Numerous species were subsequently given the identification *greggii*.

Gregg's memoranda books accompanied him to California. They were the ones he kept in Mexico after the *Commerce of the Prairies*. He intended to work them into another book. Arriving in San Francisco he had a premonition and left his belongings, including the memoranda, with a merchant friend, with instruc-

21

tions to send them to his brother John should he fail to return.

His was a fatal premonition. Gregg made his way to Rich Bar, a mining camp on the Trinity River. It was far north of San Francisco from whose harbor supplies for the northern mines had to be transported overland. The Pacific Ocean was only eighty miles west through coast ranges called the Trinity Alps. There were rumours of a harbor bay on that northern coast.

Gregg sought to recruit volunteers for an exploring expedition to cross the mountains. Family tradition was that he had received a government commission to carry out the venture. It was not a wise one. The time was winter, with rain along the river and snow at the higher elevations. Most of the men declined to go. Gregg was able to persuade only seven to accompany him.

The result was disorganization and death. Although they reached the coast after a month of exhausting hardships and discovered what was later named Humboldt Bay, there proved to be no feasible staging route through the maze of mountains. Gregg's determination to make scientific observations and scribble memoranda impeded their progress and aroused his companions' scorn and ire. While he employed his precious quadrant to measure the coast redwoods, the little band of "prisoners of the forest" groped and axed their way through groves of soaring sequoias.

At a tongue of land on the coast which they named Gregg's Point, their leader ascertained their position and inscribed on a large tree the latitude, barometrical reading and temperature at high noon, the date, and his own name. Subsequent logging has left few large trees, not including Gregg's, and the point was later named Trinidad Head.

The party gave lasting names to the Eel and the Van Dusen rivers, as well as to the Mad in recognition of a bitter quarrel they had on its banks. More disputes led to a split-up. Gregg led three men back over the snowy mountains toward Sacramento. They had come to despise his impersonal objectivity, and at one point they nearly left him to be swept away by a river. Although he was only forty-four, the younger men called him "the old gentleman." He was kind of a Don Quixote, lacking a faithful Sancho Panzo.

Things worsened. When they ran out of meat and bread, they ate acorns and herbs. Doctor Gregg had no prescription for himself. He grew steadily weaker, and on the 25th of February 1850 somewhere near Clear Lake, he fell from his horse and soon died without speaking a word—died of starvation. The men dug a hole with sticks and buried him under a rock cairn. It was precisely the kind of burial he had described in *Commerce of the Prairies*.

What became of his possessions, his memoranda and measuring instruments? Were they cached with him, jettisoned, or carried on to Sacramento? We do not know, yet I find myself pondering the words of Professor Maurice Fulton: "I suppose all the records for the trip to Northern California have been lost, although I never give up the hunt for missing papers. They are likely to be preserved in strange ways and places."

Years passed before his brother learned the details of Josiah's end, when one of the party published an account of the luckless expedition. Upon hearing of her wandering son's death, his mother had only this to say: "He overtaxed his energies that time."

Gregg's friend in San Francisco did not fail to carry out Josiah's instructions. The Mexican memoranda and belongings were sent to John Gregg. Somehow they survived the vicissitudes of time—fire, flood and insects—and of being passed around among a large family. They came at last into the possession of Claude Hardwicke, the grand-nephew of Josiah Gregg, and in the 1930's they were brought to Arizona when his widow, Antoinette, moved to Tucson.

Outside of the family no one knew of their existence. Then by inspired detective work a scholar tracked them down. Maurice Garland Fulton of the New Mexico Military Institute in Roswell proved ideally prepared to edit the Gregg archives. In 1941-44 the University of Oklahoma Press published his two-volume

Diary and Letters of Josiah Gregg, with a masterful introduction by his colleague, Paul Horgan. Together with Professor Moorhead's edition of *Commerce of the Prairies,* these books are an enduring memorial to Gregg of the Prairies.

Volume I was dedicated to Claude and Antoinette Hardwicke, Volume II "To the memory of John Gregg, 1800-1887," with these words from Josiah's letter of November 1, 1849: *Place my effects and memoranda . . . at the disposition of my brother John.* This volume witnesser of a trust well held."

The eight travel-stained booklets of Josiah Gregg came to a final haven in the Thomas Gilcrease Institute of American History and Art in Tulsa, a locale not far from the Santa Fe Trail.

READING LIST

JOSIAH GREGG (*1806-1850*)

Commerce of the Prairies. New York, Langley, 1844; Norman, University of Oklahoma Press, 1954. Edited by Max L. Moorhead.

Diary and Letters. Norman, University of Oklahoma Press, 1941-1944. Edited by Maurice Garland Fulton. Introduction by Paul Horgan.

R. L. DUFFUS

The Santa Fe Trail. 2d ed. Albuquerque, University of New Mexico Press, 1971.

JACK D. RITTENHOUSE

The Santa Fe Trail, a Historical Bibliography. Albuquerque, University of New Mexico Press, 1971.

Photograph of Josiah Gregg drawn from an old daguerrotype, courtesy of University of Oklahoma Press.

Wah-to-Yah and the Taos Trail
LEWIS H. GARRARD

The Year of Decision, Bernard DeVoto called it, and looking back on 1846 we see it as a supreme moment in our history. President James K. Polk had committed the country to its Manifest Destiny of expanding to the width of the continent. With the Army of the West, General Stephen W. Kearny was on the march for New Mexico and California. The Southwest was soon to fall to the United States of America.

If History was in the making, so was Literature. The latter comes from the impact of strong forces on sensitive natures who also have a command of language. The forces that were focusing in 1846 to bring about the acquisition of a vast territory by the American republic had also brought west two young persons: a man of seventeen, Lewis H. Garrard, and a woman of eighteen, Susan Shelby Magoffin. Unbeknownst to one another, each was destined to go west with the tide of expansion and to create enduring literature from the experience. They were at Bent's Fort only a couple of months apart. From that traders' rendezvous on the Arkansas River, they turned southwest, Garrard to Taos, Magoffin to Santa Fe.

After his return home a year later, Garrard wrote of his trip in *Wah-to-Yah and the Taos Trail*, which proved to be his only book of consequence. Although he lived for another forty years

27

as a farmer, banker, and country doctor, his literary activity produced only two undistinguished family memoirs.

Here he resembles Dana and more closely than did Gregg. Each experienced a transcendent western adventure. Each recalled it in fresh and vigorous prose, followed by a long, socially useful life without any literary development. Perhaps that was the best way. They were never subjected to the pressures that often corrupt writers who achieve success too early.

Garrard's book made no stir and was soon forgotten, not to be reprinted for nearly a century. Its title was unfortunate. There were only three great western trails and that to Taos was not one of them. The Taos Trail was merely a Santa Fe detour of uncertain pronunciation. Coupled with the also strange Indian name, *Wah-to-Yah*, it told the potential reader nothing. It is an example of the importance of the title in a book's fate.

Hector Lewis Garrard (he changed the order to Lewis H.) was well-born at Cincinnati in 1829. For a boy with wanderlust the river at his door was an irresistible lure. At sixteen he was off and away down the Ohio to the Mississippi and on to New Orleans. From there he beat his way along the Gulf coast to Galveston and back to Louisiana "where I stayed until the middle of May, visiting friends, riding horses, and shooting alligators, duck, and rail, from the bow of a long canoe in the cypress swamps."

Back in Cincinnati where he had been schooled in the classics of literature and history, a reading of Frémont's *Report* of 1845 on his Rocky Mountain explorations re-aroused the boy's wanderlust. His father had died when Lewis was six, and his mother was remarried to John McLean, an associate justice of the United States Supreme Court. They proved understanding parents.

Furnished with letters of reference and credit, cash, a pocket Bible and a book on the stars, a rifle and a few calico shirts, Garrard took to the river again in the heat of July, his destination St. Louis and points beyond. At Planters' Hotel he met the great Cérain St. Vrain, partner with William Bent in one of the fore-

28

most Santa Fe traders groups, and was taken into their party, due to leave soon for Bent's Fort. Garrard proceeded by steamer up the Missouri to the point of departure at Westport Landing, site of the future Kansas City. In mid-September "wagons west" began their long haul over the prairies.

The young Ohioan's sole purpose was adventure. It was only at his elder brother's urging that he kept a journal. Garrard tells of how each night after the caravan had bedded down, he would lie by the fire wrapped in a blanket and "scrawl a few words in a blank book," or read and indulge in reveries. "Anyone in the Far West," he declared, "is romantically inclined." From those scrawls came his book, even as Josiah Gregg's scribbles led to his classic work.

Garrard quickly adapted to the rough life of the traders. He did not worry about sanitation or the cut of his clothes. It was not long before he was in buckskin "Californy" pants and moccasins. He learned to like raw buffalo liver and marrow, and to sleep double with another man in buffalo robes for warmth. If it had not been for an educated mind and a fond family, he might easily have "gone native" for the rest of his days.

Upon reaching Bent's Fort after fifty days of travel, Garrard seemed content to remain based there in southeastern Colorado at the foot of the Rockies. The fort's doctor had a well-stocked library to supplement the few books of his own. There he had his first sight of the landmarks that were to give his book its title. *Wah-to-Yah* was their Indian name, meaning the Breasts of the World. The Spanish called them *Las Cumbres Españolas*, the Spanish Peaks, twin mountains which heralded the Rockies.

"I arose early in the morning," Garrard wrote, "and going on top of the fort, had a good view of the Spanish Peaks to the northwest, apparently fifteen miles distant—in reality *one hundred and twenty*. They were of a dull gray color; while a lower range was dazzling white, all perpetually covered with snow. To the north-east a faint outline of a mountain was descried—James' or Pike's Peak."

29

From the fort Garrard accompanied William Bent on a trading expedition to the friendly Cheyennes. He took to the Indians, they to him. "Young Whiteman," they called him. His youthful ardor was reciprocated by the maidens. A few of them he found comely. We recall Dana's joy with the Indian girls on the beach at San Diego. The difference is that Dana told nothing, and we know of it only from a shipmate's letter after reading *Two Years Before the Mast*, in which he chided Dana for his omissions.

Although Garrard does not tell all, he tells more than Dana did. Society in Cincinnati was probably more tolerant than that in Boston. What he does tell is delightful—of how when the chief's daughter ran to hide from her friends she slid under Garrard's buffalo robe and snuggled up against him. This was one of the passages cut from the school edition of 1927. Garrard was grieved when he heard later that one of his dusky mates had run off with a brave. He consoled himself with the knowledge that there was more than one pretty Indian girl in the world.

Although we lack Garrard's journal to compare it with his book, I doubt that he either toned it down or dressed it up for publication. His is the most rapturous of all western works, a lusty poem in prose to youthful freedom and adventure.

The dynamics of Manifest Destiny set Garrard on the Taos Trail. When New Mexico fell to General Kearny as a result of Governor Armijo's defection, the American leader was able to proceed to the conquest of California. He named William Bent's brother Charles as governor. While he was on a mission to Taos, a bloody uprising cost Charles Bent his life. From his brother's fort a party of vengeance took the trail for Taos. Garrard joined it.

His narrative heightens in exuberance, interest, and historical importance. From the top of Raton Pass as he stood guard with rifle and a comforting smoke, Garrard gazed back on the Spanish Peaks. Sight of them gave him a sense of security. "This is the acme of life," he exulted, "with fat, sleek mules, plenty of

30

provision and tobacco, and the undisturbed possession of our scalps."

In the novels *Wolf Song* and *Grant of Kingdom*, Harvey Fergusson describes at second-hand the emotions of the mountain men on returning to Taos. In *Wah-to-Yah* Garrard's is a first-hand view of the locale from Taos Canyon as they came down out of the Sangre de Cristos onto the idyllic plain. Here is what they saw:

"On emerging from the canyon, the view expanded to a valley nearly circular to the casual glance, hemmed in by a snowy range, while *El Rio Grande del Norte*, a few miles distant, rolled between sandbanks to the southwest. The level plain below wore a cultivated, civilized aspect. Reposing quietly at our very feet was the hamlet of El Rancho; to the west the village Ranchita, and toward the northwest, San Fernandez de Taos, its walls, as well as those of the minor towns, mica lime-washed to a dazzling whiteness. To the northeast at the base of a contiguous mountain was the dismal Pueblo de Taos, but a few weeks since the scene of the fiercest strife."

By the time they arrived, Taos had been retaken by the Americans and justice was being rendered the rebels. Garrard's is the only eyewitness account of the trial and the hanging. His was a compassionate eye, for his sympathy lay with the rebels—the Mexicans and Indians who had sought only to regain what they had lost. "It certainly did appear to be a great assumption on the part of the Americans," he wrote, "to conquer a country and then arraign the revolting inhabitants for treason."

His report of the hanging is an artful blend of the pathetic and the grotesque, the more extraordinary for being the work of a youth. The characters are sketched in a few vivid words. We are convinced that Garrard set it down the way it was, the drama heightened by his selection and arrangement of the details. Here is an example:

"We were cutting a rope from one man's neck—it was in such a hard knot—when the owner (a government teamster), stand-

31

ing by waiting, shouted angrily, at the same time starting forward—

"Hello there! don't cut that rope; I won't have anything to tie
my mules with."

"Oh, you darned fool," interposed a mountaineer, "the palous' ghost's be after you if you use them 'riatas—wagh! They'll
make meat of you, sartain."

"Well, I don't care if they do. I'm in government service; an'
if them picket halters was gone, slap down would go a dollar
apiece. Money's scarce in these diggins, an' I'm gwine to save all
I kin, to take home to the old 'oman and the boys."

"In accordance with the fellow's earnest request we spared the
ropes, on which was soap enough for a dozen good washings,
which he much needed."

Although the result was both history and literature, Garrard
was not consciously writing either. He was filtering life through
his own sensibilities. We see the Taos world as it was during
those wild days of 1847—the sights and smells and the salty
lingo to which his ear was so faithful. How he relished it all! A
bed with sheets for the first time since Missouri, coffee with fresh
milk, the fragrant warmth from a fire of piñon logs. And the
women, always the women, took Garrard's eye. Thus he observed them in the courtroom during the trial:

"Señora Bent was quite handsome; a few years since she must
have been a beautiful woman—good figure for her age; luxuriant
raven hair; unexceptional teeth and brilliant, dark eyes, the effect
of which was heightened by a clear, brunette complexion. The
other lady, though not so agreeable in appearance, was much
younger. The wife of the renowned mountaineer, Kit Carson,
also was in attendance. Her style of beauty was of the haughty,
heart-breaking kind—such as would lead a man with a glance of
the eye to risk his life for one smile. I could not but desire her acquaintance."

Taos is the high point of *Wah-to-Yah*. Garrard quit it reluctantly as back up Taos Canyon he rode with his fellows. "The green cedar and pine, the mellow light of the sun gleaming through the branches, and the twittering of dusky-colored birds, induced a dreamy state; for long intervals naught but the pattering of our mules' feet or the quick, metallic clink of the flint and steel of Louy lighting a pipe broke the silence. We were under the influence of the harmony of nature, tobacco, and Taos whiskey . . . That night I with a bunch of cigarillos from a Castillian-descended señorita, and they with pipes, sat by the blaze in a decidedly musing mood. In my dreams rebozos, black eyes, and shuck cigars were mixed in admirable confusion."

Garrard returned to Bent's Fort, meeting Kit Carson and Lieutenant E. F. Beale on the way, and then went back down the Arkansas, across the prairies to St. Louis, and on up the Ohio to home in Cincinnati. He had been gone nearly a year.

"Abominable chills and fevers greeted my return to civilization," he wrote. It was during recuperation from illness that Garrard expanded his "scanty pencillings" into a book. "Then, the request of friends coupled with the bidding of a pardonable vanity produced them in the present form." It bore this dedication: "To Mr St Vrain, the leader of our party, the traverser of the plains, the revered of the Cheyenne nation, this book is respectfully inscribed, by one who holds in grateful remembrance his many kind services."

Garrard realized that he would be charged with grossness, as when he told of feasting with the Cheyennes on dogmeat and liking it. A lack of piety might also have been held against him in the passage (one of the great frontier folk-yarns) where he lets the brandy-warmed mountain man, John L. Hatcher, recount his hilarious meeting with the Devil. "I have set down naught in malice," Garrard explained, "and it is no more my prerogative to exclude than to add." At twenty-one Lewis H. Garrard was a sophisticated man of letters.

Wah-to-Yah was not entirely ignored when it appeared in

May 1850. The literary editor of the *New York Tribune* tossed the author a crumb when he said that he had "acquired a nimble use of the pen at an early age."

Garrard's remaining thirty-eight years were full of varied activity. In 1855 he graduated in medicine from the University of Pennsylvania. He made at least one trip to Europe. With his brothers he settled in a community on the Mississippi River below St. Paul. At thirty-three he married Florence Van Vliet by whom he had five children; two of their daughters were still living in 1938. Garrard was at once a farmer, banker, member of the state legislature, and a doctor. At an old settlers' meeting in the seventies he jokingly remarked that most of his patients got well because of the recuperative influnce of the climate. He belonged to the historical societies of Minnesota, Ohio, and Pennsylvania.

Should we judge him for not having written more nor having left a mature work to match his youthful masterpiece? Only *Wah-to-Yah* has kept his name alive. A man's personality and social work fade and are forgotten. Garrard's book seemed likewise fated. It was in limbo for a long time.

Then in 1927 an expurgated school edition appeared, followed in 1936 by a handsome Grabhorn Press printing, prefaced by Carl I. Wheat. When this was facsimiled in 1968 there was perpetuated a typesetter's error by the usually impeccable Grabhorns which had omitted an entire three and a half pages of the original text of 1850. In 1938 Garrard's classic was finally given definitive scholarly editing by Ralph P. Bieber. To him we owe our knowledge of Garrard's later life. In 1955 A. B. Guthrie introduced an inexpensive edition which remains in print.

READING LIST

LEWIS HECTOR GARRARD (*1829-1887*)

Wah-to-Yah, and the Taos Trail. Cincinnati, Derby, and New York, Barnes, 1850.

———— Oklahoma City, Harlow, 1932. Abridged by Walter S. Campbell (Stanley Vestal).

———— San Francisco, The Grabhorn Press, 1936. Introduction by Carl S. Wheat.

———— Glendale, Arthur H. Clark Co., 1938. Edited by Ralph P. Bieber.

———— Palo Alto, American West, 1968. Facsimile of the Grabhorn ed.

———— Norman, University of Oklahoma Press, 1955. Introduction by A. B. Guthrie, Jr.

Memoir of Charlotte Chambers. Philadelphia, Printed for the Author, 1856.

Chambersburg in the Colony and the Revolution. Philadelphia, Printed for the Author, 1856.

BERNARD DE VOTO

The Year of Decision, 1846. Boston, Houghton Mifflin, 1943.

DAVID LAVENDER

Bent's Fort. Garden City, Doubleday, 1954.

Photograph of Lewis H. Garrard, courtesy of Arthur H. Clark Co.

Down the Santa Fe Trail

SUSAN SHELBY MAGOFFIN

What of the young woman who also went west in the Year of Decision and likewise left a lasting literary memorial?—she of whom J. Frank Dobie wrote that "she was juicy and a bride and all life was bright to her."

Her name was Susan Shelby and she was born in Kentucky in 1827, two years before Lewis Garrard saw the light across the river in Ohio. Hers was a distinguished Blue Grass family. Married at seventeen to Samuel Magoffin, twenty-seven years her senior, she was barely eighteen when they set out on an extended honeymoon over the Santa Fe Trail. He was a veteran Santa Fe trader. His brother, James, who was high in the esteem and confidence of President Polk, had preceded the newlyweds on a secret mission which brought about the overthrow of the Mexican government. Manifest Destiny at work!

The diary kept by Susan Magoffin, and which lay unknown and unpublished until 1926, illuminates her brother-in-law's far-reaching accomplishment. As such it is a primary historical document. It is also literature, for it embodies a young woman's perceptive account of life on the trail from Independence, Missouri to Santa Fe and beyond to Chihuahua.

Resurrection of Susan's diary was the achievement of Stella M. Drumm, Librarian of the Missouri Historical Society in St. Louis. She discovered the diary in the possession of Susan's daughter, Mrs. Jane Taylor, and persuaded her to allow its transcription, annotation, and publication by the Yale University Press. It took place as a first-hand source on the events of

37

that time and as a Southwest classic. A subsequent Yale paperback has the added value of a foreword by Professor Howard R. Lamar, in addition to Miss Drumm's copious, informative, and readable notes. The original diary is preserved in the Beinecke Library at Yale University.

Whereas Garrard gave no evidence of having read *Commerce of the Prairies*, Susan Magoffin held Gregg next to her Bible in importance. Her description of the journey as far as Bent's Fort is a kind of replay of Gregg. She travelled in what was for the Santa Fe Trail great luxury. Her doting husband provided his pregnant bride with a carriage, a boudoir tent (it leaked), a maid and two boys. She once remarked, "It is the life of a wandering princess, mine."

Upon reaching the trading post on the Arkansas, life closed in on Susan as she fell ill and aborted. It was a painful ordeal and a cruel disappointment, yet she displayed no self-pity. In the next paragraph of her journal, after describing this loss, she wrote,

"My situation was very different from that of an Indian woman in the room below me. She gave birth to a fine healthy baby, about the same time, *and in half an hour after she went to the River and bathed herself and it*, and this she has continued each day since. Never could I have believed such a thing, if I had not been here, and *mi alma's* own eyes had not seen her coming from the River. And some gentleman here tells him, he has often seen them immediately after the birth of a child go to the water and *break the ice* to bathe themselves. It is truly astonishing to see what customs will do. No doubt many ladies in civilized life are ruined by too careful treatments during child-birth, for this custom of the hethen is not known to be disadvantageous, but it is a *hethenish custom*."

A week later the Magoffin caravan left Bent's Fort, crossed the river and, with the Spanish Peaks in view, began the ascent of Raton Pass. A detachment had gone ahead to make a semblance of a road. There was not much to show for their work; it was still too rough for Susan to ride in her carriage. She either walked or

38

rode on horseback, as the company crept upward at the rate of half a mile an hour.

Her eyes were open to all around her. "Sometimes this is a curious little pebble, a shell, a new flower, or the quill of a strange bird." She had her first taste of piñon nuts and the sweet bitterness of wild cherries. Camped at The Hole in the Rock for its well of clear, cold water, she wrote in her diary, "So we have lain here in the hot sun with the tent *windows* raised, and eating roast-hare and drinking wine for dinner. In brevity we are quite patient under the circumstances."

It was the same route through the Sangres which only a few months later was to thrill Lewis Garrard. Susan too was moved by the sublime scenery. She wrote, "From the greatest hight to which I have yet ascended on horse-back, mountains far more lofty than any I have seen, deep vallies below that looked blue so great was the distance to them; the clouds seem resting on the mountains around us." It is still the most dramatic of entries into New Mexico.

While Garrard bore west here and descended onto the Taos plain, the Magoffins pressed on to Santa Fe via Mora, Las Vegas, Bernal, San Miguel, and the ruins of Pecos Pueblo. On August 31st she rejoiced in being at last in her own house in Santa Fe, safely under the Stars and Stripes, "the first American lady who has come under such auspices, and some of our company seem to make me the first under any circumstances that ever crossed the Plains."

Her diary tells of social-military life of Santa Fe, of callers on the Magoffins, the balls, meals, clothing, and personalities, including the fabulous Gertrudes Barcelo, "principal montebank keeper in Santa Fe, a stately dame of certain age, possessor of a portion of that shrewd sense and fascinating manner necessary to allure the wayward, inexperienced youth to the hall of final ruin."

Susan was given to religion and moralizing, at the same time that she revelled in the sensuous life of Santa Fe. She recorded it all—the gallant young American officers who paid their re-

39

spects to her, as well as the drunken ones who staggered around her parlor until taken in charge by Samuel. And she was delighted when all eyes were on her as she entered the ballroom wearing a Canton shawl of scarlet silk. She picked up Spanish rapidly, referring lovingly to her husband as *mi alma*.

General Kearny himself paid homage to Susan. On one of his calls the roof began to leak from a sudden thunder-shower and he had to jump to keep from getting soaked. On horseback the two of them rode through Santa Fe to inspect the newly-built Fort Marcy.

And so down river the Magoffin caravan wended, past Sandía and the village of Albuquerque, to El Paso del Norte and into Chihuahua. Her diary faithfully recorded the fluctuating alarms of the conflict with Mexico and the relief of final victory. Hers is a unique view of the Mexican War which ended with the vast enlargement of the United States.

In August 1847 she met General Zachary Taylor, Old Rough and Ready, and wrote in her diary of being "agreeably disappointed . . . I had not thought to find him possessed of so mild manners, such apparent high regard for female character . . . He wore his uniform which I am told is *no common custom* with him, and I should think so from the number of wrinkles in it, the work of many weeks packing. I am told the honor is worth remembering."

Her diary ended on September 8, 1847, on the eve of a siege of yellow fever at Matamoras during which she gave birth to a son. The baby died. She and Samuel returned to Kentucky and settled later in Missouri where he prospered in farming and real estate.

Two girls were born to them. To the one who lived we owe the preservation of her mother's diary. Susan died in 1855 at only 28. She was buried in Bellefontaine Cemetery, St. Louis.

In the beginning she was all that Dobie said of her. That journey down the Santa Fe Trail and into Mexico in time of war was too much for the tender girl she was. It dried up her juices, carried off her progeny all but one, darkened her day, and in the end it cost her life.

All that was long ago. What matter now her cruel fate? Time has taken away the pity. Her diary is as fresh as ever. She lives in it, in love with her husband, brave in the face of danger, suffering hardships unknown to us who travel in cool comfort.

Seventy-one years came and went between her death and the appearance of her diary. Once again have we evidence of the triumph of the written word.

I find myself toying with the thought that Susan Magoffin and Lewis Garrard might have met at Bent's Fort. Only a scant few months in time separated them. They would surely have recognized one another as kindred souls. Each has left us a little classic as testimony to a love of life that lasts to this day, made only more precious by the passage of time.

READING LIST

SUSAN SHELBY MAGOFFIN (*1827-1855*)
Down the Santa Fe Trail and Into Mexico; the Diary of Susan Shelby Magoffin, 1846-1847. Edited by Stella M. Drumm. New Haven, Yale University Press, 1926; with a foreword by Howard R. Lamar, 1962.

MAX L. MOORHEAD
New Mexico's Royal Road; Trade and Travel on the Chihuahua Trail. Norman, University of Oklahoma Press, 1958.

SHIRLEY SEIFERT
The Turquoise Trail. Philadelphia, Lippincott, 1950. A novel based on the Magoffin diary.

ELLIOTT ARNOLD
The Time of the Gringo. New York, Knopf, 1953. A novel of the Armijo period, documented in part by the Magoffin diary.

Photograph of Susan Magoffin, courtesy of Yale University Press.

June 24,
1904.

The Land of Poco Tiempo
CHARLES F. LUMMIS

The view from afar of a distant mountain range is always dramatic, whether it be the Himalayas from the Bengal plain, the Pyrenees as the road climbs through the hills of Aragon, or the Rockies seen from the rising Colorado uplands. Even as it thrilled Susan Magoffin and Lewis Garrard on their way west in the 1840's, so did this latter spectacle enthrall another youngster a generation later. Not long out of Harvard and the editorship of an Ohio newspaper, Charles Fletcher Lummis was tramping to Los Angeles to rejoin his wife who had gone ahead by rail. There he hoped to land a job on the newly-founded *Times.* His first sight of what was to prove his Promised Land moved him to these words:

"For more than fifty miles I had been walking without apparent effect straight at two great blue islands that rose from the level distance of the plains. They were the Spanish Peaks, lonely and glorious outposts of the superb Sangre de Cristo range. Under their shadows we stepped into a civilization that was then new to me—that of the swarthy Mexicans and their quaint adobe houses, with regiments of mongrel curs and flocks of silken-haired Angora goats."

Although there have been more polished writers on the Southwest than Lummis, none has equalled his genius for seeing, un-

43

derstanding, and popularizing the region. It was he who first called it "The Southwest." This smaller than average man —he stood only 5 feet 6 and weighed 135—was a wiry bundle of energy, intellect, learning and zest, and above all, a compulsion to communicate and educate. To the end of his life in 1928 at sixty-nine, he aggressively used these gifts in expressing his own ego, as well as in working for the common weal. Whatever faults of character and behavior he had—and he was domineering, egotistical, and oversexed—they were outweighed by his creativity which left enduring monuments.

In my earlier *California Classics* my subject was Lummis and his *Land of Sunshine-Out West*, the magazine that ranks with *Overland Monthly* as the greatest of western periodicals. After the turn of the century, Lummis left literary pursuits and became a crusading journalist, an innovative librarian (he headed the Los Angeles Public Library for five exciting years), and a founder of conservationist and philanthropic institutions, including the Landmarks Club, the Sequoyah League, and the Southwest Museum.

These activities were directed from his base in Los Angeles out in what was then the country, along the stream bed of the Arroyo Seco at the time before Devil's Gate Dam had subdued the wild spring floods. There beneath the hill whereon he was to establish the Southwest Museum, Lummis and his youthful Indian protegés from New Mexico toiled for twenty-three years to build El Alisal, the great stone house in the sycamore grove. "What are you wasting your time for?" a visitor asked of Lummis who, clad in his customary white overalls, was mortaring up a wall, "when you could be writing another book." "Any fool can write a book," Lummis replied, "and most of them do. It takes brains to build a house." He believed it would stand for a thousand years and hoped it would be inhabited by a Lummis dynasty—a reasonable belief, a vain hope.

My concern here is with the Lummis of an earlier period, in the 1880's and 1890's, during and after the time of his long walk.

Attachments formed on this first *entrada* into the Southwest brought him back to live in New Mexico while recuperating from a paralytic stroke. Based for four years at Isleta, southernmost of the river pueblos, he wrote books that rank among the classic literature of the Southwest.

On his way west in the fall of 1884, Lummis first met the Rio Grande at Alamosa in southern Colorado, not far from its source in the San Juan Rockies. The river soon bends south into New Mexico to form that land's arterial lifeline. He followed its course until it became engorged, then regained it at Embudo where it waters the orchards of peach, apple, and cherry that grow there to this day.

The Southwest straightway taught Lummis two things: that land there is worthless without water and that the color of a man's skin does not determine his nature. "In this country of free and brave men," he wrote, "race-prejudice, the most ignorant of all prejudices, must die out. We must respect manhood more than nationality. The deeds that hold the world up are not of any one blood."

Below Española he came to his first river pueblo, that of San Ildefonso. There he was received with courteous dignity by the people of a culture antedating that of his natal New England. Then in Santa Fe he met the man who was to be a lifelong bond between him and New Mexico. He was Amado Chaves, son of Colonel Manuel Chaves, the great Indian fighter and *patrón* of a sheep-raising hacienda at San Mateo. Young Chaves, a member of the territorial legislature, was married to an Ohio woman whom he had met while at school in the East; and to her, Lummis's Ohioan wife, Dr. Dorothea (she was an M.D.), had written a letter to introduce her husband.

Chaves insisted that Lummis stop over at the family domain west of Albuquerque. Although he stayed there for only four days, it was long enough to confirm Lummis as a Southwesterner. There he heard the songs that he loved to his dying day— "there," he said of New Mexico, "where everybody sings and

45

almost nobody can sing." He also saw vestiges of the vanished cliff-dwellers and witnessed the flagellant ceremonies of the self-crucifying Penitente brotherhood.

These were the great determining days of his life. The youthful Lummis and Chaves were henceforth blood brothers. The American named his first son after his friend and dedicated his book of stories, *The Enchanted Burro*, "To Amado and Amado" with these lines:

The name that stood for such a friend is tall enough for two—
My oldest friend on the old frontier, my newest one on the new.

The Chaves domain lay beyond Mt. Taylor, easternmost of the Navajos' Sacred Mountains, over then unknown uranium beds. Not far south was Ácoma, the Sky Pueblo, the Enchanted Mesa, and El Morro, which Lummis detoured to see before continuing along the tracks of the A.T. and S.F. They were to become places of veneration, celebrated throughout his writings.

On his roundabout walk of 3500 miles which took 143 days, Lummis carried a tiny notebook in which he had cut and pasted the railroad route he mostly followed. It also contained the names of people to call on. To entertain himself he carried a harmonica which was useful in playing for his supper when he sought shelter at a trackworker's section shack. Along the way he wrote letters ahead to the *Times*, which appeared under the by-line "Lum." (*Don't* call him Loomis.)

After his arrival in Los Angeles and reception by Editor Harrison Gray Otis who drove out to San Gabriel to escort him triumphantly into town, Lummis worked himself nearly to death as city editor of the young newspaper. He gloried in his strength and recuperative power. In 1886 the paper sent him to Arizona to cover the pursuit of Geronimo. As he was always to do, Lummis took the Indians' side. Unscrupulous traders who debauched the Apaches with whiskey, he declared, were the cause of Geronimo's latest outbreak.

In 1887 Lummis broke under his spartan regime. Paralyzed on the left side, his mind confused and mostly speechless, he lay abed while his wife sought to heal him. Never a good husband, he was a worse patient. "From first to last," he recalled in *My Friend Will*, "he refused all doses and treatment, which indicates that, despite that disaster in the brain, the skull retained most of its hardness."

It was Lummis who finally prescribed what was to prove his remedy—a return to the Chaves hacienda and there in the outdoors to let nature heal his crippled body. And so it came to pass. Each day he dragged himself about and learned to handle a rifle with his good right arm in hunting small game. He was unable to write. His mind was still disoriented by the stroke, his speech impaired. Thus he learned to listen. "So the evenings he passed with the family, playing quaint Spanish games, learning sweet Spanish songs—and something of the Spanish heart which he will never forget."

As he slowly improved, Lummis ranged wider, roughing it in the sheep camps, learning the new art of photography, and finally moving not far away to Isleta Pueblo to study the Tiguan language and culture. There he formed lasting friendships with the governor, Pablo Abeita, and with the priest, Padre Docher, who served at Isleta for nearly half a century. He aided the Indians in their resistance to Agency domination, as later he aided the Moquis (Hopis) in their fight to preserve their religion and customs.

A decade later when President Roosevelt came west, Lummis urged him to stop over at Isleta. They had been fellow students at Harvard. "I want him to see the Indians in their full humanity. I could teach him more in two hours in Isleta than he is likely to learn in his whole life about the real insides of Indians." Although he did not accede, Roosevelt did invite Lummis to join him at the Grand Canyon and ride the rest of the way to Los Angeles.

While at Isleta another stroke felled Lummis, precipitated by a letter from Dorothea, saying that she was divorcing him. He also ran out of what little money he had, which was not wholly unfortunate, for his desperate need made him a writer again. While in hospital at Santa Fe he began to write jokes and jingles which he sold to eastern magazines for a few dollars apiece. He improved enough to struggle onto a horse and go fishing in the Sangres.

Back at Isleta he benefitted from that blessed therapeutic agent, Love, ". . . one good fortune that he did not hew out for himself. A pair of very beautiful blue eyes, that had been first to bend over him when he was paralyzed for the third time, came to be the daily light of the humble adobe, where he had taken care of himself over two years."

The eyes were those of Eva Frances Douglas, newly come from Connecticut as the instructress in the pueblo's Roman Catholic school. She was twenty years old. They went to Los Angeles, bearing gifts for Dorothea, and were married in San Bernardino on March 27, 1891. In that day's entry in his curious bi-lingual diary Lummis wrote, "Eva llega y nos casamos en residencia Rev. Merlin-Jones. See Lewis, Indian Agent, who used to be sweet on her, at station, before. Vamos en #2 tourist sleeper. Cielo."

At home in Isleta they set up housekeeping in his adobe. On the 1st of April he wrote, "Pongo estufa y pinto shelves, kitchen door, silla, cajon de carbon, cajas etc. todo el dia. Leyo 'The Land of Poco Tiempo' a Eva. Cielito."

They honeymooned in the field on horse and on foot, "ransacking the out-of-the-way corners of New Mexico." His left arm and hand were still paralyzed. Then one day at a friend's house in Bernalillo he found himself unconsciously stroking his wife's hair—*with his left hand*. The clot in the brain had dissolved. Although he suffered other illnesses, never again was he paralyzed. Four children came from this union.

Their relationship with Dorothea remained amicable. Two years later when *The Land of Poco Tiempo* was published, it bore the dedication "To Eva and Dorothea." Lummis was fortunate in his wives, "Dolly" a scientist, Eva a humanist. Under his tutelage Eva learned Spanish and became a noted translator

48

of Blasco Ibáñez, Concha Espina, and other Spanish writers.

From turning out snippets for paltry sums, Lummis went on to a prolific production of stories, travel sketches, and history. He began with *A New Mexico David*, a book of stories and pieces about the Southwest intended for young readers gained through his contributions to *St. Nicholas* and other eastern magazines. It bore a frontispiece portrait of him in frontier garb, posed in an Albuquerque studio, as well as illustrations from his own photographs. In this book of firsthand experiences and observations was sounded his life's theme:

"I hope someday to see a real history of the United States . . . a book which will realize that the early history of this wonderful country is not limited to a narrow strip on the Atlantic seaboard, but that it began in the great Southwest; and that before the oldest of the Pilgrim Fathers had been born, swarthy Spanish heroes were colonizing what is now the United States."

Between 1891 and 1898 Lummis wrote ten books. Inspired by Captain Mayne Reid, the Englishman whose adventure stories of the Far West had excited his early years and helped lure him west, Lummis aimed first at juvenile readers. In the book about his long walk, *A Tramp Across the Continent*, he employed a style that could be enjoyed by all ages, although its melodramatics tax the mature reader's credulity. Derived from his travels with Eva, *Some Strange Corners of our Country: the Wonderland of the Southwest* was embellished with woodcuts from *Century*, the magazine that did more than any other to familiarize the East with western landscape.

This was followed by *The Land of Poco Tiempo*. Its opening sentence, "Sun, silence, and adobe—that is New Mexico in three words," is often quoted as the motto of the Land of Enchantment. In it he extended and refined his knowledge of the land in language both lyrical and precise, so that it is the best of all his books about the Southwest. Although rhapsodical, this passage is nevertheless abidingly true:

"Landscape and life are impressionist and will submit neither

49

to photography nor to figures. Years of study and travel do not itemize the picture—there still remains in the memory but a soft sweet haze of shifting light and shade, a wilderness of happy silence, an ether of contentful ease, wherein we live and die and are glad." Many a New Mexican today would subscribe to those words as the quintessence of what holds him resident of that land.

Two men were responsible for the development of Lummis as an authority on the Southwest. They were Amado Chaves and Adolphe Bandelier, the Swiss archaeologist. From the one, Lummis gained insight into the Hispanic community, from the other into the Indian. He met Bandelier in 1888 when the scientist blew into camp in a sandstorm. They journeyed on foot to various sites loaded down with equipment, Bandelier digging and classifying, Lummis photographing. Although he became a good photographer, Lummis recognized the limitations of the medium saying "New Mexico, like the dearest woman, cannot be adequately photographed. One can reproduce the features, but not the expression." In 1893 he accompanied Bandelier on an expedition to Peru. Lummis's works on the Southwest derive their authority from Bandelier.

This he never failed to acknowledge. To his first son Amado he gave the middle name of Bandelier and to a posthumous edition of the Swiss's pueblo novel, *The Delight Makers*, he contributed a glowing introduction. Among his scholar friends was also Elliott Coues, the ornithologist and translator of Garcés' journal. Just before his death in 1899, Dr. Coues wrote to the editor of *The Nation*, "I met our friend Lummis among his Indian protegés of Isleta . . . Lummis, Hodge, Winship, and your humble servant, squatting around a campfire, represented, no doubt, more Spanish history of the Southwestern United States from 1539 to date, than had ever before been bunched! (Though we looked like a seedier set of tramps than ever stole a ride on a freight train.)"

These fertile 1890's in which Lummis also began his editorship of *Land of Sunshine*, saw publication of *The Spanish Pio-*

neers, prefaced by Bandelier, a recognition of the Hispanic contribution to the Southwest. It won Lummis the Order of Isabella, conferred on him by the King of Spain, a decoration he proudly wore while dressed in his green corduroy suit. Several more volumes of pueblo folk tales rounded out this productive decade, although Governor Abeita was annoyed with Lummis for his indiscretion in revealing what were intended as confidences about the Tiguan ceremonials.

Lummis's later works have been well described by Edwin Bingham and Dudley Gordon in their books about Don Carlos. Into *Land of Sunshine* its editor poured riches on the Southwest —articles and photographs by himself and others, documents and translations—at the same time that he encouraged new writers and artists such as Mary Austin, Sharlot Hall, Eugene Manlove Rhodes, Ed Borein, and Maynard Dixon. Nearly all remained devoted to their patron. Although Mrs. Austin often called on Lummis for material to use in her books, she snubbed him by dedicating *The Land of Little Rain* "To Eve, *The Comfortress of Unsuccess.*"

Lummis always kept moving ahead, leaving his pioneer works to be continued by others; thus he headed the Public Library only for a time, and although he founded the Southwest Museum, he never directed it. He broke with the trustees of the Southwest Museum when they would not embrace his grand plan for satellite museums throughout the Southwest. He refused ever to compromise, never sought to accumulate money, and deeded his valuable books and papers to the Museum. His visionary enthusiasm never waned. In 1922 he prepared an exhibit for the State Fair in Phoenix, and in an accompanying pamphlet *Save Arizona's Romance,* were included these timeless words: "The higher the intelligence of a state, the more jealously it cherishes and preserves its monuments, its archives, and the tangible relics of its history. The only way is in a museum."

After twenty years of marriage, his second wife divorced Lummis in 1911, although she had left him earlier to stay with Phoebe

Apperson Hearst on her hacienda at Pleasanton and later at the Hotel Victoria in San Francisco. Until her death in 1918 the kindest of the Hearsts sent Eva a monthly check. Mrs. Lummis charged extreme cruelty in the form of abusive language and his refusal to carpet the cold stone floor of El Alisal. The real cause was his infidelity. He was not meant for a monogamous life. At the time of her separation a woman friend wrote to Eva, "What Lummis needs is a master; some Amazon of quiet voice and strong arm to physically conquer him. His amatory nature would grow decent were he well whipped regularly."

His beloved Amado died in childhood of pneumonia, eliciting many expressions of sympathy, including sensitive letters to Eva from Mary Austin. Three other children survived—Turbesé (Tiguan for Sunburst), who went away to Catholic school in the East, Keith who lived with his mother, and Jordan (called Quimu) who stayed with his father at El Alisal and helped with the clerical work. He also attended his father's lectures. Of one to clubwomen on Peru, illustrated with artifacts including a shrunken head, he reported in a letter to his mother in San Francisco that "I guess they liked it but they looked sort of scared." When his father left the Los Angeles Public Library in 1910, Quimu loyally wrote to his mother, "Yes, papa has resigned and I think he is classy to do it. I know he is very glad to be out of that mess of cheap politicians. Of course it will make it pretty hard for him for a long time because of the debts, but he will have a better time and work at the things he likes and work with me and we will be together more here in the place."

Lummis never stopped working, although he gradually wore out from the strain he put on his body. In 1912 he went temporarily blind from jungle fever contracted in Guatemala. *Mesa, Cañon and Pueblo*, published in 1925, was an enlargement of his earlier books. A year before his death from cancer he paid a last visit to New Mexico, and upon his return he wrote to Edgar L. Hewett, the archaeologist, "It was an unspeakable benediction to me to be in my Own Country—among the scenes which have meant so much in my life, and among the peoples whom I love so dearly." Later he wrote of his inability to attend the annual meeting of the School of American Research which he had helped found, "I have had a busy life, an eventful one, a fairly fruitful one. It is crowded in these my last months with innumerable golden memories. I can count the months that are left me, practically on the fingers of one hand."

He knew whereof he wrote. The end was near. The final weeks were spent in compiling a book of essays on the influence of Spain in the New World, published posthumously as *Flowers of our Lost Romance*, and one of his poetry called *A Bronco Pegasus*. A single advance copy of the latter reached him just before he died.

His death and his life were equally courageous. Turbesé and a nurse tended him, and his other children also were there at the last. On November 5, 1928 he wrote for the last time in his journal. "Up at 12:15, blind shower, shave. Fine letter from Amado Chaves. Century announcement of royalty, mostly on Mesa, Cañon and Pueblo, not very big. Belden, director of the Boston Public Library, very apologetic letter, and ordering my Benavides." The reference was to his edition of the New Mexican historical memoir of 1630, translated by Mrs. Edward E. Ayer and illustrated from photographs by Lummis and Vroman and annotated by Hodge.

He rallied and asked his daughter to play the guitar and sing the songs he loved. "Suddenly," she recalled, "he began singing Cinco Años Hace, almost with the old force and vigor. He loved the singing and I played several times afterward. Only about three nights before he died he sang the last verse of 'Believe me if all those endearing young charms' with me."

If death is ever good, his was a good death. His funeral at El Alisal was enlivened by the music he loved, as José Jarias and his men played *Adios Amores*. His ashes were mortared into the granite of the house he built.

What of Dorothea and Eva? They had long since gone their

own ways. Dr. Dorothea married Dr. Ernest Carroll Moore, director of the Normal School which became UCLA. Theirs was a long, happy marriage. Upon her divorce in 1911, Eva settled in Tucson and there two years later she married Courtenay de Kalb, a prominent mining engineer. In 1933 the University of Arizona conferred upon her an honorary doctorate of letters in recognition of her scholarship in Hispanic literature. She lived into her 99th year, surviving Turbesé by a year and survived in turn by Keith and Jordan. Her papers and those of her daughter, rich in memorabilia of the man who so profoundly affected their lives, are in the University of Arizona library.

There I found a book of poems, *For Whispers and Chants*, inscribed to Lummis in the year of his death by the poet, a young Texan who had also come to Los Angeles to seek his fortune. In presenting his book, Jake Zeitlin wrote in it these words: "To Charles Lummis, far out on a trail that I am trying to follow. Native trees and stones should be named for him. Native songs should be made of his long walks and towns should grow up where he made stories. He will never be off the map."

A good epitaph for a great man.

READING LIST

CHARLES F. LUMMIS (1859-1928)

A New Mexico David and Other Stories and Sketches of the Southwest. New York, Scribner, 1891.

A Tramp Across the Continent. New York, Scribner, 1892; Albuquerque, Horn, 1969. Facsimile edition with Introduction by Dudley Gordon.

Some Strange Corners of Our Country; the Wonderland of the Southwest. New York, Century, 1892.

The Spanish Pioneers. Chicago, McClurg, 1893.

The Land of Poco Tiempo. New York, Scribner, 1893; Albuquerque, University of New Mexico Press, 1952. Foreword by Paul A. F. Walter.

The Man Who Married the Moon. New York, Scribner, 1894; reissued as *Pueblo Indian Folk-Stories*, Century, 1910.

The King of the Broncos and Other Stories of New Mexico. New York, Scribner, 1897.

My Friend Will. Chicago, McClurg, 1911; Los Angeles, Cultural Assets Press, 1961. Introduction by Dudley Gordon.

The Enchanted Burro and Other Stories. Chicago, McClurg, 1912.

The Memorial of Fray Alonso de Benavides. Translated by Mrs. Edward E. Ayer. Annotated by Frederick Webb Hodge and Charles F. Lummis. Photographs by Lummis. Chicago, Privately Printed, 1916; Albuquerque, Horn and Wallace, 1965. Facsimile edition.

Mesa, Cañon and Pueblo. New York, Century, 1925.

A Bronco Pegasus. Boston, Houghton Mifflin, 1928.

General Crook and the Apache Wars. Edited by Turbesé Fiske Lummis. Foreword by Dudley Gordon. Flagstaff, Northland Press, 1966.

Bullying the Moqui. Edited by Robert Easton and Mackenzie Brown. Prescott, Prescott College Press, 1968.

EDWIN F. BINGHAM

Charles F. Lummis, Editor of the Southwest. San Marino, Huntington Library, 1955.

W. W. ROBINSON

The Story of the Southwest Museum. Los Angeles, Ward Ritchie Press, 1960.

DUDLEY GORDON

Charles F. Lummis, Crusader in Corduroy. Los Angeles, Cultural Assets Press, 1972.

Photograph of Charles F. Lummis and Turbesé, courtesy of University of Arizona Library Special Collections.

Wolf Song
HARVEY FERGUSSON

All generalities about writers are suspect. And yet one keeps making them, such as The Place of a Writer's Birth is not Intrinsically Meaningful, or A Writer's Creative Arc is a Good Approach to an Understanding of his Work, or Popular Success is Bad for a Writer.

In reading the fifteen books of fiction and nonfiction by Harvery Fergusson, who died in 1971 at the age of 81, I sought the meaning of his life and work by using these generalities for measurement and evaluation.

His birth at Albuquerque on January 28, 1890, as one of four children (including Erna, Lina, and Francis, all of whom became writers), proved significant as he came to be a laureate of New Mexican letters. He found it necessary on reaching manhood, however, to leave his homeland in order to write candidly about it. He lived his remaining years in Washington, New York, and California, returning to New Mexico in the summer for the only things that rivalled writing and women: hunting and fishing.

His creative arc was one of long ascent, reaching zenith in 1954 with his fifteenth and final book, followed by seventeen years of declining powers.

As for popular success, he never knew it. Although several of his books were made into movies and his last was a Literary Guild selection, none brought him wide acclaim or substantial monetary reward. He was thus spared the kind of popular success that destroyed many of his contemporaries—F. Scott Fitzgerald, Sinclair Lewis, Thomas Wolfe, Ernest Hemingway and John Steinbeck.

Yet he was not without recognition. Mencken launched him, Knopf published him. He was praised by his peers, Conrad Richter, Paul Horgan, J. Frank Dobie. For twenty years I kept pointing to his best work at the pinnacle of Southwest literature. This included the novels *Wolf Song, Grant of Kingdom,* and *The Conquest of Don Pedro,* and the nonfictional *Rio Grande* and *Home in the West.*

In these five books is the essential New Mexico. No other writer equalled this achievement. Read as romance or read as history they are true to landscape, life, and love. More than fiction, more than facts alone, they are literature.

I knew Harvey Fergusson during the last two decades of his life. On trips to Berkeley I stole time from University duties to make my way to his book-filled upper flat in a redwood house near campus that had once belonged to Phoebe Apperson Hearst. There over afternoon refreshment we talked of books, writing, and the landscape of New Mexico. His thoughts were orderly, his speech gentle, his judgments balanced. He appeared to have gained the serenity of advancing age.

How little we really know of one another! It was not until after his death when I came to study his papers in the Bancroft Library, that I perceived the inner man concealed behind the calm exterior. In journals kept throughout his life was revealed the heroism of his achievement, his persistence as a writer to whom fame and fortune (perhaps blessedly) never came. Apparent were the points on his arc. Figuratively speaking, *Wolf Song* (1927) came in the springtime, *Grant of Kingdom* (1950) at midsummer, and *The Conquest of Don Pedro* (1954) in the autumn.

His novels represent a triumph of literature over life, their

58

maker dead and gone, his books alive and here. This indeed is the true role of the artist, his personality a transient thing, his work a transformation of the mortal into the lasting.

When I ask who was Harvey Fergusson and how came he to write as he did, my answers come from sources other than his literary remains. Not only from library research, they come from travels in his native land, up and down the Rio Grande and into the Sangre de Cristos, from talks with his sister Erna and with his surviving sister, Lina, and with a friend, and from the reading of reviews and critiques of his work. And from meditation, high in a grove of eucalyptus during restful pauses from pruning the trees.

No writer had a more genuine New Mexican heritage. His maternal grandfather, Franz Huning, came from Germany in 1850 with a Santa Fe caravan, then settled in Albuquerque and founded a mercantile business. His Scotch-Irish father was from Southern planter society, a graduate of Washington and Lee University when General Robert E. Lee was its president. He arrived in Albuquerque as a young lawyer in 1883, two years after the railroad, and became a leading orator and politician, then served in Washington as the Territorial Delegate to Congress.

Home in the West is an autobiography of Harvey Fergusson's early years. It recalls the one described by Lincoln Steffens in *Boy on Horseback*. Both boys loved to escape from family and town and explore the countryside, to ride and hunt and fish. Both were banished to military school and then broke away, Steffens to Europe, Fergusson to his father's alma mater in Virginia. Likewise they disappointed their fathers in their choice of careers, preferring newspaper work to the mercantile business and the legal profession. There the parallel ends. Steffens became a journalist, Fergusson a novelist.

Literary careers don't just happen. They occur because of powerful conjunctions. Such was Harvey Fergusson's with H. L. Mencken, leading writer of the *Baltimore Sun*, editor of *Smart*

Set, and founder of the *American Mercury.* It came about when Fergusson went to Baltimore for his newspaper syndicate to get a story on Mencken's interest in the American language. When the interview was over, interviewee turned on interviewer and learned that he was writing a novel. Mencken's subsequent criticism helped Fergusson to complete it. Mencken also bought an excerpt for publication in *Smart Set.* And finally, he sent the manuscript to his publisher, Alfred A. Knopf who with his wife Blanche was on the way to becoming America's finest publisher.

Thus in 1921 Harvey Fergusson's first book, *The Blood of the Conquerors,* bore the Borzoi imprint which ensured widespread distribution and recognition. It is a novel of contemporary New Mexico where the Hispano and Anglo cultures struggle for dominance. Its modest success was a springboard via New York to screenwriting in Hollywood, enabling Fergusson to bid farewell to journalism. For the next half-century, up to the time of his death, he was a free-lance writer.

Washington was the setting of his next two novels, *Capitol Hill* and *Women and Wives,* satires respectively on public service and private lives. The second is a parable of Fergusson's marriage to a Virginia society girl with the enchanting name of Polly Pretty, which ended when she divorced him. Although he always drew on his own life for material, Fergusson was never baldly autobiographical. He was able to stand aside and see himself as objectively as he saw his other characters. He was also a good craftsman.

In his fourth novel, *Hot Saturday,* he returned to contemporary Albuquerque and succeeded in stirring up a hornet's nest. Thus he learned the dangers of writing novels about his hometown. It proved politic to live elsewhere, in New York for eight years after he left Washington, with summers in the Sangre de Cristos and periodic assignments in Hollywood.

These first four novels were competent, unoriginal books. If he had written only them, Harvey Fergusson would be unread today. They served as apprentice work, leading to the book which

60

catalyzed his powers in a masterpiece of historical-poetical prose. He called it *Wolf Song*. The publication year of 1927 proved to be one of the highest peaks of his life. He married Rebecca Mc-Cann, author of the popular newspaper feature, *The Cheerful Cherub*, only to lose her from pneumonia before the year was out.

Wolf Song was written as a love poem, not to her (although it is the only one of his books to bear a dedication: *For Rebecca*), but rather to the Sangre de Cristos, in the time of the beaver-trapping mountain men who rendezvoused in Taos and at Bent's Fort. His earlier books served to purge Fergusson of the need to deal with himself and to satirize his contemporaries. Now he could go back in history to a wilder, freer time, to a familiar landscape and people it with strong men and women joined in strife and love.

"I approached the past first with a romantic impulse—a wish to create a world out of my own longing," Fergusson wrote later, in an Introduction to *Followers of the Sun*, a reprint in one volume of "A Trilogy of the Santa Fe Trail," including *Wolf Song*, *In Those Days*, and *The Blood of the Conquerors*. "*Wolf Song* was the high point of that romantic impulse in my effort as a writer. This short and simple story is in outline a typical Western romance . . . I aspired to capture something of the heroic drama without sacrificing the real. I pitched my story in a high key, set it to swinging music, let it range the whole gamut of Western adventure—of battle, flight, and rescue, of the struggle of man against the wilderness and man against man. Here, again, one more redskin bit the dust when the hero's trusty rifle cracked, but both the hero and the redskin, I like to believe, are living creatures, born of the earth and not of the literary tradition."

Did he write *Wolf Song* in a cabin high in the Sangres? No, he created it in a back-hallway New York apartment, writing in his lifelong habit of only two to three hours in the morning. Because of his newfound love and a longing for his homeland, and because at age thirty-six he was in the prime of manhood, he was able to infuse his prose with passion and power, so that of all his books, *Wolf Song* is the most ecstatic, although strictly controlled. The writing was spread over seventeen months of 1926-27 in "the greatest burst of mental energy I have ever known."

It was the hardest work he had done, interspersed with anguished diary entries, such as "Confusion and uncertainty are the maladies of my spirit," and "I seem to have lost the shine and swing of the thing." He followed morning writing with afternoon research in the Public Library on Indians and in the Museum of Natural History on wild animals: "Like Lincoln and Poe," he wrote, "I suffer from remorse and apprehension falling into melancholia and rising into ecstasy. The same psychosis is in every creative worker."

By the end of summer he was out of the woods and safely home. On October 5, 1927, he noted, "The Knopfs sent me the advance on *Wolf Song*, so I can live for a few months at least." His wife died in December, having caught cold as they drove in a snowstorm from Salt Lake to spend Christmas in Albuquerque. Guilt for her death haunted Fergusson for the rest of his life.

Mencken did not fail his protégé. In a review in the *American Mercury* he bracketed *Wolf Song* with that other masterpiece of the same year, *Death Comes for the Archbishop*. "The Old Southwest," he said of the former, "is made to palpitate with such light and heat that they are felt almost physically, and the people that gallop across the scene are full of the juices of life."

Years later in a letter to me, Dobie conferred a similar accolade. "I had occasion last night to look for something in Harvey Fergusson's *Wolf Song*, which I rate above Guthrie's *The Big Sky*, as a novel of the mountain men. It is easily among the best half dozen novels of the west, in my estimation. Willa Cather, Conrad Richter, nor anyone else has equalled Fergusson in the swiftness, economy, and prose rhythm of chapter one in *Wolf Song*."

Among the few letters that Harvey Fergusson kept is one from Dobie, written in 1950 after reading *Grant of Kingdom*. "I guess the first book of yours I read was *Blood of the Conquerors*," Dobie reminisced. "I have had my classes in *Life and Literature of the Southwest* buy and read *Rio Grande* year after year. Always when my class got to the Mountain Men I would read aloud Stanley Vestal's ballad *Fandango* and the opening chapter or so of *Wolf Song*. One summer I had a class of 150 or so, mostly school teachers, a few of them rather elderly. When I got to 'Hump yourself, you goddam mule,' I saw one of them stiffening. When I got to 'Is that all she can do?' I saw her stiffen more. At the last 'Is that all she can do?' she got up and walked out as if she were going to experience an immaculate conception. Nobody will ever surpass the rhythm of *Wolf Song*. It is a classic in the purest sense of the word."

Where can a writer go after reaching such a peak? Fergusson was not written out, although twenty-three years were to pass before he again equalled this work. In two more novels, *In Those Days* and *Footloose McGarnigal*, he dealt with New Mexico's past and present on a level below that of *Wolf Song*. Those two decades, racked by Depression and War, saw him continue to live quietly and write steadily, eight more books of an extraordinary variety. Though he lived fully, Fergusson never wasted himself. The $500 a week paid him intermittently by Hollywood he prudently invested. This enabled him in 1931 to settle in Berkeley, drawn there by the climate, the city across the bay, and the library of the great university. His wants and needs were modest and few.

Although he never lived there again, his native state was always in his blood. "The history of my own region became as real to me as my own experience." Combining historical research and personal knowledge, he wrote *Rio Grande*, his first work of nonfiction. He saw that the Great River *is* New Mexico, the determinant of that land's past, present, and future. The book stands as one of the best works about New Mexico, and it is the only one of his books that remains in print.

The 1930's were not profitable years for most publishers and authors. The Knopf-Fergusson combination was no exception. Fergusson's next book was unexpected. *Modern Man: His Belief and Behavior* was a philosophical essay. When Alfred Knopf read it in manuscript, he was puzzled, and so was Mencken. Whereupon Knopf wrote to Fergusson a strong, friendly letter, declaring that the book would interest few people, least of all readers who wanted more Southwest books from the author of *Wolf Song,* and that its publication would be a mistake for both publisher and author. Fergusson rejected his publisher's advice to put it aside and write another novel. Knopf yielded in what was decidedly an indulgence. *Modern Man* appeared in 1936, failed to sell, and was remaindered. When his next novel, *The Life of Riley,* saw Fergusson dealing again with contemporary characters in a New Mexican setting, a vein that he had mined out, his relationship with Knopf came to an end.

Eight years passed before Fergusson published another book. *Home in the West: an Inquiry into my Origins* proved that they had not been sterile years. It is one of the best autobiographies of a writer's formative years.

Then with an odd detour in *People and Power: a Study of Political Behavior in America,* came another publishing dud, although it did have a *succès d'estime.* Fergusson was determined to please himself rather than the public (albeit a small one) who wanted more books in his Southwestern mode. We admire his determination to fulfill his creative destiny in his own way. That he had reached a low point in sales prospects did not deter him.

"It were better to read, think, and look until I am broke," he confided in his journal, "than to write a half-baked book. Start no book until one has been urgently conceived in a period of mental excitement. One ought to come sometime in the spring or early summer. If it doesn't, I can only try some other way to make a living." And then, defiantly, "It will not do to be thrifty, industrious, or provident." Which of course he really was.

His time of triumph came when the longed-for period of excitement arrived. Thoughts of his natal state were responsible. "Whenever I think of New Mexico (and my own youth)," he wrote, "I feel that haunting, nostalgic sadness that lives in the long past—the sadness of vanished worlds, of former selves, of finished things living only in memory."

Success followed when he left the present and plunged into the history of his region, to return again to the Sangre de Cristos. For thirty years he had been carrying the seed of his next book, the novel he was to call *Grant of Kingdom*. As far back as 1920 he had begun to make notes on the Maxwell Land Grant (the two million-acre holding in northeastern New Mexico granted originally by the King of Spain) unsure whether to use them in writing history or fiction.

Wolf Song had ended with the hero's getting this land along with Lola Salazar as her dowry. What had he done with it? What had it done to him? There was the story. The new novel thus became a sequel to *Wolf Song*, the springtime tale expanded in midsummer. Whereas the first novel was short and swift like a mountain stream, its successor flowed longer, fuller, more complex, and extended in time, epic rather than lyric: The foreword to *Grant of Kingdom* tells of its conception:

"More than twenty years ago I visited a beautiful valley at the foot of the Rocky Mountains and found there the crumbling ruin of a great house. Its walls were then still standing a few feet high, with great roof beams rotting in the rubble. I could count the rooms and there were thirty-eight of them, including a dining hall that might have seated a hundred guests."

"When I learned that a man had ridden into a wilderness where no human habitation had ever stood before, had built that great house, founded a society and ruled it as long as he lived, my imagination was stirred."

Fergusson had found the house built by Lucien Maxwell on the dowry land brought to their marriage by Luz Beaubien of Taos. Its ruins still stand in Cimarrón.

On a library shelf are footnoted, bibliographed, and indexed histories of the Maxwell Grant and its violent dissolution after the death of its ruler. In them are the facts. On a nearby shelf is the novel, a romantic fleshing of the skeleton of history. What riches, to be able to choose between fact and fiction, better yet to read both; and best of all, to go up river to Taos, then cross the Sangres to the lands of Lucien Maxwell and Harvey Fergusson and there, in the highest heart of the Southwest, to savor *Grant of Kingdom* and *Wolf Song*.

Their setting is not fictive. It is the novelist's homeland, beloved from boyhood. Between college and journalism, Harvey worked as a timber cruiser for the Forest Service. The Sangre de Cristos were his domain. When he came to write of them, he was more than a historical novelist, he was a man whose authority derived from the earth itself in a grant of power.

Grant of Kingdom is told by a narrator, and it ends with his return to the scene long after to talk with the surviving inhabitants. The closing paragraph expresses the author's credo, couched in grave, musical prose: "To me the droning tales of these old-timers had the quality of elegy. I felt as though I were witnessing the process by which the past becomes a beloved myth, simplified in memory so that one may see the meanings that are always obscured by the noise and dust of the present. The sleepy inertia of the little town made its past seem truly heroic. In the days when I had known it and before, a great gust of passion and energy had struck this place and blown itself out and left in its wake the ruin of a proud house and a legend in the memories of aging men."

At age sixty Harvey Fergusson had reached his second creative peak. He did not attain it alone. The faith of his new publisher, William Morrow and Co., was a factor. Another was his friendship with Quail Hawkins, a writer of children's books. Since the death of his second wife, Fergusson had not married again. From 1949 until his death he was sustained by the devotion of this younger woman.

In his last book, a novel called *The Conquest of Don Pedro*, he came down from the mountain to the river valley, left the trapper to write of the trader. It is his ripest book, his last harvest. This novel can be criticized as weaker in form and structure than its two best predecessors. It is a loose series of episodes and chronicles. Strong books make their own rules. We read it for its wisdom, its colorful setting along the lower river between Albuquerque and El Paso, *el rio abajo*, in the years after the Civil War before the railroad came.

Once again Fergusson drew on his own background as well as on the history of New Mexico. The story is of Leo Mendes, a Jewish peddler who came west for his health and "conquered" the river village of Don Pedro with a store that grew into a mercantile empire. Fergusson had models: one was Charles Ilfeld, whose trading company a century after its founding is today one of the Southwest's greatest. Another was his own grandfather, Franz Huning, the non-Jewish German immigrant who prospered as clerk, trader, merchant. There was a third: himself, as he was and as he dreamed of being. "Experience and wish fulfilment," he once wrote, "seem to me always inextricably mingled in the material of fiction."

Mendes' wisdom, his belief in nonviolence, his feeling for the river-lands, and the passion and tenderness of his loves—these are hallmarks of the novelist's genius. "My whole growth and progress as a novelist," he wrote, "has been a growing power to portray women." This power reaches its height in *The Conquest of Don Pedro*, in the portrayal of three very different women.

Don Pedro proved to be his most financially rewarding book. Choice by the Literary Guild earned $30,000, shared equally by author and publisher.

All triumph is at a cost. That of *Don Pedro* was high. What reads easily and flows serenely was written over two years in pain and anguish. "I start easily, often with material that has deep nostalgic appeal," he declared, "but my characters carry me always toward difficulty and doubt."

Completion of his books left Fergusson depleted and de-

67

pressed. From that which followed *Don Pedro*, in spite of its sales success, there was no recovery. Illness and operations brought a part of his life to an end. Creative decline followed, though he never stopped writing. One final novel was completed, its subject women. It was the sad lot of a few friends who read it in manuscript to tell him that it should not be published. Wise as he was in women's ways, it was only when he related them to the landscape and lore of their native country that they flamed into life.

For a paperback edition of *Rio Grande* he wrote a new Preface called "Albuquerque Revisited" in which he declared, "If I were young and had strong legs, it would please me now to live once more in my native town. . . . It is a great city in the making, and I know of no other place where the wilderness is so close to the city, or where the primitive survives so close to civilization. This would make it a congenial home to me."

As his strength waned he could no longer climb the stairs of his home. Writing became difficult. He brought his journal to a close, those faithful notebooks that contained his hopes and fears all through his creative life. On the 29th of December 1965 he pencilled these final words: "This is no longer either a diary or an account book because I have not the energy to keep it up."

Harvey Fergusson's last years brought widening recognition. Critics in California, Arizona, New Mexico, Texas, and as far away as South Dakota, hailed him as the dean of Southwestern novelists. Although this pleased him, he had gone beyond praise or blame. He died on August 27, 1971. At his request Whitman's "The Last Invocation" was read at a memorial service in Berkeley. His sister and his friend chose Harvey's only published poem, "Timberline," to accompany it.

Article III of his Last Will and Testament bequeathed to kinfolk and friend his guns, rods and reels, his boots and waders.

> *Home is the sailor, home from sea,*
> *And the hunter home from the hill.*

68

READING LIST

HARVEY FERGUSSON (*1890-1971*)

Wolf Song. New York, Knopf, 1927.

Rio Grande. New York, Knopf, 1933; with a new preface, "Albuquerque Revisited," New York, Apollo, 1967.

Followers of the Sun, a Trilogy of the Santa Fe Trail: Wolf Song, In Those Days, The Blood of the Conquerors. New York, Knopf, 1936.

Home in the West; an Inquiry into My Origins. New York, Duell, 1945.

Grant of Kingdom. New York, Morrow, 1950.

The Conquest of Don Pedro. New York, Morrow, 1954.

JAMES K. FOLSOM

Harvey Fergusson. Austin, Steck-Vaughn, 1969.

Photograph of Harvey Fergusson by Cedric Wright, courtesy of Lina Fergusson Browne.

Edge of Taos Desert; Winter in Taos
MABEL DODGE LUHAN

Although Taos was not at the end of the great historic trails, the cultural trails of a later time led there, as in California they led to Carmel. Garrard was the first to sense and describe the charm of Taos, and he nearly succumbed to it. Kit Carson fell lastingly under its spell. "No man who has seen the women, heard the bells, or smelled the piñon smoke of Taos," he swore, "will ever be able to leave." Kit didn't. He took an Hispano wife, died there, and is buried in the cemetery that bears his name.

Taos of fifty years ago differed little from the Taos of long ago when the first Spaniards emerged onto the plain from the gorge of the Rio Grande and saw the twin pueblos at the base of the Sangre de Cristos. The whiskey-roaring Yankee trappers changed it not. The painters of the 1890's found it the perfect hideaway.

Remoteness, idyllic setting, altitude of nearly 8,000 feet, and the rhythmic way of life of the Taos Indians, formed an ambience similar to the one the early artists and writers found in Carmel. Such an atmosphere is a delicate thing, destroyed by crowds and commerce. Today Carmel and Taos prosper in the tinsel aftermath of their golden age.

For nearly half a century from her arrival there in 1916 until her death in 1962, Taos was dominated culturally by a single woman—Mabel Ganson Evans Dodge Sterne Luhan. Her love for Taos was deep, abiding, and true, her books about it the best that she wrote. No one has written better about Taos. Her influence was strong and widespread. It was she who summoned D. H. Lawrence to New Mexico, and although she did not succeed in replacing Frieda as Lawrence's inspiration, she did set the scene for some of his best work, a novel, stories, and essays.

Her spacious home became a sanctuary for writers and artists. She was ever hopeful that they would give voice and image to the timeless Taos she loved. She even drew the recluse Robinson Jeffers from Carmel. He did not reroot in Taos. Although he and his wife and their twin sons spent several summers as her guests, his was a genius that required ocean granite, cypress and fog on which to thrive. Only a single poem came from his visits, called "New Mexican Mountain," and it was not to her specifications, for it described the white tourists (such as she) as "pilgrims from civilization, anxiously seeking beauty, religion, poetry; pilgrims from the vacuum."

To the public she was known as the rich woman who married a blanket Indian. It was her fourth marriage and though the most unlikely it lasted forty years until her death. He died a year later. "I always loved the slightest appearance of masterfulness in a man," she wrote before coming to Taos, "because it hinted at an opportunity for me to exercise my strength." In Antonio Lujan of Taos Pueblo she met her master. He retained the original spelling of his surname, whereas she phoneticized it.

I was long prejudiced against Mabel Luhan. It began in 1932 with her book about Lawrence called *Lorenzo in Taos*—a willful work more about her than him. Although he recognized her gift of New Mexico, he could not abide her bullying, she who by the power of money and will had always succeeded in getting what she wanted. Here is how Lawrence damned her in a letter written in 1922, after his arrival at Taos and escape to a mountain ranch, a dozen miles distant. It was written to his German mother-in-law.

"You have asked about Mabel Dodge: American, rich, only child, from Buffalo on Lake Erie, bankers, forty-two years old, has had three husbands—one Evans (dead), one Dodge (divorced), and one Maurice Sterne (a Jew, Russian, painter, young, also divorced). Now she has an Indian, Tony, a stout chap. She has lived much in Europe—Paris, Nice, Florence—is a little famous in New York and little loved, very intelligent as a woman, another 'culture-carrier,' likes to play the patroness, hates the white world and loves the Indians out of hate, is very 'generous,' wants to be 'good' and is very wicked, has a terrible will-to-power. She wants to be a witch and at the same time a Mary of Bethany at Jesus's feet—a big, white crow, a cooing raven of ill-omen, a little buffalo."

I came upon that description in *Not I but the Wind*, Frieda Lawrence's reply to Mabel's book, and then upon meeting Frieda herself a few years later, I was even more prejudiced against Mabel Luhan, so that when I first came to Taos we did not pause but hurried on to the Lawrence ranch on the aspened shoulder of Lobo Mountain. By then Frieda and Mabel had made peace.

"Would you like to meet her?" Frieda asked.

"No, thank you," I replied. "One Valkyrie is enough."

That jovial frau laughed from the pit of her stomach and exclaimed, "Ja! Ja!"

Mabel Luhan's tasteless book on Lawrence was followed by a massive four-volume set called *Intimate Memories*. The first, *Background*, was about growing up in Buffalo and marriage which ended when her husband was killed in a hunting accident, leaving her with baby John. I found it of minor interest.

The second volume, *European Experiences*, was better reading. It told of her next marriage and years of *fin de siècle* living as the mistress of a Florentine villa. It came alive when she wrote of Duse, Stein, Toklas, Picasso, Matisse, and Craig; of neurotic orgies of clothes-buying in Paris, and of that river city's fragrance of coal smoke and Chanel.

73

In 1912 she returned to America to give her son an education in his native country. It was Lincoln Steffens who suggested that she hold weekly free speech gatherings in her New York apartment. She was willing, admitting that she had "always known how to make rooms that had power in them." Her open house discussions proved exciting. The police had to be called to control the crowds that wanted in.

It was a restless time of popular radicalism which she recounted in her third volume, *Movers and Shakers*. In addition to Steffens, her salon welcomed other angry young men including Walter Lippman, Hutchins Hapgood, Max Eastman, and John Reed with whom she had a passionate affair. It was she who wrote the first article on Gertrude Stein, although she thought there was truth in the suspicion that Miss Stein's style had originated with a typist's warming-up exercises. Mary Austin and Isadora Duncan were among her friends.

She married Maurice Sterne as an afterthought, for they had been living together for some time. After the ceremony she reported this conversation:

"Shouldn't we have a little honeymoon, darling?" He gave a gusty, involuntary laugh, half-nervous, half-tender.

"Oh Maurice! *You* go. I'd rather stay here and go on with what I'm doing. Where do you want to go?"

Maurice wanted to go west, to a friend's camp in Wyoming where his stepson was also summering. So off he went on his honeymoon, while she stayed at home on hers. When he returned to New York, she was even less inclined to a connubial existence.

"It's no use, Maurice," she said. "We can't make a go of it here. One of us must leave. And *I* want to stay here. I'm going to send you out to the Southwest. I've heard there are wonderful things to paint. Indians."

So the obedient Maurice packed up again and went off to Santa Fe, bearing letters of introduction from Mabel, including one to Lorenzo Hubbell, the great trader, at Ganado.

Mabel continued with psychoanalytic therapy administered by the celebrated Dr. Brill. She also frequented mediums and masseuses. She was at a loose end of living.

Then a medium saw Indians in her life. She dreamed of an Indian face in some green leaves. The climax came when Maurice wrote from Santa Fe,

"Dearest girl, do you want an object in life? Save the Indians, that art-culture—reveal it to the world! It would be the easiest thing in the world to get a number of Indians from different parts of the country to perform at New York and above all at Washington, and to make the American people realize that there are such things as other forms of civilization besides ours. I saw a wonderful dance yesterday."

Mabel was intrigued. She sensed a new mission in life. She decided to go and see what Maurice was up to. What was planned as a 14-day trip lasted forty-six years. The Southwest took her and held her. It also purified her and precipitated two books that are her monument: *Edge of Taos Desert* and *Winter in Taos.*

Whereas her earlier writing was primarily about herself—and she was of limited interest, except to herself—in her Southwest books, Taos was her unique concern. Santa Fe? Merely a place to which one telephoned for supplies. Albuquerque? I don't believe she mentions it anywhere in her writing. Taos was her sole domain.

Edge of Taos Desert tells of her coming to the Southwest and the transition between Russian and Indian husbands. It was 1923 before she was actually married to Antonio Lujan, for he too was married, to a fellow Taoseña. Her writing about him is restrained and discreet, as her earlier writing about men was not, for, she said, "I feel increasingly obliged to leave most of it unwritten, not only the secret aspects of his religious life and experience, but the secret intimacies of our own personal life together."

How came she to Taos when Santa Fe was her objective? Upon rejoining Maurice in the capital, she discovered that she had been preceded there by other cultural arbiters. She could not tolerate competition. "I'm going to Taos," she declared. "Why?" her husband asked. "Because someone in New York said I should see Taos," she replied. She couldn't remember who it was.

Then when everyone told her that nothing was there except a dusty plaza and a few saloons opening on to it, she was determied to go to Taos. And so she hired a local driver and his Model T, and with Maurice for ballast they set out on a long day's drive over the primitive road to Taos, seventy-five miles to the north.

Her first view of Taos came at sundown, as they switchbacked out of the river gorge on the dangerous road and gazed over the sage and rabbit-brush plain to the purple Sangres. It was dark when they reached the village. The winter night was cold. Accommodations were wretched. And yet this woman who had known every comfort and luxury was undeterred. Even as Jeffers came without knowing it to his inevitable place at Carmel, so came she to Taos.

That same night she ventured forth by flashlight to seek a place to live. The eccentric Doc Martin passed her on to his even queerer neighbor, Mr. Manby, an Englishman who had come to Taos with a dream of transforming it into a stately domain. With an Indian's help he had transplanted thousands of cottonwoods along the road to the pueblo, careful to select only the male trees. When another man planted female cottonwoods nearby, Manby was furious because of their litter of flying fluff.

Mabel persuaded Mr. Manby (against his will) to rent half of his rambling house to her, and there she settled and there she stayed, until eventually Tony led her to buy land adjoining the pueblo and build thereon a house that grew by rooms and stages into an hacienda. Over the years many writers came and went, including Mary Austin and Willa Cather, both of whom drew on the Taos scene.

Whereas *Edge of Taos Desert* presents the outlines of her coming to Taos, *Winter in Taos* is a homely book, filled with the simple details of daily life; of birds, dogs, and cats, the grains in the fields, the system of water rationing, the communal rhythm of the pueblo, and above all the seasons and weathers—the explosion of spring, the summer fragrance of goldenrod and wild plum, the aspen colors of autumn, and finally the blanket of winter. It is quite simply a beautiful book. In it Mabel Luhan came finally to the world outside herself.

A last book, *Taos and its Artists,* reproduces paintings and biographies of the men and women who gave the village its fame. She also used the work of photographers to embellish her books. Thus we see that Ansel Adams, Edward Weston, Ernest Knee, and Laura Gilpin, employed their camera lens with artistry equal to the painters'.

Taos has been many things to different peoples down through the centuries since the first puebleños settled at the foot of Taos Mountain for its unfailing flow of water from Blue Lake. No wonder that snow-fed body of water was deemed sacred.

I don't know whether Mabel Luhan recognized it—probably not—but the best of all books about the Taos Indians came from a maverick writer, Frank Waters, who remained aloof from what Lawrence called "Mabeltown." His *The Man Who Killed the Deer* is the classic novel of the pueblo and its conflict with the Anglos.

Throughout the years after my first visit to Taos in 1940, I returned time and again to that upland village and saw it becoming a town. In the summer of 1956 I had a farewell tea with Frieda Lawrence, six weeks before she died. I never met Mabel Luhan. Her net allowed such little fish as I to swim freely in and out of Taos' waters. My place of rendezvous was the nook that seemed to me the village's heart of hearts, the tiny Taos Book Shop. There I came to know its owners, Claire Morrill and Genevieve Janssen, who have partnered the shop for a quarter century.

In later years Mabel Luhan grew withdrawn and more eccentric, living strictly on her own terms. The gate to the Big House, crowned by a bronze Indian head by Maurice Sterne, bore a sign which declared that tourists were not welcome. When she drove out in a curtained car with white-sheeted Tony and driver up front, Mrs. Luhan occupied the back seat alone. Only she received curb service from the Taos Book Shop. When invited to parties, she came not; when uninvited, she came.

After the 1930's she wrote no more about Taos, at least not for publication, except for letters on civic matters to *El Crepusculo*, the weekly newspaper. She deplored the deterioration of Taos into a modern town, lit by neon and deafened by jukebox and swarming with tourists. A proposal to cut down the cottonwoods on the road to the pueblo provoked her to eloquent ire.

Her novelist son John Evans (*Andrew's Harvest* and *Shadows Flying*) had attended Yale and it was there that his mother's papers and correspondence, her published and unpublished manuscripts, were deposited. They weighed three-quarters of a ton. Her Taos benefactions included a hospital, a bandstand, a collection of santos and thousands of books to the Harwood Foundation, and many anonymous private charities. More lasting than all are the books she wrote about the place she loved.

Mabel Luhan lies in the Kit Carson Memorial Cemetery, Antonio Lujan in the graveyard within the pueblo church's walls. In spring the wild iris blooms in both.

READING LIST

MABEL DODGE LUHAN (1879-1962)
Lorenzo in Taos. New York, Knopf, 1932.
Winter in Taos. New York, Harcourt, 1935.
Edge of Taos Desert. New York, Harcourt, 1937. Vol. 4 of her *Intimate Memories*.
Taos and its Artists. New York, Duell, 1947.

CLAIRE MORRILL
A Taos Mosaic; Portrait of a New Mexico Village. Albuquerque, University of New Mexico Press, 1973.
Photograph of Mabel Dodge Luhan by Edward Weston, courtesy of Beinecke Library, Yale University.

The Plumed Serpent

D. H. LAWRENCE

Half a century has passed since a correspondence began between a woman of determination in Taos, New Mexico and a writer of genius in Taormina, Sicily. She had read his book, *Sea and Sardinia*, and knew it for one of the best travel books ever written—an unpretentious account of a week's trip across the Mediterranean island, yet charged in every line with electricity.

"I wanted him to know Taos," she recalled after the writer's death, "before it became exploited and spoiled, before good roads would let in the crowds."

Thus was set in motion the machinery that brought D. H. Lawrence to the Southwest and enriched the literature of the region. "I called him there," Mabel Dodge Luhan continued, "but he did not do what I called him to do. He did another thing."

This he did—and the writing that came from his Southwest experience as a result of his own vision was a greater thing than to have become a lackey of that rich manipulator whose meddling with writers and artists created what a wag once called Chaos in Taos.

The credit is hers, however, for having lured Lawrence to the Southwest. In some ways it became his Promised Land, the refuge that he had vainly sought the world around and to which he tried in turn to bring disciples. He responded to it with a wealth of creative work—poems, essays, stories, novels—that climaxed his prolific career before it ended at age forty-five. If he had lived, northern New Mexico would probably have been his final home. He died in France in 1930, kept by illness from returning to his ranch northwest of Taos. It was a property he had accepted from Mrs. Luhan, paid for with the manuscript of *Sons and Lovers*.

Persuading Lawrence to come to New Mexico proved difficult even for the magnetic Mabel. He was mulish. At the point of coming he backed away, turned about and went off in the opposite direction, first to Ceylon and then to Australia. She bided her time, however, knowing the world to be round; and so eventually he arrived in California by ship from Down Under. The train brought him and his wife Frieda to Lamy, and thence to Santa Fe.

"The moment I saw the brilliant, proud morning shine high up over the deserts of Santa Fe," he wrote, "something stood still in my soul, and I started to attend. There was a certain magnificence in the high-up day, a certain eagle-like royalty. In the magnificent fierce morning of New Mexico one sprang awake, a new part of the soul woke up suddenly, and the old world gave way to a new."

As a writer, D. H. Lawrence was the opposite of Mary Austin, who said that it took her years to assimilate a region before she could write about it. Not Lawrence. He had the power of instantaneous perception and assimilation. It was said of him, in essentially truthful exaggeration, that he could arrive in a city for the first time, take a taxi from station to hotel, draw the curtains of his room, and then sit down and write a perceptive essay about the place. His brief stay in Australia produced the novel *Kangaroo*, hailed by Australians as one of the best about their land.

Lawrence was in the Southwest—including New and Old Mexico and Arizona—only part of the time between 1922 and 1925, and yet his work about those places remains of lasting value. He never settled down. And he was ever a storm center. Designing women such as Mrs. Luhan competed with Frieda for his attention. Neurotic men were also attracted. He grew increasingly ill. World War I had destroyed whatever idealistic hope he had once had for a peaceful world. He was driven by genius on what he called a "savage pilgrimage."

And yet nothing kept him from writing. He was the author of scores of books and hundreds of articles, essays, and poems. He was a voluminous letter-writer and a good painter. He could cook and sew and keep house. In the years since his death a vast biocritical literature has grown up around his life and work. He is in the pantheon of English literature.

Lawrence was a born writer and by constant writing he made himself a better one. His compulsion to write was as reflexive as his breathing. Yet this alone does not make a great writer. He also had something meaningful to say about life, about men and women, and of both the visible world of the senses and the invisible world of the mind. He was a student, a critic, a philosopher, and also a good botanist.

The Southwest's impact on him was immediate, strong, and creative. And yet he was not overwhelmed by it nor moved to rhapsodizing. He had both near and far vision, and was able to observe the minute details against the panoramic background.

I mentioned the electrical charge that is found in Lawrence's writing. This brings us to the mystery of style. What is it? Or rather, why is it? We can analyze the components—a writer's choice of words, his rhythms of phrase and paragraph, we can study his carpentry and craft. That's the *what* of it. *Why* Lawrence wrote as he did, whether of England, Italy, Sardinia, Ceylon, Australia, or the Southwest, so that regardless of place or subject, the prose is unmistakably his and no other's—aye, there's the mystery.

Lawrence's first writing about the Southwest was inspired by the Indians. He arrived at Taos in September 1922 at the time of the annual fiesta on the Jicarilla Apache Reservation. Hardly before he could unpack, Mabel sent him off to the event in the charge of her husband, Tony.

This was the greatest of all Southwestern Indian ceremonials, to which the Jicarillas invited their fellow tribes, including Utes from Colorado and Navajos from Arizona. Their reservation in northwestern New Mexico was not far from Taos, yet because of the rough country and primitive roads, the round trip took five days.

The barbaric spectacle, especially the hypnotic drumming, had a profound effect on Lawrence. Henceforth nearly everything he wrote about the Southwest bore evidence of this. Later Lawrence witnessed the Antelope and Snake dances on the Hopi Reservation in Arizona and the Corn and Deer dances at the Taos and Santo Domingo pueblos.

In the beginning he hoped to write a novel of northern New Mexico. "I shall be so glad if I can write an American novel from that centre," he had replied to Mrs. Luhan in the course of their correspondence. This he never did. When later they quarreled, she believed it was to spite her that he made Old rather than New Mexico the setting of *The Plumed Serpent*. He probably did want to spite her, but his reasons for choosing Old Mexico were deeper than that.

As is often true of writers, Lawrence wrote best when he was able to withdraw from social involvement and then distill the essence of the experiences he had undergone. Here is how Frieda put it: "Our lives, Lawrence's and mine, are so easy if nobody makes any mischief."

Mabel Dodge Luhan was a great mischief-maker.

The Lawrences' Kiowa Ranch, twenty miles from Taos, was a sanctuary—in the temperate times of year. At an altitude of 8,500 feet, it was snowbound in winter. This was a reason for their seeking the sun in Old Mexico, as well as to get away from "Mabeltown." The ranch appears in much of his New Mexican writing, in essays and poems, and it serves as setting for the final part of the short novel called *St. Mawr*.

A story entitled *The Princess* is the masterpiece of his New Mexicana and is also one of the finest of his tales. Its origin was ordinary enough—merely a horseback trip he took into the

Sangre de Cristo range. This wilderness setting he used for a symbolic story of a maiden lady and an Hispano guide. Here is the essence of his genius for the description of nature and the sexual conflict between a primitive man and a sophisticated woman, between the native and the foreign, instinct and intellect. It is a touchstone for all Southwestern writing.

A passage from it will illustrate my meaning when I said that Lawrence had both near and far vision. Here is how he described the land in autumn: "They emerged on a bare slope, and the trail wound through fragile aspen-stems. Here a wind swept, and some of the aspens were already bare. Others were fluttering their discs of pure, solid yellow leaves, so *nearly* like petals, while the slope ahead was one soft, glowing fleece of daffodil yellow; fleecy like a golden foxskin, and yellow as daffodils alive in the wind and the high mountain sun.

"She paused and looked back. The near great slopes were mottled with gold and dark hue of spruce like some unsinged eagle, and the light lay gleaming upon them. Away through the gap of the canyon she could see the pale blue of the egg-like desert, with the crumpled crack of the Rio Grande canyon. And far, far off, the blue mountains like a fence of angels on the horizon."

When it came to characters for his fiction, Lawrence was uncreative. He used people at hand, usually those he disliked. Thus the woman of *The Princess* is said to have been suggested by the Honorable Dorothy Brett, a titled Englishwoman who followed Lawrence to Taos. Of all the disciples, she is the only one left, still living there in old age and enjoying a considerable reputation as a painter.

Lawrence's "revenge" on Mabel was to carry her off fictively to Old Mexico and in a masterful story called *The Woman Who Rode Away* offer her up as the sacrificial victim of a remote tribe of Indians. To compound this injury to his erstwhile hostess, Lawrence used as the final ceremonial setting a cave Mrs. Luhan had once showed him in the Arroyo Seco near Taos. This story ranks with *The Princess* at the zenith of his Southwest writing.

Lawrence and Frieda first went to Mexico in the early part of 1923. The first month was spent in sightseeing in and around Mexico City, all the while he was absorbing new material, including a bullfight. His disgust at the spectacle came into the opening episode of his Mexican novel. A Mexican diplomat and an American woman archaeologist served as "sources" for him. At the same time he read avidly in the literature of Aztec and Mayan religion and the history of Mexico and its revolutions which never ceased to threaten the country.

When he became saturated, they found a house on Lake Chapala, near Guadalajara. "I felt I had a novel simmering in me," he wrote to a friend in England, "so came here, to this big lake, to see if I could write it."

He did indeed. In a month of sustained creativity, he had written ten chapters totalling 250 pages. Lawrence preferred to write out of doors, seated on the ground, with his back against a tree. He used a big barreled, red fountain pen, rapidly filling the pages of student exercise books with beautifully legible script. Thus it was that he worked each day on the lakefront, under a willow or pepper tree, while the village life teemed around him. He was annoyed only when his red beard and gaunt face caused peons to whisper "Cristo! Cristo!"

Frieda's memoirs recall their life at this time: "My enthusiasm for bathing in the lake faded considerably when one morning a huge snake rose yards high, it seemed to me, only a few feet away. At the end of the patio we had the family Lawrence describes in the novel. I tried my one attempt at civilizing those Mexican children, but when they asked me one day, 'Do you have lice too, Niña?' I gave up."

Whatever conflicts may have disturbed his inner being, Lawrence's writing flowed from his pen in unbroken serenity. Seven years after his death I had the experience of cataloging the mass of his manuscripts that had been left to Frieda. It was clear in perusing those thousands of pages that writing was for him a triumphant act, a kind of daily purification ritual.

By the end of June the novel was finished "near enough to leave." He and Frieda went to New Jersey to be near his publisher in New York, and then she proceeded alone to England. She had become alienated by his continual involvement with followers. It was their first and last serious separation. Lawrence went to California and spent several weeks in Los Angeles and Santa Monica, then drifted back to Guadalajara, via Palm Springs, Nogales and Alamos, travelling by train, Model T Ford, and horseback. He was at a sterile loose-end without Frieda.

He finally yielded and rejoined her in Europe, and then persuaded her to return with him to the New Mexican ranch. There the summer of 1924 proved to be one of his supreme creative periods, during which he wrote *The Princess*, *The Woman Who Rode Away*, and *St. Mawr*, any one of which would have been a good season's work.

Once again, however, there was trouble with Mabel. She was determined that Lawrence write about *her* Taos. He resisted by fleeing again with Frieda to Mexico. The weather was the reason he gave. "I want to go south, where there is no autumn, where the cold doesn't crouch over one like a snow-leopard waiting to pounce."

This time, deciding that Lake Chapala was too touristy, he went instead to Oaxaca, a goodly distance south of Mexico City, where he rewrote his Mexican novel. By January 1925 he informed his agent that "it will probably make you open your eyes —or close them; but I like it very much indeed."

He called it "Quetzalcoatl," but his publisher, Alfred A. Knopf, preferred translation to *The Plumed Serpent*. This was the ancient god and legendary ruler of the Toltec and, in a poetic sense, the symbol of Mexico. Lawrence's theme was a revolutionary revival of the archaic religion.

This stay at Oaxaca, during which he was photographed by Edward Weston, proved to be the last great creative period of Lawrence's life. Even the long novel was not enough to contain his abundance. He also wrote essays on their everyday life which, together with pieces on the Indian dances of Arizona and New Mexico, form the volume called *Mornings in Mexico*, a book to shelve alongside his other travel classics, *Twilight in Italy* and *Sea and Sardinia*.

Except for the autumnal *Lady Chatterley's Lover*, written in Tuscany and filled with nostalgia for his English origins, *The Plumed Serpent* was Lawrence's last big work. Its creation nearly cost his life. Upon finishing it he was laid low by what he variously called malaria, grippe, or typhoid. It was something more serious—tuberculosis in the third stage. In her memoirs Frieda tells of how near he came to death.

" 'You'll bury me in this cemetery here,' " he would say, grimly."

"No, no," I laughed. "It's such an ugly cemetery, don't you think of it. And that night he said to me, 'But if I die, nothing has mattered but you, nothing at all.' I got him better by putting hot sandbags on him, that seemed to comfort his tortured inside."

The doctors gave him a year to live. He lived another five.

The Plumed Serpent was published in 1926. It provoked violent criticism, and angered the Mexican diplomat Lawrence had drawn upon in the book. "Genius?" he exclaimed later in reviewing Witter Bynner's memoir of Lawrence entitled *Journey With Genius*, "Second-rate idiot!"

The usual verdict has been that the novel is an ambitious failure, although there have been those who disagreed, notably Katherine Anne Porter, herself the author of classic Mexican stories, who hailed it as a great work. The failure, critics said, was that Lawrence did not do what his heroine did—remain in Mexico and embrace the old religion of the feathered serpent which his plot symbolizes and his characters personify. In other words, that he didn't practice in his life what he preached in his books.

Such criticism, even when enunciated by his loyal friend, Aldous Huxley, is irrelevant. The truth lies deeper, beneath the surface of the plot. There we discover, as poet Jascha Kessler has observed in an essay on Lawrence, a mytho-poetic view of Mexico, seen in Lawrence's luminous vision and set forth in glowing prose.

The best critique of *The Plumed Serpent*, and of Lawrence in Mexico, is in L. D. Clark's *Dark Night of the Body* (a title suggested by St. John of the Cross's *Dark Night of the Soul*). Professor Clark of the University of Arizona went over Lawrence's trail in Mexico City, Chapala, and Oaxaca, and to illustrate his book, his wife, LaVerne, photographed the sites and residences which marked the writing of *The Plumed Serpent*.

To be a classic a book need not have unanimous or even majority acceptance. Certainly Lawrence is not for everyone, although it is true that the variety of his work offers readers the opportunity of choosing something to their taste. To fully enjoy Lawrence, there must be an initial surrender *on his terms*, a suspension of belief upon entry into the Lawrentian world, and then a reading of him as poet, mystic, and prophet of earth rather than sky.

The Mexican earth and its peons are in the *The Plumed Serpent*. Not only the people; the "birds, beasts, and flowers," to use words Lawrence gave to a volume of his poetry, are there in vivid profusion. Mud-hens on Lake Chapala, the loading of cattle into a barge for transport to market, festive scenes, banditry and the violence of revolution; the heat and smells and barbaric squalor of rural life are there, charged with that voltage which makes Lawrence's prose so recognizable and readable, even when the reader rejects his doctrine of the mindless blood.

That *The Plumed Serpent* is a Southwest, as well as a Mexican classic, comes from Lawrence having embodied in it material from north of the border, particularly when he described the ceremonial dances of the followers of Quetzalcoatl. Thus did he use what he had first seen at the Jicarilla reservation, at Hotevilla in Hopi land, and at the Santo Domingo and Taos pueblos. In reading it Mabel must have been newly annoyed at the way Lawrence persistently refused to write to her order.

Back at the ranch a final time in the summer of 1925, Lawrence once again revised *The Plumed Serpent* and then sent it off to be published. He was only thankful to have survived its creation, an extraordinary achievement in view of his physical condition. On June 10 he wrote to a friend,

"I am about my normal self again—but shall never forgive Mexico, especially Oaxaca, for having done me in. I shudder when I think of that beastly church, with its awful priests and the backyard with a well-ful of baby's bones. Quoth the raven: *Nevermore*. But this *Nevermore* is a thankful, cheerful chirrup, like a gay blackbird. Nevermore need I look on Mexico—but specially Oaxaca. Yet my Quetzalcoatl novel lies nearer my heart than any other work of mine."

The Lawrences left New Mexico in September. It was not without regret. "It grieves me to leave my horses," he wrote to a friend, "my cow Susan, and the cat Timsy Wemyss, and the white cock Moses—and the place."

From the safety of Italy, he resumed correspondence with Mrs. Luhan. He showed his gratitude by dedicating *Mornings in Mexico* to her, "since to you we really owe Taos and all that ensues from Taos. Reading the New Mexico essays gave me a desire to come back—made me feel that, as the wheel of destiny goes round, it will carry us back. I should love to see the dances at Santo Domingo and the winter dances at Taos again—and go to Zuni where I've never been."

He never did. Those last years that it took him to die were spent in a vain quest for health—to Spain and to France, always in search of the sun. There on the French Riviera the end came on March 2, 1930. "The minutes went by" Frieda recalled, "Maria Huxley was in the room with me. I held his ankle from time to time, it felt so full of life, all my life I shall hold his ankle in my hand."

He had never stopped hoping and planning. Only two months before he died he declared in a letter to Mrs. Luhan that if only he could summon the strength to get started on the long journey, he would surely recover at the ranch. He even talked of founding a school there under the pines, like the Greek philosophers in their gardens. "I feel I might perhaps get going with a few young people, building up a new unit of life out there, making a new concept of life."

Does his spirit ever wander back and encounter the young people who have established communes in the Taos region? It would please him to know that the ranch was given by Frieda to the University of New Mexico as a retreat for young writers and artists.

Forty-odd years ago I grieved to read of Lawrence's early death, and in 1933, while on the French Riviera, I made a pilgrimage to where he died and was first buried, inland a few miles at Vence, an ancient Roman stronghold in the rocky foothills of the Maritime Alps. Later through my work on the manuscripts I came to know Frieda, the incomparable Frieda, on visits to the New Mexican ranch to where Lawrence's remains had been transported and where she too was to find her last resting place. Once I brought her and Aldous Huxley to a meeting at UCLA where they talked about Lawrence to the delight of an enthralled audience.

Frieda Lawrence lived until 1956. When I saw her a last time, a few weeks before her death, she was old and gray and thin and yet her exuberance was undiminished. One had only to be with her to know that Lawrence was right: he did indeed owe it all to her. Without her vitality, he would probably have died much earlier, never having written the Southwest classics, which were crowned by *The Plumed Serpent*.

She was not one to take credit. Her memoirs were called *Not I, But the Wind*.

READING LIST

D. H. LAWRENCE (1885-1930)
Sea and Sardinia. New York, Seltzer, 1921.
St Mawr. New York, Knopf, 1925.
The Plumed Serpent. New York, Knopf, 1926.
Mornings in Mexico. New York, Knopf, 1927.
The Later D. H. Lawrence. Selected by William York Tindall.
New York, Knopf, 1952. Includes the American novel, stories, and essays, 1925-30.

WITTER BYNNER
Journey With Genius. New York, Day, 1951.

L. D. CLARK
Dark Night of the Body; D. H. Lawrence's The Plumed Serpent. Photographs by La Verne H. Clark. Austin, University of Texas Press, 1964.

JASCHA KESSLER
Ashes of the Phoenix; a Study of . . . The Plumed Serpent. Ann Arbor, University Microfilms, 1957.

FRIEDA LAWRENCE
Not I, But the Wind. New York, Viking, 1934.
Memoirs and Correspondence. Edited by E. W. Tedlock, Jr. New York, Knopf, 1964.

MABEL DODGE LUHAN
Lorenzo in Taos. New York, Knopf, 1932.

Photograph of D. H. Lawrence on Azul, courtesy of UCLA Library Special Collections.

The Land of Journeys' Ending

MARY AUSTIN

What book would I pick if asked to choose a single work to represent the creative literature of the Southwest? Now in the '70's my choice remains the same as the one I made in the '50's in *Books West Southwest*. It would be *The Land of Journeys' Ending* by Mary Austin. Because it was written about lasting things, the book remains as fresh now as it was when published in 1924.

Rereading it for the first time in twenty years, I am even surer that it is the book that best embodies the essences of the region whose heartland is Arizona and New Mexico. It was written in her prime by a wise and indomitable woman who synthesized history, anthropology, mythology and religion, flora and fauna, the seasons and weathers, in strong and poetic prose. In it she reached again the pinnacle attained in her first book, *The Land of Little Rain*, that California classic of 1903.

Neither book was an accidental achievement. Classics never are. They derive from the impact of vital experiences on writers with the strength and talent to refine them into literature. By the time she came to write *The Land of Journeys' Ending*, Mary Austin had perfected her ability to assimilate and transmute experience. Thus it is the ripest, richest book of all the many that she wrote.

Hers was a long hard way of learning. Born in 1868 and

schooled in Illinois, she arrived in Southern California during the Boom of the Eighties. Her family took up a homestead on the lonely northern edge of the Tehachapi Mountains in Kern County. School teaching and marriage to an unsuccessful rancher led to the sagebrush land east of the Sierra Nevada, the land she was to exalt in her first book.

A determined drive for literary recognition led her in turn to Los Angeles, San Francisco, and Carmel. She wrote and published prolifically. After leaving her husband when he proved unable to support her, she reluctantly placed their mentally abnormal daughter in an institution and lived alone until her final years, when a niece shared her home. What Mary Austin lacked in beauty she made up in a commanding presence. She was prone to quarrel with all who did not defer to her.

When her publisher wanted a successor to her first and most popular book, she replied that it would take a dozen years of living in a given land and at least $10,000 for support during that time, before she could produce a similar work.

What also stood in the way was her ego, a humorless, prophetic ego that drove her on a long detour via Europe and New York before she found that her genius could flower again only when rooted in the colored earth of the Southwest.

Before that could happen, she had to gain recognition in New York. As a zealous pre-Women's Liberation advocate, Mary Austin was a formidable person, possessed of a power for which she demanded intellectual recognition. Her use of this power she called "sparking." Once when unable to obtain a Pullman berth between Chicago and Denver, she reported having "sparked" the conductor at such high voltage that the poor man cried out, "Lady, I see that you are determined to have a berth, even if it means my dropping someone off the end of this train." She got her berth.

Another victory came on January 8, 1922, when the National Arts Club gave her a testimonial dinner. She wore a flame-colored dress, and over it a mantilla and a tortoise-shell comb in her heaped-up hair. Of the laudatory speeches she was critical for failing to recognize her many books. Still, her end had been achieved; after a twelve-year struggle, New York was subjugated.

Thereupon she wisely left town. She had always felt like a transient in the East. "I liked the feel of roots," she wrote of her move back west, "of ordered growth and progression, of continuity, all of which I found in the Southwest."

Mary Austin came to Santa Fe in the fall of 1918 at the suggestion of her friend, Frederick Webb Hodge, whom she had first met at Los Angeles in 1899. She was finishing *The Trail Book* and needed first-hand details of the Pueblos. She wrote to Hodge from Los Angeles, knowing that he was at work on the excavation of Hawíkuh, near Zuñi, saying she would like him to show the place to her. He replied that he was closing down for the winter and that she should go to Santa Fe and see Edgar L. Hewett at the School for American Research. The next we hear, she was celebrating the end of the war by joining the dancing in the streets of Santa Fe to the measures of "Lupita" played by the band.

When after the first of the year Mary became ill, Mabel Luhan invited her to Taos to recuperate. They had first met in New York at Mabel's free-speech salon.

The chemistry of personal attraction is mysterious. Two such prima donnas should have clashed. Instead they proved amicable. Not that Mabel was uncritical of Mary. After Mrs. Austin's death she wrote in a mostly generous memoir, "She was one of those women whose legs are too short for their top side, but she never saw herself whole and did not feel over-balanced. She felt like the tall, dominating queenly type."

"Taos was her first experience of New Mexico," Mabel wrote later, "and one day she paced up and down behind the house along the calvary between the morada and the great wooden cross. When she came in she said, 'I believe I am going to owe you a great deal. I think I will settle somewhere here.'" When she did, she prudently chose Santa Fe. Taos could have only one queen.

Her first visit in 1918 led to Mary Austin's receiving a Carnegie grant to study the Americanization of Taos County. Tony and Mabel Luhan and the painter, Gustave Baumann, drove her about in a wagon. Nothing tangible resulted. In the following year she lectured at the Normal School in Las Vegas and to the Tucson Art Association. Her creative life was coming into focus again, as it had once before at the turn of the century when she wrote *The Land of Little Rain*.

The Southwest was a twin gift to her—New Mexico from a woman, Arizona from a man. The man was a distinguished botanist, Dr. Daniel Trembly MacDougal, of the Carnegie Institution of Washington's Department of Botanical Research, and head of the department's two field stations, the Coastal Laboratory in Carmel and the Desert Laboratory in Tucson. They had met in Carmel through her lifelong interest in his subject.

Correspondence between them which began in 1914 grew in volume and meaning and led to her visits to Tucson in 1919, 1922, and 1923. *The Land of Journeys' Ending* was dedicated "To Daniel T. MacDougal, of the Cactus Country."

Mary Austin did more than dedicate her book to Daniel MacDougal: she wrote it for him. I quote from only one of her many letters, in which, after referring to having re-read *The Land of Little Rain* for the first time in 15 years, she went on to say,

"I have always thought it a much over-rated book. But I see now that where I came wholly into the presence of the Land, there was a third thing came into being, the sum of what passed between me and the Land which has not, perhaps never could, come into being with anybody else.

"Now I see what you mean by your insistence that I should come to the Southwest until the same transaction takes place between my spirit and the spirit of the Land.

"And I know that I shall die unsatisfied if that does not happen. I have been enough in the Southwest to understand that

98

what would come to me there would be immensely more radiant and splendid than what came in California. I long for it with all my soul, as if it were something I was dedicated to before I was born, and can not fulfill myself without having.

"It doesn't take long to know a land of which I already know so much. And I can take from you, I can use your experience exactly as freely as I use my own—how few people there are of whom we can say that!"

While writing *The Land of Journeys' Ending* she told Mac-Dougal "This book must be, in a sense, a monument to our common delight in the Southwest."

This it was, written from love and delight, from an emotion formed of intellect and spirit, of thought and feeling. She ardently wished to please him from whom she had received so much of his knowledge of the cycle of life in the arid lands. Her letters to him, beginning always "Dear Friend" and in which she revealed herself as to no other correspondent, were love letters in the platonic sense.

Theirs was the kind of friendship she had once begun to have with Charles F. Lummis when she was his protégée in *Land of Sunshine*. Their egos thwarted its growth. He also scolded her for her faulty use of Spanish. In her autobiography, published after Lummis's death, she dealt with him in ungenerous terms.

Dr. MacDougal was more tolerant than Lummis of her demands on him. "You were to carry a little book," she reminded him, "in which to jot down the things you were to remember to tell me for my Arizona book." His replies, which came also to be headed "Dear Friend," were more restrained than hers. Three years older, he outlived her by twenty-four years, dying at Carmel in 1958 at 93.

By 1923 Mary Austin was ready to settle in Santa Fe and gather knowledge and feeling in the book she planned to be published uniformly with *The Land of Little Rain*. She chose Santa Fe because of the ancient capital's mountainous setting and nearness to the desert, for its native culture and intellectual sophistication as a gathering place of creative people. On the Camino del Monte Sol she built her Casa Querida, her Beloved House, and there she lived until her death in 1934 in her sixty-sixth year.

At first it was a lonely street. Mabel thought she would enliven her friend's house with the gift of a radio. She showed her a set. Mary stared at it solemnly for a moment, then asked, "Where do I talk?" Mabel abandoned the idea.

Mary Austin became the dominant cultural personality of Santa Fe. This was no mean feat in a city which harbored such a high percentage of literary and artistic egos. Yet there was no challenge to her position so imperious was her manner. At first she welcomed Willa Cather, letting her use her home to finish writing *Death Comes for the Archbishop*. When the book appeared, Mrs. Austin was perversely outraged by Miss Cather's having made her protagonist what he was—a French priest. This, she protested, was a betrayal of Santa Fe's Spanish heritage.

If Mary Austin usually put down her peers, she was always helpful to younger writers. Erna Fergusson and Peggy Pond Church testified to her kindness. She was tolerant of Santa Fe's unconventional liaisons. Tourists and curiosity seekers were rebuffed. She led a benefactor to purchase the privately owned Santuario de Chimayó and give it to the state. The native arts and crafts received support even beyond her lifetime; her modest estate provided for the Indian Arts Fund.

Before she could finish her Southwest book, she felt the need of another field trip. It was taken with a Santa Fe couple, the Cassidys, whom she had met by chance on the boardwalk while attending a suffrage meeting at Atlantic City in 1916. Inez Cassidy's husband, Gerald, was an artist whom Mrs. Austin wanted as the illustrator of her book. The field trip was for him to make sketches, as well as for her to make notes.

Alas for her plan. The publisher rejected his drawings and used instead illustrations by John Edwin Jackson. Though accurate, they are lifeless. An integral part of the beauty of *The Land of Little Rain* was the marriage of E. Boyd Smith's drawings with the text and the publisher's format, although Mrs. Austin characteristically never acknowledged this. The Century Company's design was dull. The reason her regular publisher, Houghton Mifflin, did not issue the book was that she contracted with Century to serialize some of the chapters in their magazine before publication in book form. They failed to keep it in print, and it has never been republished.

On April 3, 1923, Mary Austin and the Cassidys set out by car from Santa Fe, following the pueblos down river from Santo Domingo to Isleta, then over the mountains to Tucson where she stayed with the MacDougals. They explored first the great forest of cactus, palo verde, and ironwood between Tucson and Florence now traversed by the Pinal Pioneer Parkway. Then a journey through the Papaguería, guarded by the sacred peak of Baboquívari, resulted in a breakdown at Santa Rosa, deep in the desert a hundred miles from Tucson. The agent drove them to the Shrine of the Children's Sacrifice, known to her from Lumholtz's book. She thrilled to an arroyo of palos verdes in flower. Shower of gold, the Spanish called them. When the car was repaired they drove north to Casa Grande and the Gila, and on to Phoenix.

Governor Hunt placed his car at her disposal. Never inactive she addressed a business men's lunch and organized a chapter of the Indian Defence League. There in the Salt River Valley she pondered the vestiges of the irrigation system of the Hohokam, the Indians who had mysteriously vanished long ago. She theorized that the Papagos were their descendants. It was here in 1887 that Hodge did his first field work, as the young secretary of the Hemenway Expedition from Harvard.

Their destination was Zuñi. There a dust storm had driven the inhabitants indoors. In a letter to Dr. MacDougal, Mrs. Austin reported wrapping herself in a blanket and making medicine with all her might. It worked. The storm abated.

They went on to Inscription Rock where she made friends with Ranger-Custodian Voght. When he was called away his assistant, a young Princetonian, led her to the top of El Morro, leaving the Cassidys to sketch below. To this day it is still a rough trail. In her time it was a dangerous one for a novice climber. She had to use rock-hewn toe-holds and hang on to the branch of a pine tree. What a picture!

She knew now that she had come to the heart of hearts of the Southwest—there at the buff-colored battlement beyond Zuñi and Hawíkuh where the first Spanish penetration had climaxed under Coronado four centuries before. What she gained on that transcendent day enabled her to exalt the chapter "Pasó por Aqui" to the summit of all she ever wrote. It was truly journeys' end for Mary Austin.

They slept that night at Grants in the lee of Mount Taylor, noblest of the sacred peaks, then drove south through the *malpais* to Ácoma. And so back to Albuquerque and Santa Fe, completing a journey of 2500 miles—a fateful journey that determined the nature of her remaining life. In it, she said, were gathered all the years of her life, her experience and intentions. Although exhausted, she had still another trip to make, to the Grand Canyon.

Her book was written under the difficulties of ill health and unsettled abode. All creation is at cost. She poured into her masterpiece essences of her being never to be restored. Her autobiography *Earth Horizon*, eight years later, though densely factual and not always accurate, was unleavened by any lyricism or lightness of spirit. She also wrote a novel, stories, sketches. Never again, however, did she attain the level of her two masterpieces, those classic books of the lands she loved. Letters to MacDougal told of her struggle to control her material. Leisure and freedom from anxiety,which she lacked,were needed to give charm to her work. She kept listening for the inner voice that told her when her work was right.

Among her papers in the Huntington Library is the journal kept by Mary Austin on this trip, from April 3 to May 19, a bare narrative of when, where, and what, designed to serve as a remembrancer when she came to write the book. To compare it with the finished work is to marvel at the creative process. Apparent is the power of this indomitable woman in transcending the limitations of circumstances and of her own lonely nature. "I have never been taken care of," she once said in words of profound sadness.

A woman of genius and no talent, one critic cruelly called her. Although this may apply to some of her work, it is not true of this Southwest classic.

Mabel Luhan did not fail her. "Dear Mary," she wrote, "your book came and I devoured it and find it full of beauty. It seems to me to be an evocation—something mesmeric about it. The phrases call up so vividly what I have seen and carry within me. I think you should sell a lot of it—it is sure to be liked. I don't like the drawings much. Otherwise it is a handsome book and so full of knowledge."

Mrs. Austin's Spanish, as Lummis pointed out, was never perfect; and this was true also of her topography. And yet, as her letters to MacDougal and Lummis show, she sought always to be informed and accurate.

Old-time Southwesterners have criticized the brevity of her stays in New Mexico and Arizona before she wrote her Southwest classic. How irrelevant is such criticism! Like Lawrence and Stevenson, for example, Mary Austin had a poet's power of swift and sensitive perception and retention. The end, not the means, is all that matters in literature. She ended on target.

To be lastingly read a book must be about lasting things. Mary Austin knew this to be true. She avoided ephemera—politics, economics, personalities—those transitory things that change from age to age. What she saw in 1923 was what Coronado saw in 1540 and what we see today—"the flow of prevailing winds, the succession of vegetal cover, the legend of ancient life; and the scene, above everything the magnificently shaped and colored scene." The chapters of her timeless book are a processional of the past that is also present and future.

She was ever poetically responsive to the land, to "old settle-ments, low, earth-colored, like fowls dusting themselves in the sun." She read the weather in the distant mountains by the color of the Rio Grande. She knew that "not all the fine and moving things in American history were done in English." She saw what Ross Calvin was to expand a decade later in *Sky Determines*, that "the location of forests in Arizona and New Mexico is largely a matter of the force and direction of prevailing winds." Water also determined, for although rain falls on radicals and conserva-tives alike, the mother ditch makes communists of them all. She was aware of the residue of personality left in all places once inhabited by man, of "some trace that human sense responds to, never so sensitively as where it has long lain mellowing through a thousand years of sun and silence."

Protestant missionaries and the Indian Bureau (their alien, inappropriate buildings like a pox on the land) angered her as they did Oliver La Farge. She anticipated Erna Fergusson's *Dancing Gods* in her perception of the pueblo ceremonials as a way of life rich with lessons unlearned by the Anglo barbarians. "Yet still in that dust, blossom and smell sweet, concepts for the lack of which our age goes staggering into chaos."

She despised the violence and destruction by frontier riff-raff. The despoliation of the environment led her to declare, "Go heedfully where you go, then, along the trail borders. Break no bough heedlessly, and uproot no seeming weed." It was life that she celebrated, the wholeness of life in balance and beauty. She was ahead, far ahead, of most writers of her time and place in her perception and adoration of an ancient, abiding Southwest. She still is.

If you seek only facts about the heartland, Mary Austin is not for you. If prophecy and mysticism are beyond you, then read her not, for in her opening words she takes her stand: "This be-ing a book of prophecy, a certain appreciation of the ritualistic approach is assumed for the reader. The function of all prophecy is to discern truth and declare it, and the only restriction on the prophet is that his means shall be at all points capable of sustaining what he discovers. Anybody can write fact about a country, but nobody can write truth who does not take into account the sounds and swings of its native nomenclature." To clinch her point, she provided a glossary of Spanish words and phrases.

Although her ashes were cemented into a rock in the Sangre de Cristo range above Santa Fe, her spirit is elsewhere. At El Morro, the place of her heart's desire, she knew that the law would prevent her burial. "Here, at least, I shall haunt," she wrote in the peroration to "Pasó por Aquí." And then these solemn words:

"You, of a hundred years from now, if when you visit the Rock, you see the cupped silken wings of the argemone burst and float apart when there is no wind; or if, when all around is still, a sudden stir in the short-leaved pines, or fresh eagle feathers blown upon the shrine, that will be I, making known in such fashion as I may, the land's undying quality."

Go to El Morro and take her book with you. There in that haunted place you will find landscape, history, piñon and juniper, sheep, an eagle, a bluebird—and the spirit of that indomitable woman.

READING LIST

MARY AUSTIN (*1869-1934*)
The Land of Little Rain. Boston, Houghton Mifflin, 1903.
The Land of Journeys' Ending. New York, Century, 1924.
Taos Pueblo. Photographs by Ansel Adams. San Francisco, Grabhorn Press, 1930.
Earth Horizon; Autobiography. Boston, Houghton Mifflin, 1932.

HELEN MACKNIGHT DOYLE
Mary Austin, Woman of Genius. New York, Gotham House, 1939.

T. M. PEARCE
The Beloved House. Caldwell, Idaho, Caxton Printers, 1940.
Mary Hunter Austin. New York, Twayne, 1965.

WILLARD HOAGLAND, *editor*
Mary Austin, a Memorial. Santa Fe, Laboratory of Anthropology, 1944.

JOE W. LYDAY
Mary Austin. Austin, Steck-Vaughn, 1968.

Photograph of Mary Austin and Daniel T. MacDougal, courtesy of Arizona Historical Society, Tucson.

Interlinear to Cabeza de Vaca
HANIEL LONG

In the life of Haniel Long, Santa Fe played a role similar to Carmel's in that of Robinson Jeffers. Each proved to be the inevitable place.

There are other reasons for linking the two. Each was a minister's son, compelled by the Christian ethic to become essentially a religious writer. Each was identified originally with Pittsburgh. Jeffers was born there on the North Side, January 10, 1887. Although Long's birthplace was elsewhere (in Rangoon, Burma, March 8, 1888, where his father was a Methodist missionary), he was raised from the age of three in the East End of Pittsburgh; and after schooling at Exeter and Harvard, he returned to teach literature for twenty years at Carnegie Institute of Technology. The name Haniel (pronounced Han-éye-el) is Hebrew, meaning "The Grace of God."

The acrid atmosphere of the Steel City drove Long away in search of health. With wife and son he went to France and to California. He was in La Jolla, Los Angeles, and San Francisco in 1919-20. He fished for tuna off Catalina Island. A friend wrote to him from Pittsburgh, "California, with its atmosphere and its outline, must be wonderfully helpful to you. Surely in such an environment, your poetic strength should come to its fullest."

It didn't. What worked in the Golden State for Pittsburgher Jeffers failed to fire Pittsburgher Long's poetic furnace. The congestion of Los Angeles, population 600,000 displeased him. The downtown streets, he observed, were not prepared to handle the traffic. They still aren't.

And so the Longs headed for home on the Santa Fe. The train was delayed for two hours near Laguna Pueblo, between Gallup and Albuquerque. There it was that Haniel Long fell under the spell of New Mexico. For him it proved truly the Land of Enchantment.

"I stepped down into the freshness and vastness of the diminutive piñon forest," he recalled later, "and as I walked about among the blue-green odorous trees, I felt like a giant, for over their heads was the horizon of the mountains. On a near-by hill was the ancient town, the first pueblo I had ever seen. I was pleased that houses could be so unpretentious, built simply of the earth and leaving nothing to be improved upon. So with the little trees: they gave me the pleasure that comes of small perfect things which adapt their forces without scattering or waste."

Thus even as Jeffers had come to his journey's end a few years earlier, so Haniel Long came to his. The poet Witter Bynner had settled in Santa Fe early in the 1920's. He had also preceded Long at Harvard. Poetry was their bond, linking them as young writers and years later as old men when, at a memorial service for Long, Bynner read his friend's poems.

It was Bynner's invitation that first brought the Longs on visits to Santa Fe. In 1929 Long finally broke down from conflict between teaching and writing. He resigned his professorship at Carnegie Tech and took his family to live in Santa Fe. There he spent the remaining twenty-seven years of his life. He soon had "impressions of a very different kind of life from any I have ever known, a much older one, in many ways a better one."

Although Long had written two books, *Poems* (1920) and *Notes for a New Mythology* (1926), before the final move to New Mexico, his best work was done as a Southwesterner. He became the leader in a renaissance of regional writing centered in Santa Fe. There he wrote half a dozen books and thousands of words in the form of journalism, letters, and diaries.

Such literary bulk is impressive, and yet, like sand castles, it is subject to early erosion. In a small work of only thirty-eight pages, with the unusual title, *Interlinear to Cabeza de Vaca,* Long fashioned something hardier, a small book that will, I believe, outlast all the rest of his work. Now a generation old, it wears well, a jewel of a book.

First published at Santa Fe in 1936 by a cooperative guild founded by Long and others called Writers' Editions, the *Interlinear* has been reissued by New York and London publishers as *The Power Within Us,* and more recently by the Frontier Press. It has also been translated into German and French. The Encyclopedia Britannica's *Gateway to the Great Books,* edited by Robert M. Hutchins, Mortimer Adler, and Clifton Fadiman, reprinted it in full in "Man and Society," Volume 6 of the 10-volume set. There it takes place with the writings of Xenophon, Tacitus, Prescott, La Bruyère, Emerson, Hawthorne, Whitman, and other great figures of the western world. Its latest appearance, under the original and happier title, is owed to a young Pittsburgher, Ron Caplan, who found Long's memory still green at Carnegie Tech.

My discovery of *Interlinear to Cabeza de Vaca* happened thirty years ago on the shelf of a Los Angeles bookstore which had a supply of unsold copies. I bought one at the published price of $1.50, more for its desert-colored format, I must admit, than for its contents. A reading of it led me to return and buy the rest of the copies—a dozen, I recall—to give to friends, including Henry Miller, our neighbor in Beverly Glen, who was moved to write a foreword for the English edition.

I kept rereading the book, and once after I had crossed the continent, not in eight years and on foot as did Cabeza de Vaca, but swiftly in a Hillman Minx, I was moved to write about the book in an essay on Southwestern literature. I sent a copy to

Haniel Long. He responded with an invitation to visit him in Santa Fe.

There I pilgrimaged annually in the three years of life that remained to him. The friendship between us led to his bequeathing his literary archives to the UCLA Library.

Sky Determines, Ross Calvin said. *Books Determine*, I add. Their ability to do so is determined neither by size nor length nor publisher. The very course and character of my relationship with the Southwest and its literature was determined by Long's little book since it first drew me to him and his newfoundland.

That writer is fortunate who finds his inevitable place, and who also finds the subject which unites his gifts in a work that abides after all else of his has been eroded by Time. Why does this promise to be true of Haniel Long's *Interliner to Cabaza de Vaca*? Let me begin to answer by quoting what the Britannica editors said in prefacing their 1963 reprint:

"*The Power Within Us* may be characterized as an adventure story, as history, anthropology, as religion; and it will stand up under the scrutiny of all these disciplines. But its place as a classic is assured first of all by its beauty. It is a piece of prose that had to be written by a poet. It was."

As partial as I am to poetry and as much as I loved Haniel Long, I must say that his poetry alone would not win him immortality. It is not that he was a bad poet. He was a good one. That is not enough. Only great poets live forever.

As a poet Long was introspective and romantic, concerned with his own feelings and with nature, often moved lyrically by subjective, private concerns. Only when he came to grips with greater, stronger themes did his language take on power and tension and vitality. At such times when his subjects drew him out of himself, he found that he required prose, albeit of a poetic caste, to express himself to the fullest.

Such instances occurred in a Whitmanesque prose-poem called *Pittsburgh Memoranda*, in a critical work, *Walt Whitman and the Springs of Courage*, and in a philosophical essay entitled *A*

112

Letter to St. Augustine after Rereading His Confessions, also in a regional book, *Piñon Country,* of the American Folkway series; and finally in the *Interlinear to Cabeza de Vaca* and a kind of companion sequel to it, a prose poem about Cortés's Indian interpreter and lover called *Malinche (Doña Marina).* In a posthumous novel, *Spring Returns,* with a preface by Anne Morrow Lindbergh, the power was gone, the tension lost, the vitality waned. Its setting is upper New York State, far from the Southwest.

Unlike Carmel, which was only the creative capital of California, Santa Fe was also the political capital of New Mexico. This made it a more rewarding place for a writer to live in than Taos to the north. Santa Fe had the resources of newspapers, printers, patrons, and readers with leisure. It was officially bilingual and also tricultural, blessedly off the railway and highway that disturb Albuquerque to the south. In the 1920's Santa Fe was a town of 20,000 inhabitants, a community with more virtues than vices, more assets than liabilities. Its high, dry climate was a basic attraction for the literary people who colonized it.

The Chicago poet, Alice Corbin, had come early and set up base camp at the foot of the Sangre de Cristos. She invited Witter Bynner to make it a stop on his lecture tour. There he fell ill and stayed on to recuperate—a stay that lasted the rest of his life. Disgust with Los Angeles and New York led Mary Austin to Santa Fe. She too remained until she died. Paul Horgan came upstate from Roswell, Oliver La Farge from Rhode Island via Cambridge, New Orleans and New York. Others followed.

By intellect, sympathy, and idealism, Haniel Long became a cultural leader of Santa Fe and all of New Mexico. Unlike Mary Austin, an egocentric "loner," Long was a cooperator. Two decades of teaching had taught him fellowship. He was the dominant force in Writers' Editions, "a cooperative group of writers living in the Southwest, who believe that regional publication will foster the growth of American literature."

This idealistic venture resulted in seventeen publications be-

113

fore World War II cut off its paper supply. Designer-printer Walter Goodwin, Jr., owner of Santa Fe's Rydal Press, gave its books style and beauty.

Another fruit of the 1930's was the New Mexico Writers page edited by Long, and assisted by Witter Bynner, Erna Fergusson, Paul Horgan, and Frieda Lawrence, featured in the weekly *New Mexico Sentinel*, a newspaper founded by wealthy Cyrus McCormick.

Haniel and Alice Long and their son Anton lived at the heart of Santa Fe in a restored adobe with a walled garden and orchard. From the branch of a peach tree hung a wind-bell from Kyoto. Their water allotment came from the *acéquia madre* outside the wall, the mother ditch which flowed from Santa Fe's Sierra Madre. Their house was furnished with early American pieces, its walls bright with regional paintings and drawings. Books were in every room. And music.

As he aged and his eyesight worsened, Long was sustained by music. He was a tall and rangy man who wore whipcord pants, a wide belt with silver and turquoise buckle, flannel shirt and stetson, and soft low boots. I found in him all the best in the culture of eastern education and experience, harmonized with the elements of Indian-Hispano civilization. He was widely read in contemporary and classical, local and international literature. He communed with friends roundabout Santa Fe. Erna Fergusson often took him to ceremonial dances at the river pueblos. He loved the Grand Canyon and the Mesa Verde.

Much before it was fashionable Long was an ecologist, a conservationist, and a spokesman for Southwestern minorities. His *Piñon Country* is a meaningful book on the Upper Sonoran life-zone of New Mexico-Arizona, written with personal charm in a casual style that conceals the labor that went into its creation. It reads as though its author were speaking to us from knowledge and wisdom gained after much experience and reflection. Facts are present, the history is true; and the cultural material is seen with a poet's vision, which resulted in prose illumined by concern for modern people in an ancient setting.

When I came to him in his mid-60's, I found Haniel Long a grave and kindly sage. In words he gave to Alvar Nuñez Cabeza de Vaca, Long might well have been speaking of himself and for those who have survived their fevered years. "In youth the human body drew me and was the object of my secret and natural dreams. But body after body has taken away from me that sensual phosphorescence which my youth delighted in. Within me is no disturbing interplay now, but only the steady currents of adaptation and of sympathy."

As his life drew to a close and his creative arc descended, Long enjoyed being read to. On visits I read from his St. Augustine and Whitman books and from the manuscript of the novel he was trying to finish. We also listened to music—Mozart and Mahler —and talked of the conflict between a man's public and private life. "If you would achieve your best as a writer," he counselled me, "you must do as I did and leave the administrative life." When I finally did, he had been dead for ten years.

Haniel Long's life exemplified for me something of what Whitman's did for him. Here are Long's words, taken from his book about the Quaker poet: "All men in one way or another feel the need of the mystery which is much the same under the names of corroboration, self-justification, benediction, and which means the courage to be oneself. Down into this life of ours, this succession of daily emergencies each filled with the need of reality, certain men can thrust their roots deeper and deeper. Others cannot. When one examines the careers of men, something of the greatness of those who are truly great may dawn on one like a white-crested mountain, K2 or Everest, so far away that it seems to be a white sheep lying down in a pasture."

When he came to write his *Interlinear to Cabeza de Vaca*, Long was ready for the challenge of compressing his learning, thought, and feeling. The several drafts preserved in his papers

115

reveal his efforts to bring the book to its final form. As early as 1915 he had become interested in the history of the Andalusian conquistador. As a poet and expositor, a Christian idealist and resident of a land whose native culture goes back to the pre-Columbian era, Long entered the 1930's in command of the elements which went into the composition of his masterpiece. He knew what he wanted to do and how to do it; and when it was done, he knew what he had wrought.

"This book is the dearest to me of all my books," he wrote to his German translator, Hildegard von Barloewen, "and I believe that it expresses best the key idea of all my writing, namely: that each of us has, in a degree, the power of giving health and happiness to others."

The books's reception told him he had succeeded as never before (and would never again) in writing a work with both mystical and universal appeal. Letters from readers among his papers prove the *Interlinear's* power to move all manner of people.

What does it mean, *Interlinear to Cabeza de Vaca*? It is simply Long's poetic utterance of the unsaid meaning of the report the Spaniard wrote to his King, Charles V, after returning from years of wandering from 1528 to 1536. His odyssey took him and his companions, the survivors of an expedition of 600 men, from Florida to northern Sonora. They were the first white men to cross the North American continent. During their ordeal, reduced to nakedness and enslaved by the Indians, the three Spaniards and one Moor came to find that they had the power of healing. Thus they were accompanied by bands of natives, imploring to be cured of their illnesses.

The meaning of this "power within" and of the nature of true Christianity—"If ye would find your life, ye must first lose it"—is what Long perceived between the lines of the Spaniard's laconic narrative published in 1542 after his return to Spain.

The *Interlinear* is a great original in Southwestern literature. It took Long outside of himself, drew his gifts and his power unto

116

itself, so that although it is the least personal of all that he wrote, it is also the most truly his.

"Your Majesty," the *Interlinear begins,* "I am that Nuñez Cabeza de Vaca who lately sent you a Relation of his shipwrecks and mischances during the eight years he was absent from your dominions. In painful doubt whether my words were clear enough, I write again."

And it ends with these words: "If one lives where all suffer and starve, one acts on one's impulse to help. But where plenty abounds, we surrender our generosity, believing that our country replaces us each and several. This is not so, and indeed a delusion. On the contrary the power of maintaining life in others, lives within each of us, and from each of us does it recede when unused. It is a concentrated power. If you are not acquainted with it, Your Majesty can have no inkling of what it is like, what it portends, or the ways in which is slips from one. In the name of God, Your Majesty, Farewell."

Publication and republication of the book enriched Long's life with new friends. He was magnetic to both men and women. The man-woman relationship was for him a source of meditation and creation. And it was the inspiration of the book I have called a companion to *Interlinear*. This came from his loving friendship with a fellow New Mexican writer, and its dedication acknowledged the debt: "Gratefully to Erna Fergusson who first acquainted me with Malinche."

When she proved unable to write an historical novel about Malinche, Erna Fergusson persuaded her friend to write of the Yucatan girl in his own way. Long cast his work poetically in the form of a monologue by Malinche, in which the girl becomes an image of the ideal woman all men bear in their hearts. Although it too is a moving and beautiful work, it does not attain the level of the *Interlinear*. Perhaps the reason is the ambiguity of the woman's nature, a loving woman driven by a desire to fulfill her country's destiny by aiding Cortés in the destruction of its people and their culture. Unlike Nuñez, Malinche left no narrative for Long to interline. She lives only as a shadowy figure in the histories of Bernal Diaz, Las Casas, and Gomara, the sources used by Long in his interpretation of her character and motivation.

Did Erna Fergusson approve of what her friend had done? She did indeed. From Guatemala she wrote to Long, "I adore her. It's strong and deep and true and full of well-digested thought. Yes, Mexico had to accept her conqueror however brutal and stupid he was. And he was, and still is, and the day Malinche looked forward to has not come yet, but when it does it will be because the wisdom of women and blind old men knows that it's through love that the thing has to be done."

Haniel Long died in 1956 in his sixty-ninth year, preceded in death three days by his wife. He also was in hospital at the time and never knew of her passing. Thus ended their marriage of forty-three years. Did he have a premonition that it would end as it did, when three years earlier he wrote in his journal of how they had read in Ovid of the old couple, Baucis and Philemon? Here is what he wrote: "'Since we have passed our years in harmony,' the man said, 'let me never see the tomb of my wife.' It was granted him; he became an oak and she an elm in the same hour, and you can still see them growing if you travel in Asia Minor."

READING LIST

HANIEL LONG (1888-1956)

Interlinear to Cabeza de Vaca; His Relation of the Journey from Florida to the Pacific, 1528-1536. Santa Fe, Writers' Editions, 1936; Pittsburgh, Frontier Press, 1969.

The Power Within Us. New York, Duell, 1944; London, Drummond, 1946, with a foreword by Henry Miller. A reissue of the Interlinear with a changed title.

118

Malinche (Doña Marina). Santa Fe, Writers' Editions, 1939.

Piñon Country. New York, Duell, 1941.

If He Can Make Her So. Pittsburgh, Frontier Press, 1968. Selected Writings, with an Introduction by Ron Caplan.

ALICE LAVINIA LONG

The Poems. Naples, N.Y., Privately Printed for the Haniel Long Fund, 1967. Contains "Selections from the poetry of Haniel Long, made by Witter Bynner and read by him at the memorial services for Alice and Haniel Long on October 21, 1956, at Santa Fe, New Mexico."

Photograph of Haniel Long by Harriet Burkhardt, courtesy of UCLA Library Special Collections.

Death Comes for the Archbishop
WILLA CATHER

Twenty years had passed since I had read *Death Comes for the Archbishop*. Would I rank it as high now as I did then? Tastes and standards change—or should. Life appears differently at sixty-seven than it did at forty-seven. I first read Willa Cather's other books and the biographies and memoirs that have appeared since her death in 1947. Then with everything else read, I came back to the *Archbishop*. This time I brought to it two decades of increasing familiarity with the Southwest—its landscape and literature, its culture historical and contemporary, and its literary personalities.

The book was the same volume I had read before, having long stood on the shelf awaiting my return. I had placed in it a colored postcard of the bronze likeness of the Archbishop that stands before his cathedral in Santa Fe. It was this statue that first aroused Miss Cather's curiosity about Jean-Baptiste Lamy, the French priest from the Auvergne who came to New Mexico in 1851 and labored there to civilize the vast episcopate until his death in 1888.

Every book has its inevitable time and place to be read. They were conjoined for me when I reread the book in a rocky garden in the foothills of the Santa Catalinas, overlooking Tucson. It was a magical experience, as I brought to the book all I had gained from the passing years.

I ask more of a book than the bare bones of plot, narrative, and characters. It must breathe, be chromatic and full of murmurous overtones, so that it goes on pulsing, glowing, and echoing after it is put back on the shelf. Willa Cather's is such a book. From a submersion in her life and work, I perceived the stages which led to *Death Comes for the Archbishop* and that it justly ranks in the highest realm of American literature.

Some have denied her authority as a Southwesterner. One, an otherwise knowing man of letters, declared that her knowledge was gained from auto trips between the Harvey Houses in Lamy and Santa Fe. Obviously he did not know of her long familiarity with the region. Because of the *Archbishop*, New Mexico has claimed Willa Cather. Arizona has a prior claim. Winslow was her home for three months on her first visit to the Southwest in 1912. She went there to live with her brother, Douglass, who was a brakeman on the Santa Fe. Later she returned on long visits to Arizona, New Mexico, and Colorado. Her work was cumulatively enriched by these Southwestern experiences.

Although her fame was established by elegiac novels of the Nebraska prairie, *O Pioneers!*, *My Ántonia*, and *A Lost Lady*, it was the Southwest that brought her genius to zenith. Here is how her biographer, E. K. Brown, put it: "The persistence and the diversity of the references to the Southwest suggest—what is indeed the truth—that the discovery of this region was the principal emotional experience of Willa Cather's mature life."

The map of her life is wide and colorful. She was born in Virginia on December 7, 1873, and taken to Nebraska when she was ten, where her family and other Virginians formed a colony of pioneers among German, Scandinavian, and Bohemian farmers. Christened Willela, she liked to be called Bill or Billy, and eventually changed her name to Willa. She was a tomboy and the oldest child in a large family. Her first interests were in nature and science. She said she intended to be a doctor, and sometimes jokingly signed herself "William Cather, M. D."

At the University of Nebraska in Lincoln, an influential

teacher diverted her to literature. Thus she was introduced to Stevenson, Maupassant, Flaubert, Mérimée, and Henry James. When she proved a fluent, perceptive writer, she became the drama and literary critic for local papers. This led upon graduation in 1895 to a newspaper job in Pittsburgh and then to teaching English literature in high school there. During the decade of her life in the birth town of Robinson Jeffers and Gertrude Stein, she kept on writing.

Isabelle McClung, the beautiful, art-loving daughter of a wealthy family, persuaded her parents (against their will) to let Willa live with her in a studio apartment in their home. From this haven came Willa Cather's first books, one of poetry, *April Twilights* (1903) and one of stories, *The Troll Garden* (1905). She and Miss McClung travelled together in Europe.

Willa Cather never married, although she did not lack proposals. She dedicated herself to her art—and to two women, Isabelle McClung and Edith Lewis. With the latter, a friend from the Lincoln years, she came eventually to share a home until her death. Masculine traits were strong in her. She was short and stocky and given to plain dress. Her hair was the color of bronze, her eyes blue-grey.

From Pittsburgh her destiny led to New York. Publication of *The Troll Garden* brought her into the ken of S. S. McClure, the foremost magazine publisher of the time. When the great muckrakers, Lincoln Steffens, Ida Tarbell, and Ray Stannard Baker, quarreled wth McClure and quit his magazine in a body, the publisher began to recruit anew with the appointment of Miss Cather. Within three years she became the managing editor of *McClure's*.

She impressed those around her with her forceful ability. The young poet Witter Bynner, joined the staff of *McClure's*, and years later in a review of three books about Willa Cather, he recalled an incident during their tenure on the magazine when a story in manuscript by Miss Cather, based on a friend's life, was judged by the editorial staff to be fraught with emotional peril for the friend if printed. She refused to withhold it. "I can hear her now," Bynner wrote, "saying briefly, 'My art is more important than my friend.'"

Her early stories of Pittsburgh and the East were influenced by Henry James and Edith Wharton. Prairie and Southwest lay below the horizon. The forces that brought them higher were set in motion by a meeting in 1908 when, on an assignment in Boston, Willa Cather became friends with Sarah Orne Jewett, dean of New England writers and author of *The Country of the Pointed Firs*. She was twenty-five years older than Miss Cather. Her pleasure in *The Troll Garden* was not increased by the stories Willa Cather wrote while managing *McClure's*.

Whereupon Miss Jewett wrote Miss Cather what was probably the most important letter the younger woman ever received. Its counsel turned her toward her ultimate fame. "If you don't keep and guard and mature your force," the older woman wrote, "and above all, have time and quiet to perfect your work, you will be writing things not much better than you did five years ago. . . . Your vivid, exciting companionship in the office must not be your audience, you must find your own quiet centre of life, and write from that to the human heart. . . . To work in silence and with all one's heart, that is the writer's lot; he is the only artist who must be solitary, and yet needs the widest outlook on the world."

It is one thing to receive advice, another to embrace it. Although Willa Cather doubtless already knew it for the truth, Miss Jewett's was the confirmation she needed. This became her credo, and by adhering to it for the remaining thirty-nine years of her life, Willa Cather achieved greatness as a writer.

The first step toward it was that maiden journey to the Southwest, to Arizona in the spring of 1912. Even before she went there, however, the Southwest had appeared in her work in a story called "The Enchanted Bluff," published in *Harper's Monthly* in 1909. Unlike the conventional tales Miss Jewett had warned her against, it went back to her girlhood and the local

124

legend that Coronado had come as far as the prairies near Red Cloud, Nebraska in his search for the Seven Golden Cities of Cíbola. The story she wrote was of some boys camping on a sand-bar in the river who fall to talking of the Mesa Encantada in New Mexico.

The immediate inspiration of the story was the controversy that had raged in the magazines and newspapers over whether or not the Enchanted Mesa had been inhabited; and particularly an article in *Century* by Frederick Webb Hodge called "The Ascent of the Enchanted Mesa," with "Notes on Old Mesa Life" by Fernand Lungren, illustrated from photographs by A. C. Vroman of the Hodge party surmounting the Mesa.

Winslow, Arizona in the spring of 1912 was a rough division point on the Santa Fe, between Gallup and Flagstaff. It served Willa Cather as place of departure, by horseback to the Painted Desert and by train to Flagstaff, "deadheading" with her brake-man brother; and from there north to the Grand Canyon and south to Walnut Canyon and its prehistoric cliff dwellings. Re-membered landscapes, especially of old cottonwoods and Navajo hogans along the Little Colorado in a sandstorm appeared later in the *Archbishop*.

This was the Southwest before its transformation by the auto-mobile. By one of those strange coincidences, this same place and time—Winslow in 1912—was to serve as the setting for Oliver La Farge's *Laughing Boy*.

It was not landscape, archaeology, or history, however, that most excited Willa Cather. It was a man—a young Mexican from Vera Cruz named Julio, a singer of songs to his own guitar accompaniment. Julio took her to the Painted Desert and to a *baile* in the *barrio*. He was apparently the only man ever to in-fatuate this strong woman. She poured out her feeling in letters to a friend at *McClure's*, urging her also to come to the South-west and find herself a Mexican sweetheart.

She finally broke away, albeit reluctantly, and returned East; and yet she never forgot him. Years later, when someone asked her how Mabel Dodge Luhan could have married an Indian, Willa Cather replied, "How could she help it?"

This Southwest *entrada* was the great watershed in her creative life. She never returned to *McClure's*. Henceforth she was a novelist. She settled in Pittsburgh with the McClungs, and there the emotion of parting with Julio and reunion with Isabelle produced a "sudden inner explosion and enlightenment." From that exaltation came O *Pioneers!*, to be followed by two other prairie masterpieces. She declared rightly that she was the first, in the words of Virgil (*Primus ego in patriam mecum . . . deducam Musas*) to bring the Muse into her country.

She moved back to New York in 1915 to share an apartment in Greenwich Village with her other friend, Edith Lewis. Music and opera were strong interests, and she wrote *The Song of the Lark*, a novel based on the career of Olive Fremstad, the Swedish Wagnerian soprano—and on herself and her struggle to achieve independence and maintain integrity as a writer. It is not one of her best books. There is too much detail. In a revision years later, she cut it by ten percent. Our interest in it is the way she used her Southwest experience, including Julio who appears at the end as an old Mexican troubadour on tour in the East.

Next Miss Cather agreed to take a writing assignment in Germany for S. S. McClure. She and Isabelle McClung planned to go together. Judge McClung, who held the purse strings, said no. And so Willa Cather took Edith Lewis instead and set off for the Southwest on her first visit to the Mesa Verde which, thanks to President Theodore Roosevelt, had been made a National Park in 1906. The two women went by narrow gauge railroad from Denver to Durango, and thence by team and wagon from Mancos onto the Mesa. There for a week they camped in the Park and had the nearly exclusive attention of the ranger. They also met the brother of Richard Wetherill; the latter was one of the two cowboys who had discovered the great Cliff House in 1888. When they were lost overnight in a remote canyon, the stir made news in the *New York Times*. Ten years later this Mesa Verde adventure of 1915 became "Tom Outland's Story," an inset in her novel, *The Professor's House*.

From the Mesa Verde the two women travelled by wagon over rough roads to Taos and spent a month there in a primitive adobe hotel run by a Mexican woman. They rode horseback to nearby villages, including Arroyo Hondo. Thus was acquired material that was to give *Death Comes for the Archbishop* its concrete Southwestern imagery.

Upon her return East Willa Cather was shocked by the death of Judge McClung and the breakup of the old home in Pittsburgh where she had first opened the creative vein. An even worse blow followed. Freed of fatherly domination and with money of her own, Isabelle married. Her husband was Jan Hambourg, a foreign violinist. Willa was shattered. Writing became impossible. Again she sought solace in the West, in Taos and in Wyoming with another brother, Roscoe, then back in Nebraska where her mother needed help around the house. That was the time, Willa said, when she learned not to fear a kitchen range.

And again she found healing in her art. Back in New York she created the novel which shares with the *Archbishop* highest rank in the Cather canon. In *My Ántonia* she did not repeat her mistake in *The Song of the Lark* of overfurnishing the story. "How wonderful it would be if we could throw all the furniture out of the window; and along with it, all the meaningless reiterations concerning physical sensations, all the tiresome old patterns, and leave the room as bare as the stage of a Greek theatre ... for the play of emotions great and little."

This is what she did in *My Ántonia*. All her gifts were fused in it: knowledge of the prairie, abiding love for its pioneer Bohemians, and mastery of her medium. That she wrote prose is true, but prose intensified by imagination to the level of incandescence. Though austere in person and mannish in dress, her writing was ever distinguished by feminine tenderness.

This was the highest point she had reached. At forty-five she was beginning to feel the ills of the body. World War I and Isabelle's defection left painful scars. Her stories and succeeding novels grew sombre. She sought writing havens at Jaffrey, a New Hampshire village, and on the island of Grand Manan in New Brunswick's Bay of Fundy. She travelled again in Europe. *One of Ours*, a war novel (and one of her weakest) won the Pulitzer Prize. Honors and royalties accrued. *The Professor's House*, with its interpolated Mesa Verde story, harked back to her university years. Two short novels, *My Mortal Enemy* and *A Lost Lady*, were studies in disillusionment.

The latter is the third of her prairie masterpieces. In it she gave a last look at the land and the railroading age that followed the pioneers. Although romantic sex is a thin and pale strand in her fabric, she could when she chose to, quicken the reader's senses, the more so for what was merely implied. Such occurs when Mrs. Forrester and her lover emerge from a buffalo-robed rendezvous in the snowy cedar brake and the man returns to cut the boughs they had ostensibly gone for. One of the Blum boys had hidden by chance close to the sleigh and horses. This is what he saw:

"He reached under the seat for a hatchet and went back to the ravine. Mrs. Forrester sat with her eyes closed, her cheek pillowed on her muff, a faint, soft smile on her lips. The air was still and blue; the Blum boy could almost hear her breathe. When the strokes of the hatchet rang out from the ravine, he could see her eyelids flutter . . . soft shivers went through her body."

Was this an actual experience of roaming tomboy Billy Cather? Was she the hidden observer? Not necessarily. As well as Henry James, her master was Flaubert, to whom little happened except in the imagination.

As her fame grew, Willa Cather demanded privacy. When writing, her door was locked, telephone disconnected. Only with her friends was she gracious. She never joined groups, signed appeals, supported movements, nor became an autographing speaker. She lived by Miss Jewett's injunction, presenting to the world a blank facade.

In 1920, irked by her Boston publisher's lack of flair in design-

128

ing and promoting her books, she left Houghton Mifflin and sought out the rising young publisher, Alfred A. Knopf. He welcomed her, and until her death twenty-seven years later, hers were his distinguished Borzoi books. I once persuaded Knopf to speak to my students on his life as a publisher. He recalled Willa Cather's interest in the details of her books and that it was she who wrote the matter that appeared on the dust wrapper of *Death Comes for the Archbishop*. She was a lady of a very special kind, he said, now all but extinct. Loyalty was one of her great qualities; if she were on your side it was impossible for you to do anything that she regarded as wrong. And if she were not on your side, you simply couldn't do anything of which she approved.

Her experience with the motion pictures was similar to that of Harvey Fergusson's. After an unsatisfactory adaptation of *A Lost Lady*, she refused to grant any more movie rights even when the offers were high; and furthermore, her will forbade any movie, radio, and T.V. productions of her books. Only novels of action can be dramatized, she said; hers were chromatic books of feeling, mood, and setting, and would be destroyed in the process. She also left the restriction that her letters were never to be published. They are finding their way into libraries—Yale, Newberry, Huntington, the Willa Cather Memorial Library in Red Cloud, Nebraska—where they may be read and paraphrased, but never copied nor quoted verbatim.

Although it seems unlikely, it was D. H. Lawrence who was responsible for Willa Cather's return to the Southwest after an absence of nearly ten years, a return that resulted in her writing *Death Comes for the Archbishop*. It appears that it was Knopf who brought them together. In 1924 when Lawrence and Frieda, en route back to their ranch from Europe, twice had tea with Miss Cather in her Greenwich Village apartment, they were then Knopf authors. She promised to rejoin the Lawrences in New Mexico.

And so the following summer she returned to Taos and lived

in the house that Mabel Luhan had built for the Lawrences. Tony Lujan drove her and Edith Lewis about the countryside, sitting in the driver's seat "in his silver bracelets and purple blanket, often singing softly to himself, while we sat behind," Miss Lewis recalled in a memoir of her companion. They visited the Lawrences at their ranch on Lobo Mountain. That summer was a great creative time for Lawrence and Willa Cather, he completing *The Plumed Serpent*, she conceiving the *Archbishop*.

How did that conception come about? Preparation for it began with her knowledge of the French missionaries in the Southwest, gained from a priest on her first visit to the region in 1912, and then from reading and travel on her several returns. Finally, in that summer of 1925 while staying at La Fonda in Santa Fe where she could look out from her room on the statue of Archbishop Lamy, there occurred another of those "sudden inner explosions and enlightenments" that had yielded *My Antonia*.

In seeking information about Lamy (and, according to one writer, acting upon the suggestion of the medical doctor, Julius Tyndale, an older Nebraska mentor and friend, that she write about the pioneer archbishop) she had obtained an obscure book by a priest named William Howlett, privately printed in 1908 at Pueblo, Colorado. This was *The Life of the Right Reverend Joseph P. Macheboeuf*, who had been Lamy's vicar and lifelong friend. Enthralled by the book, she stayed up nearly all night reading the story of the old churchmen renamed in her story Latour and Vaillant. By morning, the plan of her book was clear. This recalls the origin of *Ramona*, also conceived explosively by Helen Hunt Jackson.

"From that time on," Miss Lewis wrote in her memoir of Miss Cather, "it completely took possession of her, filled all her waking thoughts. She knew exactly what material she needed in order to write the story as she wanted to write it, and she seemed to draw it out of everything she encountered—from the people she talked with—old settlers, priests, taxi-drivers, Indian traders, trainmen; from old books she found in the various libraries in

Santa Fe, and used to bring back to the hotel by the armful, and read in the evening; and from the country itself. We drove all over northern New Mexico, this time by automobile. She made notes occasionally about dates and facts she took from her reading; but I do not think she made any notes of things she herself encountered. She trusted to her memory to retain anything of real interest or importance."

Paul Horgan, who has long been engaged upon a biography of Lamy, tells of coming inadvertently upon Miss Cather and Miss Lewis in lounging chairs on a La Fonda balcony, surrounded by books and papers, at work on the *Archbishop*. ". . . the nearer of the two ladies turned upon me a light blue regard of such annoyance and distaste at my intrusion that I was gone too quickly to take more than a sweeping impression of where I had been." It was the only time he ever saw Willa Cather. Chagrin and respect mingled in an unfading memory of his intrusion.

Writing the book, Miss Cather said, was "like a happy vacation from life, a return to childhood, to early memories. As a writer I had the satisfaction of working in a special genre which I had long wished to try. As a human being, I had the pleasure of paying an old debt of gratitude to the valiant men whose life and work . . . gave me a feeling of close kinship with them."

She was wrong, however, when she declared that its writing took only a few months. Begun in New Mexico, it was continued that fall in New Hampshire and then in New York during the winter and spring. For purposes of her story she found it necessary to return the following summer to see for the first time the Mesa Encantada and Ácoma. She and Miss Lewis were detained for a week at Laguna Pueblo by cloudbursts which made impassable the clay road south.

Back at La Fonda, Miss Cather neared the end of her task. Before going into hospital at St. Louis, Mary Austin offered Willa Cather the use of her empty home, La Casa Querida, as a quiet place to write. Miss Cather found it ideally suited to her

131

need, commenting in a grateful letter to Mrs. Austin how much she enjoyed working among old Hispanic furnishings, and hoping that she had not worn out the blue plush chair wherein she wrote. Later she inscribed a copy "For Mary Austin, in whose lovely study I wrote the last chapters of this book. She will be my sternest critic—and she has the right to be. I will always take a calling-down from my betters."

The book was finished that fall during her only stay at the MacDowell Colony at Peterborough, New Hampshire. It had taken a year and a half to write.

She knew that she had wrought a masterpiece. Upon delivering the manuscript to Knopf, she predicted that after he and she were dead, his son would be paying royalties to her niece. On this book alone she shrewdly asked, and was given, an extra one percent of royalty. Now, nearly half a century after publication, Alfred Knopf is still paying royalties to her estate.

Although not a Catholic (she was converted in 1922 to the Episcopal faith) Miss Cather's book was embraced by Catholics. As noted earlier, Mary Austin was displeased that French rather than Spanish missionaries were portrayed. The author had failed to include an acknowledgement of her debt to Father Howlett's book which had been the skeleton for her work. When that aggrieved priest gently reminded her of the oversight, she contritely wrote a letter to the *Commonweal*, telling how she came to write the book and crediting Father Howlett for all she owed him. Her title came from one of the pictures in Hans Holbein's famous sequence, *The Dance of Death*.

In form and content, *Death Comes for the Archbishop* is like no other Southwest novel. "I am amused that so many reviews of this book," Miss Cather said in her letter, "began with the statement, 'This book is hard to classify.' Then why bother? Many more assert vehemently that it is not a novel. Myself, I prefer to call it a narrative."

It is a work wherein the creative imagination seizes certain facts about the people, the land and the life of the Southwest, and remoulds them in a new form on a higher level, and does this in language of crystalline simplicity. The frescoes of Puvis de Chavannes in the Pantheon inspired her, she said, to visualize the book as a tapestry peopled by a few contrasting characters. Her touch was delicate, strong, and sure. The book's configuration is like a prismatic web.

Its appeal has always been wide. Once in the 1950's I sent President Robert Gordon Sproul an article on Southwestern literature which recalled my first reading of Willa Cather. His reply came from a vacation cabin high in the Sierra Nevada. "I found what you had to say about Willa Cather especially interesting, having years ago enjoyed a similar experience. I was left somewhere in a hotel room with nothing else to read, and opened *Death Comes for the Archbishop*. I found this book full of spiritual vitamins and was refreshed by the beauty of its contents as well as its writing. And so Willa Cather was one of the first I recommended for an honorary degree when I came into the presidency." She was awarded the LL.D. by the University of California on Charter Day, 1931, one of many such honors she received. The first was in 1917 from her alma mater.

Throughout this Virginian-turned-Nebraskan-into-Southwesterner's book, there is no false note, no wrong color. It is faithful to the land and the people. She brought to it a half century of living, loving, looking and learning, and its creation was the supreme point to which she attained as a writer. This was her zenith, and is a benchmark by which creative Southwestern writing may be measured.

Willa Cather lived another twenty years and wrote several lesser books, notably *Shadows on the Rock* (1931), *Lucy Gayheart* (1935), and *Sapphira and the Slave Girl* (1940). They were years of gradual descent and dwindling energy. "A book is made with one's own flesh and blood," she lamented. "It is cremated youth." As she burned away in her writing, she had less and less to give. Yet she was ever generous with what she had. During the Depression she helped half a dozen families, including her brothers'. She settled a pension on her old friend, Dr. Tyndale.

Life closed in on her. Her parents died, followed by Isabelle and her two dearest brothers, Douglass and Roscoe. After Isabelle's death, Jan Hambourg returned the letters Willa had written to his wife. Bundle after bundle they were burned in her Park Avenue apartment's incinerator. One who knew her said that Willa Cather feared the betrayal in print of "the heat and the abundance that surged up in her."

The second World War was a final blow. She stopped writing, leaving an unfinished story of the time of the Avignon papacy. This too was burned. Although never bedridden, and lucid to the last, she knew that her end was near. Her reading was in Shakespeare and Chaucer. On April 24, 1947 death came for Willa Cather.

She lies buried on a hillside in Jaffrey, New Hampshire. Her gravestone bears these words from *My Antonia*: "That is happiness; to be dissolved into something complete and great."

READING LIST

WILLA CATHER (1873-1947)
O Pioneers! Boston, Houghton Mifflin, 1913.
The Song of the Lark. Boston, Houghton Mifflin, 1915.
My Antonia. Boston, Houghton Mifflin, 1918.
A Lost Lady. New York, Knopf, 1923.
The Professor's House. New York, Knopf, 1925.
Death Comes for the Archbishop. New York, Knopf, 1927.
Novel and Stories. Boston, Houghton Mifflin, 1937-41. 13 vols. With new prefaces and textual revisions by the author.
On Writing: Critical Studies on Writing as an Art. New York, Knopf, 1949.

E. K. BROWN
Willa Cather, a Critical Biography, completed by Leon Edel.
  New York, Knopf, 1953.

EDITH LEWIS
Willa Cather Living; a Personal Record. New York, Knopf,
  1953.

ELIZABETH S. SERGEANT
Willa Cather, a Memoir. Philadelphia, Lippincott, 1953.

Photograph of Willa Cather, courtesy of UCLA Library Special Collections.

Dancing Gods

ERNA FERGUSSON

"I wish you could sit on my *portal* now," Erna Fergusson wrote me one December. "There's a foreground of dull gold dry fields, with swatches of red willows, dark elms, silvery cottonwoods getting ready for spring, the incredible blue of the Sandias, pricked out now with snow, and the even more incredible blue of sky with sitting clouds. Come soon again to sit on my *portal*. You've never tried it in winter. Our winter coloring is better than any other season. Subtle, but deep and revealing."

Ten years passed before I responded and made a winter journey to Albuquerque. Alas, it was too late to enjoy the vista from her covered porch. She had died in 1964 in her seventy-sixth year, after a crippling illness. And there was no *portal*, there was no house. The old Armijo dwelling which she had inhabited, on the river road beneath a cathedral cottonwood, was gone, bulldozed to make way for tract houses.

If Erna Fergusson had been only a woman, albeit a distinguished native New Mexican of pioneer lineage and a magnetic person of friendships on many levels of society, her memory would vanish as her contemporaries dropped away. That she is now remembered and will be for long to come is because she was also a writer, a creative woman unneedful of marriage and children, who left a legacy more meaningful than her own flesh and blood.

Books were her gift to posterity, the first of which was her best. More than forty years have passed since *Dancing Gods* was published. It is still the best of all books about the Indian ceremonials of New Mexico and Arizona. The book was with me on my journey to the city on the Rio Grande. As well as to see the winter landscape described by Miss Fergusson, I wanted to learn what had led her to write the book and why it holds its place at the pinnacle of all that she wrote.

Although I came to friendship with Erna Fergusson in the last decade of her life, during which we exchanged many letters and drank even more cups of Darjeeling during summer and autumn visits to her river-road home, I could never draw her out about her own work. She would discuss literature in general and latterly the problem she faced of heightened awareness and increasing skill, accompanied by diminished vitality and stamina. She was a critical reader in many fields.

At tea-time her home was a kind of salon, warmly hosted by this gray-haired, blue-eyed, quizzically humorous woman. One encountered there a cross-section of Southwestern society—a senator, the governor, a university president, her gardener, a neighboring teen-ager on horseback who reined up and chatted with her on the *portal*, or a priest, a printer, a high school principal. At one time or another, I met them all at Miss Fergusson's. People were drawn by her passionate interest in them for their accomplishments and their problems. In an alcove of her study she kept a little pin-up gallery of some of her favorites, such as Eric Sevareid, J. Robert Oppenheimer, and John F. Kennedy.

A photograph of the latter evoked a story of J.F.K. during his campaign for the presidency. "I was one of a small delegation to meet him at the airport," she said, "and I made it out to the plane on my crutches with a copy of my *New Mexico* to give him. I thought the facts in it might be useful to him and anyway books are good things to have on planes. So I gave it to him and then

138

began my progress back to the terminal, when I felt a tap on my shoulder. It was Kennedy. 'I just want you to know,' he said, 'I like what you wrote in my copy.'"

"What did you write?" I tactlessly asked.

She laughed. "That's my secret."

Erna Fergusson left her voluminous papers to the University of New Mexico. I found their examination a formidable task. They fill scores of cartons and file boxes, folders and scrapbooks, and are housed in the tower of the massive pueblo-style university library.

What had gone into *Dancing Gods* to make her first book a classic of Southwestern literature? It appeared to be another instance of the unlikeliness of literary creation. Until publication of this book in 1931, Erna Fergusson gave no obvious promise of writing a work that would surpass all others on a subject—the ceremonial Indian dances—that had engaged many writers before her, including Lummis, Austin, and Lawrence.

It was not that she was untrained. Erna Fergusson had received good preparation at Girls Collegiate School in California, leading to a B.A. from the University of New Mexico and an M. A. in History from Columbia University. She had travelled in Europe and then taught school in Virginia and New Mexico. In World War I she became field director for the Red Cross in New Mexico. This latter experience took her throughout her state into contact with its three cultures, Indian, Hispano, and Anglo. It served also to perfect her Spanish. Encouraged by Kyle Crichton she began to write articles of local history for the *Albuquerque Herald* in a series called "Do You Remember?"

Her interest and training in history, a love for the peoples of her own land, and a compulsion to communicate, were the elements that coalesced in the making of Erna Fergusson as a writer. *Dancing Gods* still lay ten years ahead. She continued to write for the local paper and then for national magazines, always on New Mexican history, folklore, and ecology.

She once said that her life had followed a reasonable pattern, one thing leading logically to the next. *Dancing Gods* was no exception. It came from knowledge gained in Red Cross work that had taken her into the remote villages of New Mexico. Her familiarity with the state led to the Koshare Tours, founded in 1921 by Erna Fergusson and Ethel Hickey. The name came from the Pueblo dancers called the "delight makers," a better term than "entertainers."

These two bold ladies were the first women dude wranglers. Their venture originated when Erna had been asked by an Albuquerque group to show them the Penitente country. This led her to arrange similar tours on a paying basis. The keynote was informality.

Among her papers is a scrapbook in which Miss Fergusson preserved every piece of literature relating to the Koshare venture. It began with a 7-passenger, air-cooled Franklin sedan, a driver with a strong back and a stout shovel, and either Fergusson or Hickey as courier. The first trip was from Santa Fe to Taos, with three days in the pueblo village, at a total cost of $50 per person.

This grew into a choice of tours from Albuquerque to the pueblos of Isleta, San Felipe, Santo Domingo, Taos, Jemez, Ácoma, and Laguna, and later as far as the Hopi villages in Arizona. The tours were arranged to coincide with the ceremonial dances at the various pueblos.

Only a woman of Erna Fergusson's tact, persuasion, and sympathy could have brought it off. Her fluent Spanish helped. On her first tour to Ácoma, the chief rebuffed her fiercely until, opening her toilet kit to the mirror in the cover and holding it for him to see, she said to him, "I want you to meet a good friend of mine." He laughed and the tour proceeded. At one of the Hopi villages the Indian girls challenged her to a footrace. When she beat them, they gave her a Hopi name meaning Beautiful Swift Fox.

"I have been accused of making a living out of what I most like to do," Erna Fergusson wrote in *Sunset*, "with the implication that it is therefore no work. But that's not half of it. When we arrive at your door with a big car with a spade on behind for possible mud, a lunch kit for the inevitable famine, huge thermoses for probable thirst, a strong man for emergencies, and an expectant group of tourists in the back seat, don't get the idea that it just happened."

In 1926 Koshare Tours was sold to the Santa Fe and, with Miss Erna as chief courier, it was expanded into the famed Indian Detour. Tourists left the train at Las Vegas or Lamy, entered Packard or White coaches, and set out via the pueblos all the way to the Grand Canyon and the train again.

The basic intention of these tours was educational rather than just having fun. The advisory board would have enhanced the most prestigious university faculty. It included A. V. Kidder, Edgar L. Hewett, Sylvanus Griswold Morley, Charles F. Lummis, and Frederick Webb Hodge.

Thus it was clear that *Dancing Gods* was no accidental impressionistic book. Rather it was distilled from rich experience, involving years of field work, study, and sympathy with the Indian people.

By 1927 Erna Fergusson decided that she was ready for a full-time career as a writer. Her younger brother, Harvey, was already well established as a novelist. When she asked him if he thought that she could write a book, he replied that any fool could write a book. "And so," she said, "I proceeded to prove him right."

Dancing Gods was published in June 1931. She was fortunate in that her publisher, then and of her subsequent books, was Alfred A. Knopf. No American publisher has ever equalled him in the way his books reflected his own learning, taste, and publishing acumen. He also came to know the West at firsthand. For the ensuing thirty years the Fergusson-Knopf Borzoi books maintained the highest standards of content and format.

What led her to Alfred Knopf? He was her brother's publisher and also of Witter Bynner. It was at Bynner's home that

Erna Fergusson first met Knopf, and it was Bynner who gave her book its happy title. Its illustrations were from paintings of the ceremonials by contemporary southwestern artists, all of them friends of the author. The Knopf edition remains one of the most beautiful of all books on the Southwest.

That Erna Fergusson's prose is the best ever written about the Indian ceremonials—Pueblo, Navajo, Apache—is because it is perceptive and simple, reverent and lucid, and is also infused with qualities of character and style which remain in solution, so that the writer's personal idiosyncrasies and anthropological theories do not muddy the flow of clear prose. The result is deceptively simple, a language like crystal through which the reader sees the subjects free from the distortions of self-conscious personality.

From many possible choices to illustrate what I mean, here is her description of Zuñi Pueblo:

"Forty miles from the railroad, Zuñi Pueblo has all the charm of remoteness; and its outline, as it sits massed on a hill above the river, is probably little changed since it was settled just after the revolution of 1680. Its terraced houses mount against the sky in a terra-cotta pyramid, with ladder-poles and house-top ovens rising above the empty skull of the abandoned mission. There are too many staring white windows for pure beauty, but even they do not spoil the color tone. The river-bank is the same color as the stone and adobe houses, and where it breaks down to the sluggish stream, it is fringed with silver-gray cedar fences, which sometimes support shelters for stock or ragged green straw stacks. Puffs of gray-blue smoke always drift over Zuñi; and all these colors—terra-cotta and gray, dull green and smoke-blue—are repeated in Corn Mountain, whose sculptured buttes rise a thousand feet above the plain."

As my eyes tire and my discrimination increases, I find myself prizing brevity above all in a writer. Erna Fergusson had this quality from the beginning. Although she wrote a great deal, it was never more than enough about a chosen subject. *Dancing*

Gods is a book of just under three hundred pages, and yet it is long enough to be satisfying. The beauty of its thought and language leads the reader to savor it. It does not seek to "explain" the Indian. She acknowledges the gulf between the races. Whereas Anglos sing of love, the Indians sing of the things that matter: rain and sun and corn. Their ceremonies are for growth, for life, not for amusement or entertainment. That is the basic theme of the book.

Dancing Gods made Erna Fergusson overnight into a nationally respected writer. It was accepted as authoritative by those who knew the Indians. Knopf was eager to publish more by her. She wrote successively on Mexico, Guatemala, Venezuela, Chile, Cuba, and Hawaii, coming back finally to the southwest and New Mexico. Along the line she wrote a book on Mexican cookery that goes on selling to this day. Her books were justly described as more than guides and less than histories. There is a category in between; it is called literature.

Each book was the result of both fieldwork and scholarly reading. Her papers bear abundant witness to the methods she employed in documenting her work. Voluminous data was gathered and indexed. Scrapbooks and photographic albums were compiled. Yet most any writer can do as much. What lifted her books to the level of literature was the personal vision which illuminated her material. Her second book, *Fiesta in Mexico*, was written after she had driven alone 20,000 miles south of the border. In Guatemala she travelled with a young woman archaeologist. Her gifts were an inquiring mind, humane concern, abundant energy, and sympathetic goodwill toward our southern neighbors.

On rereading these several travel books I found that the deeper south she went the more impersonal her work became. Only *Guatemala* ranks at the pinnacle with *Dancing Gods* as having the extra dimension of literature. That small, mostly primitive country excited her imagination and brought her prose to colorful life.

143

She had an admirable practice of pasting into a "dummy" of each of her books the reviews and letters it elicited. In a copy of *Guatemala* I found two reviews that probably pleased her as much as anything ever written about her work. The first was by Joseph Henry Jackson, literary editor of the *San Francisco Chronicle* and the author of a book on the same country called *Notes on a Drum*.

"All of this is set down in an easy style that may deceive you at first," Jackson concluded, "into thinking you are reading just another pleasantly written travel book of no account. As you get into Miss Fergusson's, though, you can't help seeing that it's a great deal more. In fact, all unassumingly, she has written the best book on Guatemala since the Maudslays wrote their classic in the nineties."

The other review was by J. Frank Dobie, who ended by saying, "In a way it is a travel book; more accurately it is a book by a person with seeing eyes, understanding nature, and the information necessary for perspective, who travelled to a place, sensed out the very best coign of vantage for seeing, and bored into the land and its people."

Dobie's review led to friendship between him and Erna Fergusson. I recalled that his was one of the photographs in her "gallery." When she was preparing *Our Southwest*, Dobie wrote her a long letter of contacts to make when she came to fieldwork in Texas. Published in 1940 it remains the best general work on the region.

No two delimitations of the Southwest agree. Ed Ainsworth used to say that it was wherever the mesquite grew, until I told him I had seen it growing in London's Kew Gardens. Erna Fergusson included Texas west of Dallas, Colorado of the Mesa Verde, all of New Mexico and Arizona, and none of Southern California. "Who would recognize its gargantuan congeries of Iowa villages as Southwest?" she asked. "Who, living under a hedge of mammoth geraniums on a California farm, miscalled a ranch, knows anything of the arid Southwest?"

144

Her opening chapter, "What is the Southwest?" is still timely, its peroration more pertinent than ever, as we are coming to see the land as something to be cherished, not exploited. "The arid Southwest has always been too strong, too indomitable for most people," she wrote. "Those who can stand it have had to learn that man does not modify this country; it transforms him, deeply. Perhaps our generation will come to appreciate it as the country God remembered and saved for man's delight when he could mature enough to understand it. . . . The Southwest can never be remade into a landscape that produces bread and butter. But it is infinitely productive of the imponderables so much needed by a world weary of getting and spending."

By the mid-1950's Knopf proposed that she update *Our Southwest* for a new edition. She and I discussed it over tea on her *portal*. Repeated operations on her hip made it impossible for her alone to carry out the fieldwork that had lent such charm and authority to her books. Only half-jokingly she suggested that I be her driver and legman. Alas, I had a fulltime job back on the edge of her Southwest. The book was never revised.

In her "dummy" of it I found a letter from a man in Colorado. "I might say in perusing this publication," he wrote, "I overcame my lifelong aversion to reading a book written by a woman—my first in 35 years."

She returned finally to write about her native state in *New Mexico, a Pageant of Three Peoples*, published in 1951. With the aid of a young historian at the University of New Mexico, she revised it for a new edition in the year of her death. It is the best book on the state. In 1973 Paul Horgan prefaced a paperback of the revised edition.

Books such as hers remain valid as literature, regardless of their going out of date in some matters of fact and history. Erna Fergusson can be read now as then for her way of seeing, sensing, and saying—the old Three S's that crop up whenever I write about literature. To be read beyond a writer's time, his work must have this added dimension absent from most travel books.

145

Erna Fergusson completed nearly everything she set out to do. Lack of strength prevented her from finishing a book on the pioneer Tingleys of New Mexico. Her collection contains material assembled for an historical novel about Malinche, Cortez' native consort and liaison with the Aztecs. She sought and received advice from her brother and from her friend, Paul Horgan, and yet for some reason she never undertook the work. She was content that her dear friend, Haniel Long, did write about the Indian woman and dedicated his book to her.

My long day in the university library tower, stevedoring cartons and files, came to an end with a perusal of the diaries she kept during the final decade of her life. They are no more self concerned than was her conversation or her published work. Terse notes on the passage of the hours from early waking to sleep reveal the stoical, stricken woman which her destiny decreed that she must become before release from suffering.

It was growing cold in the tower as I sat reading. I was alone in a cubicle with a view northeast to her beloved Sandias. It was just as she had written me, years before—snow on the mountains, blue sky, cloud shadows on the land. I would read a page, gaze out, and then close my eyes and seek to bring her life and work into focus. I thought of a dead poet's line: "Crack the rock if so you list; bring to light the amethyst." Aye, there was the problem; how to reveal the essential truth of her achievement as woman and writer.

Her entries were a shorthand by which to remember the days. "4.30: Awoke depressed about finances. 11.00: Baby squirrels on the step. 3.00: Jittery. 6.00: A still gray sad day. 11.30: Lights out." And another day: "Too weary to write. Rain. Smell of autumn. Pain getting beyond endurance. Nembutal."

Right up to her death of cancer on July 7, 1964, she persisted in pencilling these notes. They became harder to decipher, until on the day before she died the last entry is a scrawl.

Brave woman, her books her monument.

READING LIST

ERNA FERGUSSON (1888-1964)

Dancing Gods; Indian Ceremonials of New Mexico and Arizona. New York, Knopf, 1931. Albuquerque, University of New Mexico Press, 1957; a facsimile of the first edition.

Fiesta in Mexico. New York, Knopf, 1934.

Guatemala. New York, Knopf, 1938.

Our Southwest. New York, Knopf, 1940.

Mexican Cookbook. Albuquerque, University of New Mexico Press, 1945.

New Mexico; a Pageant of Three Peoples. New York, Knopf, 1951; Revised edition, Albuquerque, University of New Mexico Press, 1964; paperback, with preface by Paul Horgan, 1973.

Mexico Revisited. New York, Knopf, 1955.

DAVID A. REMLEY

Erna Fergusson. Austin, Steck-Vaughn, 1969.

HAMILTON TYLER

Pueblo Gods and Myths. Norman, University of Oklahoma Press, 1964.

FRANK WATERS

Masked Gods; Navaho and Pueblo Ceremonialism. Albuquerque, University of New Mexico Press, 1950.

Photograph of Erna Fergusson, courtesy of Lina Fergusson Browne.

Sky Determines
ROSS CALVIN

To comprehend the literature of New Mexico one requires a topographic map of the state, a map which shows how the mountains, rivers, and plains determine the location and occupation of inhabitants. Dominating all is the great central valley of the Rio Grande, that immemorial lifeline along which history and culture have moved from the beginning.

Literature in New Mexico has flourished best in the upper reaches of that lifegiving river from Albuquerque through Santa Fe to Taos. The southeastern plains, watered frugally by the Rio Pecos, have few laureates, notably Eugene Manlove Rhodes and Paul Horgan.

What of southwestern New Mexico? There the land rises from the Rio Grande toward the Continental Divide, up through Apache country, silver and copper lands, to culminate in the Gila wilderness where the mountains start that river on its way across Arizona to union with the Colorado at Yuma.

Southwestern New Mexico has languished in a literary sense. Its chief settlement, Silver City, lacked a voice until in 1927 there came a young Episcopal clergyman named Ross Calvin. Neither religion nor literature but health brought him and his family to that high dry region. In him an unsung part of the state was to be given its spokesman.

Not only that southwestern part; all of New Mexico was cele-brated in the book that Ross Calvin began to write soon after his arrival and published in 1934, seven years after he first saw New Mexico. It was a land that was to be his home for the remaining forty-three years of his life.

Sky Determines was the felicitous title he gave it, with the subtitle "An Interpretation of the Southwest." What he meant was that New Mexico's history and culture were the result of its climate. This was hardly a new idea, but until Ross Calvin, no one had focussed it as relentlessly as he did on every aspect of the state, past, present, and future.

Sky Determines was an immediate success, praised by critics and relished by readers. Ernie Pyle, that wandering journalist who was to die in the war, called it his southwestern Bible. After its eastern publisher let the book go out of print, the post-war immigration into New Mexico led to a demand for its reissue. Accordingly new editions were published in 1948 and 1965.

When we examine the genesis and growth of this book which has become a classic of New Mexico and of the Southwest, we see that it grew organically out of its writer's education, experi-ence, and environment.

Ross Randall Calvin was born in 1889 on an Illinois farm only ten miles, Ernie Pyle observed, from the Indiana farm on which Pyle was born. From schooling at Depauw College in Greencastle, Indiana, Calvin went on to Harvard for graduate work, and there in 1916 he received the Ph.D. in English philol-ogy. He then taught at Carnegie Tech and Syracuse. After at-tending the General Theological Seminary in New York, he was ordained an Episcopal minister. Within three years he became a curate in Trinity Parish, New York, and then rector of St. Peter's Memorial Church in Geneva, New York.

There his health broke. He was ordered to seek recovery in the Southwest. His first fifteen years were spent in the Silver City pastorate, followed by an equal number of years at Clovis in eastern New Mexico, and finally by thirteen years of retirement in Albuquerque where he was canon honorary at St. John's Cathedral. He died on January 30, 1970. During those long years as clergyman-naturalist-writer, Ross Calvin had become truly a New Mexican.

An early interest in nature is revealed in his papers, housed in the Library of the University of New Mexico. Among them is the first tiny notebook of a series he kept throughout his life. He was only twelve years old when he began to jot down observations of birds, animals, and weather. His Log Book, he called this long project, and it shows him to be a born naturalist. Also among his papers is an unpublished manuscript entitled "Moods of Earth and Sky," composed of entries selected from fifty years of the Log Book.

This interest in natural phenomena is at the heart of *Sky Determines*—this ability precisely to see and to interpret nature. His power of description was enhanced by his literary-linguistic education. Thus we see that experience and training were brought to bear on environment, the enthralling new landscape of southwestern New Mexico. From observations made on walks and rides and from wide reading and correspondence with authorities, his book was born.

And born from necessity. As a result of doctors' orders to spend as much time as possible out of doors, Calvin rambled over the foothills of Silver City, penetrating deeper and higher into the Gila wilderness. Stopping to rest, he would observe and contemplate, and then make notes on the three by five cards he carried with him.

He also used a camera to fix landscapes for later recall. Specimens of plant life were studied under the microscope. Finding no answers locally, he sought them in the literature of earlier observers. His papers also hold replies to inquiries directed to botanists, zoologists, meteorologists, and other learned persons throughout the Southwest.

As the 1930's sank into the Depression, the Calvins' living became a meagre one. In a diary kept during those lean years we discern the outline of a frugal existence. Lacking money to pay help, Dr. Calvin often swept the church and tended the furnace. Gasoline for a second-hand car was bought in small amounts. On September 30, 1931, he entered these words: "The month lingering like an unloved guest. Infection on hands and feet and other skin trouble have made it a time of misery. Eight kinds of medicine were used, to say nothing of others for hay fever and insomnia. And the price of my stocks dropping steadily day after day."

There was always the work of the parish—marriages, births, christenings, confirmations, deaths. One entry tells of sitting all night by a dying boy's bed and then in the morning carrying the little body downstairs for burial.

He was a clergyman first, then a naturalist, and in what time was left, a writer. It was the compulsiveness of a born writer, and an obsession with an unrelenting theme, that served to advance the writing of *Sky Determines*, in spite of adversity, illness, and all other demands and interests. Once he had picked up the trail of the all-determining Sky Powers, Calvin followed it from ecology to anthropology, history, and economics, through the long range of New Mexican culture from its earliest appearance in the art of the Mimbres Valley potters.

Conceived thus in illness and economic uncertainty, what might have been a sombre treatise proved instead a hymn to life. In the opening pages, Ross Calvin sounded this high note:

"There hovers over many of the pages a shadowy ulterior purpose of pointing out to a bedevilled humanity that in the world of roots and clouds and wings and leaves there exists no Depression; that in its beauties and simples rather than from divers bewildered senates and parliaments is man's peace most likely to be derived; that as life progressively adapts itself to its background of sun and soil, it gains in wholesomeness and sincerity."

Twenty years later, Joseph Wood Krutch was to speak for

Arizona in similar language. Whether or not Calvin and Krutch ever met, by their books are they blood brothers.

The Depression rendered unlikely the publication of a manuscript by an unknown author from a remote region. At least one New York publisher rejected it before Calvin succeeded in placing it through an agent with the Macmillan Company. Even then that venerable publisher was forced by the hard times to require the author to pay half the costs of publication.

In looking for influences on Calvin's theme, his bibliography in *Sky Determines* provides clues. I lend importance to the presence there of the noted geographer Ellsworth Huntington's *The Climatic Factor as Illustrated in Arid America*, published by the Carnegie Institution in 1914. Also cited was John C. Van Dyke's *The Desert* which inaugurated a new appreciation of the arid lands.

When in 1964 I sent Ross Calvin a brief list of "Good Reading About the Desert" (which included, of course, *Sky Determines*), he wrote me,

"You must know, although few others do nowadays, the grand book which gave me my first introduction to the desert. It was the work of an eastern art critic—of all people—who lectured long ago at Harvard and Princeton. His name? John C. Van Dyke. The book? Simply *The Desert*. Scribner, 1901. What a color vocabulary he had! And he knew with surprising accuracy many of the plants and animals of the wastes. But above all, how sensitive he was to desert light and air!"

A later influence on Calvin was the early topographical explorer, William H. Emory, whose *Notes of a Military Reconnaissance from Fort Leavenworth . . . to San Diego*, published in 1848, was a field report which covered lands investigated subsequently by Calvin. In 1951 Calvin annotated the work for the University of New Mexico Press as *Lieutenant Emory Reports*.

There is no way of knowing how many people have been drawn to New Mexico by a reading of *Sky Determines*. We have specific evidence that one was—a young hospital technician named Lyle Saunders, who was to become the author of a comprehensive bibliography of New Mexico.

When *Sky Determines* was first republished, Saunders reviewed it in the *New Mexico Quarterly*. He told there of how a chance reading of the first edition had led him to quit his job in a New York hospital, burn his bridges, and set out in a newly painted bright red 1928 Chevrolet for the Land of Cíbola.

"It was with vast ignorance and great expectations," Saunders wrote, "that I came to New Mexico, sustained by the bright promise of a book which proclaimed and illustrated the thesis that in the beauties and simplicities of the world of roots and clouds and wings is man's peace most likely to be found. I was not disappointed. From the moment when I first saw the sky and earth of New Mexico from the top of Raton Pass late on a September afternoon (which is the way all newcomers should see it first), I have known that my decision was right and that Calvin had written with under- and not with over-statement."

Sky Determines was uniformly acclaimed by authoritative reviewers, including Erna Fergusson, although she also reproached Calvin for his narrow view of the Hispanos, a view that he widened somewhat in later editions and in an essay called "The People of New Mexico." The most poignant tribute was that written by Eugene Manlove Rhodes, the cowboy laureate of the lower Rio Grande, who penned it on his deathbed in San Diego. In sending his review to Ross Calvin with a covering letter, he wrote,

"Congratulations on *Sky Determines*. A charming book. The only book about New Mexico which admits that the world does not end suddenly just south of Albuquerque. Give us some more. Ave et vale. Good luck. Very sick. Excuse scrawl." The envelope was postmarked June 27, 1934. Gene Rhodes died that night. Today the framed letter hangs on the wall of the Coronado Room in the University of New Mexico Library.

Ross Calvin did indeed answer Rhodes' call for more. In 1946 there appeared his *River of the Sun; Stories of the Storied Gila*,

154

a kind of coda to Sky Determines. It was conceived on a lower level of imagination.

The Gila book was born under lenses, Calvin wrote in the foreword, and went on to say that he meant "the lens of a botanical magnifier . . . the lens of a camera . . . the lenses of a powerful pair of binoculars by which eyes see better and farther, and so give testimony not of hearsay but of a witness. The mass of material so gathered represents, in addition, of course, to the necessary reading, the distillation of hundreds of field trips— the most complete release, the richest relaxation in a fairly busy life."

Calvin observed how cause and effect operate throughout a river's course. What occurred up near the headwaters inevitably affected the lands below Gila Bend. Today the problem of river control is agitating the conservationists who see the Army Engineers' Lower Gila plan as a threat to wildlife.

Whereas Calvin's sustained prose sings throughout Sky Determines, much of River of the Sun is reportorial. Rare are such exalted passages as this hymn to the most cherished range grass of all:

"Prince of the family is the regal blue grama (Bouteloua gracilis), which bears regularly on each side of its stalks two purple spikes which in autumn ripen and curl into graceful golden sickles. The graceful grama, as its name implies, is a thing of beauty, and though it extend in an unbroken plantation miles across, each plant still seems a rarity. And where a savannah of them, nodding in the breeze and dotted with well-spaced junipers, stretches far into the distance to overlap the flank of a blue mountain, only a dolt can remain insensitive. Grasslands have always and everywhere been wealth, but they are also beauty. Such scenes, oftentimes enriched with added interest by a herd of antelope, everywhere met the eye of the early traveler in the Southwest. The sea of grass, then, rather than the desert, is the picture of the grazing country which history holds up."

In format, River of the Sun is the most attractive of Calvin's books. This was due to its having been designed for the University of New Mexico Press by Carl Hertzog, the master printer of El Paso.

In 1948 the University of New Mexico Press reissued *Sky Determines*, with minor revisions and additions. Peter Hurd's black and white drawings are a lesser substitute, however, for the beautiful photographs by Calvin and his wife which illustrated the first edition. The author's "Afterthought," a kind of booster message which anticlimaxed the first edition and was deplored by Erna Fergusson, is expanded to claim credit for being the first to propose that, in 1940, the state of New Mexico hold a Coronado Cuarto Centennial celebration. (The matter is documented in the Calvin papers, where it appears that Calvin's first suggestion in 1932 was antedated a year by Charles D. Martin's resolution presented to the Chavez County Historical Society. In conceding this priority, Calvin went down with banners flying, as he observed that although his was not necessarily the first or only seed, it was the seed that sprouted and grew. He was right.)

In 1965 the University of New Mexico Press published a third edition of *Sky Determines*. This is a photo-reprint of the 1948 version, with 74 pages of new material tacked on at the end. The additions represented the author's effort to modernize the book as a result of the two great New Mexican explosions—of the bomb and of the population. His intention was well meaning. New Mexico *had* changed. "Man Determines," Calvin observed, might well have been the sub-title of this third edition.

What was called for, however, was a new and separate book. Unable to achieve this, he succeeded only in blemishing his earlier work. There was no one to save the book from its author, and from the desire of its publisher to make it an up-to-date work on the state. It would seem that its first brilliant success had dazzled Ross Calvin. Lost was the gift of self-criticism. His power over language had weakened. He was unable to recognize that he had in him only a single inspiration which came at the summit of his prime and which never came again.

156

Ross Calvin remains an odd figure among Southwestern writers. That he did not achieve more supreme works is partly due to the demands upon him of his thirty years of devoted church labors in New Mexico. These he never slighted. His most tangible and lasting achievement occurred during the Clovis pastorate when he built the Church of St. James, an enchanting structure of adobes in the ancient manner. Parish activities, innumerable sermons, writing for church and regional periodicals, family responsibilities and ill health—all of these drained off the creative vitality that might have flowed into and ennobled successors to *Sky Determines*. By the time he retired, approaching seventy, it was too late.

He never became a part of the cultural colonies in New Mexico. Although a prolific writer, he was not a literary person in the way of Haniel Long or Erna Fergusson. Although he and Long were once on the faculty of Carnegie Tech at the same time, there was little intercourse between them when they became New Mexicans. More than miles separated Santa Fe and Silver City.

Both Long and Calvin left Pittsburghiana in their bibliographies. Calvin's is called *Barnabas in Pittsburgh* (subsidized by him for publication in 1966), a biographical history of a welfare house for outcasts founded in 1900 by Gouverneur Provoost Hance. This, home where society's totally rejected were cared for, went long unrecognized by the Episcopal Church. Dr. Calvin chronicled its dedicated existence to final acceptance by the Church as the Monastic Order of the St. Barnabas Brotherhood. Pious and moving a work though it be, *Barnabas in Pittsburgh* is a far piece from *Sky Determines*.

So what does it add up to? That among the vast number of books about the Southwest, proliferating endlessly, classics are few. That in his good long life of eighty years, Ross Calvin achieved one and one only. And also that only one is needed to place an author in our pantheon.

That *sky* does indeed *determine* is brought home to Southwesterners whenever the land withers in drought. Consolation may be found then in words which bring Ross Calvin's master-piece to a close:

"And when the last Americano in the fulness of time follows the last Spaniard and the last red man into the shadows, this will still be the same poignantly unforgettable land of beauty, its arid mesas, canyons, and deserts lying perpetually beneath an ocean of pure light, and its Sky Gods still pouring frugally from their *ollas*, the violet-soft rain."

READING LIST

ROSS CALVIN (1889-1970)

Sky Determines; an Interpretation of the Southwest. New York, Macmillan, 1934.

————Ill. by Peter Hurd. Albuquerque, University of New Mexico Press, 1948. Revised edition.

————Ill. by Peter Hurd. Albuquerque, University of New Mexico Press, 1965. Revised and enlarged edition.

River of the Sun; Stories of the Storied Gila. Albuquerque, University of New Mexico Press, 1946.

Barnabas in Pittsburgh; From Common Clay to Legend. New York, Carlton, 1966.

WILLIAM H. EMORY

Lieutenant Emory Reports. Edited by Ross Calvin. Albuquerque, University of New Mexico Press, 1951. Reprints Emory's *Notes of a Military Reconnaissance,* 1848.

Photograph of Ross Calvin, courtesy of University of New Mexico Library Special Collections.

Pasó por Aquí

EUGENE MANLOVE RHODES

"Strong natures do not willingly concentrate on poetry," Robinson Jeffers once observed, obviously with himself in mind. "They need some blindness or exile to shut them up to it."

This is the key to the character of Eugene Manlove Rhodes, who began as a "locoed cowboy" poet and ended as the prose laureate of the cattle kingdom. Rhodes is to southeastern New Mexico what Santee is to southern Arizona, and Dobie to all of Texas—the dominant creative figure of those arid rangelands.

If not forced by exile, confined by marriage, and driven by need to be a writer, Rhodes would not have lived as long as he did—to his mid-sixties—for the violence of his youth foretold an early death.

"If I hadn't met you," he said to his wife at the end of his life, "I should probably never have written any stories. I was about to engage in a life of outlawry. It looked very attractive."

He wasn't joking. From the age of thirteen when his family moved in 1881 from his native Nebraska via Kansas to the Tularosa basin of New Mexico—a *bolsón* (big pocket) one hundred fifty miles long by fifty miles wide, closed on the west by the White Sands, black *malpaís,* and the San Andrés range and on the east by the even higher Sacramentos—young Gene roughed it as a well-driller's roustabout and a wrangler on the celebrated Bar Cross Ranch.

161

Later he homesteaded and ran a few steers and horses high in the San Andrés mountains. Like Ross Santee, his Arizona counterpart, Rhodes preferred horses to cattle and never became a top hand. A daredevil rider, he also served as a volunteer guide on a hunt for Geronimo.

It was a violent frontier, scene of the bloody Lincoln County wars and the killing of Billy the Kid by Sheriff Pat Garrett. Rhodes was in the thick of it, short-fused, quixotic, standing five eight and weighing one hundred fifty pounds, a wildcat of a man, though no killer. After witnessing the violent deaths of thirteen men he said he preferred peace. Salvation lay in his abstention from alcohol. Most of the West's bloodshed he believed was due to drunkenness. The code by which he came to live was the honorable one of Chivalry. His motto was *Pay for what you break*.

Rhodes' heritage helped preserve him for literature. His parents were educated, his father a colonel of volunteers in the Civil War and a great raconteur; his bookish mother was a graduate of what was later Knox College. They encouraged their son in his late teens to leave the frontier for two years at the College of the Pacific, then located in San José. There he began to write. What money he had came from summers as a harvest hand in the Salinas Valley. In 1888 he visited Carmel and described it later as it was in that halcyon time of Robert Louis Stevenson who, incidentally, was one of his idols. Only when his money ran out did he return to New Mexico.

Soon thereafter he came upon *Land of Sunshine*, the lively new periodical edited in Los Angeles by Charles F. Lummis. Beginning in 1896 with a poem, Rhodes was a contributor of verse and prose for the next ten years. "This has red blood in it," Lummis exclaimed of Rhodes' first story. As usual he was right in his literary perception.

Although it was the *Saturday Evening Post* that eventually provided Rhodes with payments more commensurate with his worth, Lummis was the first to recognize and encourage him. Their friendship was never broken, though Lummis was unspar-

162

ing in his criticism. When Rhodes' first book appeared in 1910, it drew these words:

"You have done a very extraordinary thing. Very uneven, in places hazy. Not entirely pulled together in a final drawstring. A novel made up of episodes. But you have made the best talking book that ever came out of the mouth of the West. The language they use on occasion is frequent and painful and free. And to my surprise you have some desirable ladies. I often think back to the times I rapped your knuckles for doing just what you do now. I never saw any work of yours I didn't admire. I never saw any of it that I didn't want to kick you for not doing it better, as you are perfectly competent to do."

Exile was the result of Rhodes' marriage. Lummis's magazine set the events in motion. When Rhodes' parents moved from New Mexico to Pasadena, they met a nurse whose younger sister in New York state had been left a pregnant widow with one child. From Mrs. Rhodes the nurse heard about her literary son in New Mexico. When the nurse returned to New York to help her sister recuperate from diphtheria, she took with her a copy of *Land of Sunshine* containing a Rhodes poem about the Santa Fe Trail. She read it aloud, to the pleasure of the convalescent. "Why not write and tell him so?" she suggested.

It was that simple, romantic and fateful. After several months of silence, he replied with a twenty-page letter. A two-year correspondence ensued. No scrap remains. By his instructions, the letters were burned by his widow. In 1899, propelled by an unhappy love affair in New Mexico, Rhodes headed east to marry Mrs. May Davison Purple.

Lacking the fare, he got a job as cattle-prodder on a trainload of steers bound ultimately by ship for Liverpool. He reached New York with torn clothes and battered face from a victorious fight en route with an ex-pugilist also employed on the train. He bought a cheap suit and back-tracked to the village of Apalachin on the Susquehanna, near the New York-Pennsylvania border.

When May met the stage at a haunted trysting place called

Spooky Bridge, a man got off she saw as a mouse-colored blonde with sunburned face and piercing blue eyes, and "hard as nails and quick as greased lightning." It was Eugene Manlove Rhodes, age thirty, bringing marriage offerings of a red *papier-maché* telescope for the boys and for her a pearl-handled revolver, a volume of Kipling's verse—and himself.

"We kissed each other, a bit timidly, I'll allow," May wrote in the posthumous biography, *The Hired Man on Horseback* (the title came from Rhodes' most famous cowboy poem), "and hand in hand we paced slowly up the hill to the house." There she and her sons lived with her parents.

Marriage followed in two weeks, and four days later Rhodes returned to New Mexico—alone. He lacked the fare for his wife and stepsons. It was the following summer before he could send for them. What May did in that brief initial meeting was her supreme gift to him: she strengthened his determination to be a writer and refused to let him take an office job in an eastern city.

Back together in New Mexico they lived first in Tularosa, a town shaded by old cottonwoods—*alamosgordos*. It was an odd honeymoon. Gene left soon for six weeks on the fall roundup at his ranch twenty-five miles away in the mountains. Marriage hardly gentled him. On Thanksgiving Day in 1900 he boxed Tularosa's six best Mexicans and beat them all. His passion was also for baseball. On the day Tularosa played nearby Alamogordo, the former's first baseman refused to go, whereupon Gene left May holding the reins while he whipped the recalcitrant player and stowed him in the wagon.

Life became even rougher for May when they moved up to the ranch. She was pregnant. Any life other than Spartan, even for her, was inconceivable to Gene. Their son Alan (named for a Stevenson character) was born in Tularosa with a minimum of medical and nursing care. Their only money came from the sale of steers. To supplement it Gene took the teacher's examination in Alamogordo and passed with top grades. The certificate was denied him, however, on grounds that his "moral conduct" did not warrant it. He would have made a great frontier teacher.

In need of cash and encouraged by the rancher-writer, Agnes Morley Cleaveland of Datil, Gene turned earnestly to writing, determined to crack the eastern market. He did. *McClure's*, whose managing editor was Willa Cather, was the first to fall. They paid $40 for his story, four times as much as Lummis's lean budget had allowed.

Even with this turn of fortune their marriage was under strain. He was often away at the ranch. May's aging parents needed her. She grew homesick. And so in 1903 she and the boys went back to Apalachin.

Their separation lasted three years. He kept writing, at night by lamplight, and sending his stories for May to edit and type. In the end it was more than love that reunited them. New Mexico grew too hot for him. Legend has it that two warrants were out for his arrest, one for following the old frontier custom when hungry of killing your neighbor's beef rather than your own, and the other for assaulting the purist who turned him in. Years later at the peak of his fame, Rhodes was humorously pardoned by the governor of New Mexico and made a colonel on his staff with special license plates for his car.

Rhodes reached Apalachin on the 23d of April 1906 with three dollars, May's guitar and her favorite rug. "There was so much to tell, so much to listen to," she recalled, "we sat till late in the night and the kerosene lamp burned low. It snowed that night, and when he wakened and saw the ground white, he thought he was ruined for life. He never came to like springtime in New York. He used to say he never did *live* there; just went back and got snowed in for twenty years."

Nor did the East ever mellow his temper. When a neighbor cast aspersions on May's homemade cheeses, Gene climbed up on his wagon and fed him his words. Another time he whipped a man who persisted in blocking his sleigh. Mostly though he was peaceful and loving toward neighbors and family.

Marriage and exile thus joined to bring Rhodes to renown as

a writer. Looking back at New Mexico during those long years of absence, he found that he had miraculously brought it with him. "When I was riding that country," he said, "my mind was a fresh, blank page. Everything I saw—rock, canyon, peak, spring—is there to this day."

And to a character in one of his stories he gave these impassioned words: "You would have seen, perhaps, only a howling wilderness, but this man was to look back, waking and in dream, and to remember that brooding and sunlit silence as the glowing heart of the world. From this place alone he was to be an exile."

Eastern farming was foreign to this western ranching man, yet farm he did as May's parents declined in strength. Farming income was eating money; that from writing was spending money. He was openhanded with what he had.

After ten years at Apalachin he wrote to Lummis: "Myself, have resolutely declined to cultivate or develop artistic temperament or, if I do say it, to have my head turned by flattery. I get plenty of it; but I never write well enough to please myself. I don't like to write; I like to live. Want to go to South America, and Africa and Australia, especially the last. Am 47 going on 60. Have enormous and shackly old farm house. Am success as farmer: like it: hate climate: detest N.Y. idea of standardizing all thinking, making carbon copies of men. Family life happy but am dreadfully dissatisfied with the East, and with raising boys here. Tied down—duties—can't get away without shirking some."

In 1907 he sold his first story to the *Saturday Evening Post,* the periodical responsible for establishing and sustaining his national reputation until the end of his life. In 1910 he sent his first book, *Good Men and True,* to Lummis with these words, "I am sending you the first copy of my own first immortal monumental etc. work. And, by the way—did I ever thank you for guiding, philosophizing and friending me?"

Rhodes never became a prolific writer. Writing was drudgery and a last resort when he needed spending money. "It seems impossible for me to finish a story," he declared, "except under the pressure of want. I *work* on them all the time—but finish when broke. Every time I finish a story I am filled with astonishment. It is really a sort of miracle."

His love for baseball never cooled. When a New York editor telegraphed him to come to what promised to be a lucrative conference, Rhodes wired back that a ball game in which he was to play had priority. In 1911 he went to nearby Cornell University with these priorities: "to see baseball, boat races, and to consult the library."

Poker was another passion. At a meeting in Philadelphia with the *Post's* editors, Gene cleaned them out. Henceforth they did business with him by mail. His "The Come-On" is a great poker story.

In 1919 Hollywood lured him. He hoped to sell some of his stories to the movies. The cowboy actor, Harry Carey, starred in three of Rhodes' tales for which the writer received $2500 apiece. Most of the money went back to Apalachin. Again he was separated from his family for nearly three years.

Rhodes lived in a cottage on Marmion Way on the west bank of the Arroyo Seco, near the Southwest Museum and Lummis's rock house, El Alisal. The two men formed a congenial group, along with Will Levington Comfort, Will Rogers, Harry Carr, and Maynard Dixon, Rhodes' favorite western painter. Yet the period proved barren for him as a writer. He needed May, his indispensable muse. Wasn't his pet-name for her "Mary and Martha"?

Stewart Edward White's *Arizona Nights* had long been one of Rhodes' best-loved books, and at this time in Los Angeles there occurred a conversation we fervently wish someone had reported. All we know is from this passage in a Rhodes letter: "All morning I have been riding with Capt. McKittrick, 'The Old Cattleman' of *Arizona Nights*. And, say, we had some talk."

In 1922 Rhodes returned to Apalachin. Three years later May's parents died. In another year they sold the farm and headed for New Mexico by car. The long exile was ended. All that Rhodes ever really liked about the East, he told Lummis, was the indoor plumbing.

He and May settled in Santa Fe where Mary Austin baked them her own little cakes. Inez and Gerald Cassidy were also their friends, and they rented poet Alice Corbin Henderson's house in nearby Tesuque.

The altitude of 7000 feet proved too high for Gene's heart, weakened by influenza, and so they moved back down to his beloved range. "Youth has come back to me overnight," he exulted. Tularosa, however, was a disappointment. The old water-drinking cottonwoods had been sacrificed for shade-skimpy poplars. From down the road in Alamogordo the sheriff sent greetings by a friend, explaining that he could not pay them in person since he still held those warrants for Gene's arrest.

The land around was unchanged. Rhodes urged Maynard Dixon to come and paint its changing colors. Publishers kept asking him to write his autobiography. He never did, preferring to transform it into fiction. He planned a collaboration with another old-timer on a book about early New Mexico. He was never able to finish it.

As his health failed Rhodes grew discouraged, then despondent, leading Lummis, on the eve of his own death from cancer, to write his old protegé a stern letter of mingled reproach and sympathy. When Rhodes heard of Don Carlos' passing, he wrote to Maynard Dixon, "Lummis has left us. It is a great grief to me that I could not have seen him again."

At this time Rhodes read *Death Comes for the Archbishop* and gave it high praise. He warred constantly against the critical school of H. L. Mencken, whose Atlantic seaboard critics denigrated the West without venturing across the Hudson. Staunch allies were the rambunctious Utahan Bernard DeVoto and the Texans Walter Prescott Webb and J. Frank Dobie, all good men and true.

Winters in the Tularosa basin proved too rigorous. In 1931

the Rhodes went into what proved his last exile, to Pacific Beach at San Diego. There they lived for the remaining three years of his life, caught in the crushing grip of the Depression.

During the Apalachin years the farm had sapped Rhodes' strength in what was his writing prime, so that these anguished words were then wrung from him, "To write stories one needs some ease and *rest* when you are worn out. I am very tired, and yet I can write only at night."

Now on the Pacific shore ease and rest were his; alas, his strength was gone. The timing was wrong. Although his publisher kept advancing small sums on the Old-Timers manuscript, his collaborator had died and Rhodes was unable to finish it alone.

When Phil Townsend Hanna, that first great editor of *Westways* (then called *Touring Topics*) heard of Rhodes' straits, he commissioned him to write a monthly commentary. Six appeared, from December 1932 through June 1933. They were verbose, cranky and bitter. In his own words, he lacked the gift of brevity possessed by Will Rogers.

Rhodes never lacked friends. During the final years his especial ones were his fellow writers, Max Miller, Alan Le May, Walt Coburn, Stewart Lake, and Eddy Orcutt of the San Diego *Union*. A proposed subscription set of Rhodes' collected work, to be called the Bar Cross Edition and illustrated by Maynard Dixon and Ed Borein, died in the Depression.

In her tender book about her husband, May Rhodes tells heartbreakingly of those last years. "Not all the California sunshine could brighten the knowledge that we were old and broken and practically penniless. The fledglings were grown. They were gone. There were only a very lonely man and a very lonely woman, long, weary miles from the special lands we loved."

Their car enabled them to enjoy rides in the back country as far as Palomar Mountain where a bookish old Tularosa waddie lived. When the *Post* rejected Rhodes' last manuscript, *Beyond the Desert*, as too long for serialization, he telegraphed that

169

they were down to forty-eight cents and to please wire something, anything, that he would make any necessary cuts. They sent a $100 advance by return telegram.

As Rhodes' life drew to a close, a roadrunner came every day to their yard. "It knows I am homesick for New Mexico," Gene said to May, "and has come to comfort me." His last writing was a review for the *Union* of *Sky Determines*, mailed to Ross Calvin on the day of Rhodes' death.

He died at home of heart spasms in the early morning of June 27, 1934. He was fortunate to be spared the desolation which overtook Robinson Jeffers and Raymond Chandler, for instance, whose wives preceded them in death. By his wish, May took her husband's body back to New Mexico and buried it high and deep in the San Andrés range, up in Rhodes Canyon where he had homesteaded long before. There it rests under a great red rock on which is inscribed:

Pasó por Aquí
Eugene Manlove Rhodes
Jan. 19, 1869—June 27, 1934

The years have passed, his work endures. What is it about it that enthralls readers? Never a great number, they are known as "the passionate few." His faults are the obvious ones Lummis noted in the beginning. His plots are often too complicated and weakly motivated. His characters are never subtly drawn, his women mostly untouchable. It was Dobie who remarked truly that Rhodes' reach always exceeded his grasp.

What is it then? Of primary importance is the *setting*, the backdrop of desert and mountains that Rhodes adored. His land is southern New Mexico, from Belen in the north to El Paso and from Silver City beyond the Rio Grande to Roswell on the Pecos, a domain he made his own even as Harvey Fergusson did the landscape of northern New Mexico.

And the *characters*. Although drawn in the flat, their actions are real, for they were taken from the people Rhodes knew and often gave their true names. They talk the lingo of the range as heard by a writer with an ear for the cadence and nuance of living speech.

Harder to isolate is the *flavor* of the writer himself, his charm that he magically infused into his prose. His was a personal way of writing that led him at times to pepper his narratives with utterances quite unlike the usual *Post* style.

Still another Rhodes hallmark is his *literary allusiveness,* the flowery talk of the waddies which echoed his own reading. Many are the legends of "the locoed cowboy" who read as he rode. During his years on the range, each sack of Bull Durham smoking tobacco held a free book coupon, good for a wide range of classical literature. As a result every bunkhouse had its own library, and bookish cowboys such as Gene Rhodes were not all that rare.

Finally, there is also present throughout his work the shock of *reversed values* which came from Rhodes having been the underdog at outs with the law. His good guys are the bad guys and vice versa. His villains are the bankers, lawyers, landowners, law officers, his heroes the loners running for their lives. Rhodes perceived that a man in adversity sometimes rises to his best and becomes a Robin Hood, a Cyrano de Bergerac, a Musketeer. He did not include Billy the Kid.

All of these Rhodesian qualities are concentrated in his short novel, *Pasó por Aqui*—the story of a bank and store robber pursued by the law and seeking to escape into Mexico from the Tularosa basin. On the verge of success he encounters a poor Mexican family dying of diphtheria in their shack on the edge of the White Sands. He abandons all thought of flight and stays to nurse the family through the crisis. When the posse catches up with him and the sheriff sees what the fugitive had done, he personally escorts him to safety. If you like it, you will read more of Rhodes. If not, don't try, for this is his best.

He has been well-served posthumously. *The Best Novels and Stories,* prefaced by J. Frank Dobie, followed his widow's biography with its impassioned introduction by Bernard DeVoto. In W. H. Hutchinson, Rhodes found his ideal biographer and bibliographer who drew on his own and the collection in the Huntington Library to write a model "Life and Letters" called *A Bar Cross Man*. For thirty years Hutchinson of Cohasset Stage, near Chico in Northern California, labored to keep Rhodes in the public eye. In addition to his two scholarly books, "Hutch" compiled two anthologies, *A Rhodes Reader* and *The Little World Waddies*, and also persuaded the University of Oklahoma Press to reprint most of Rhodes in its Western Frontier Library series. His was a pious and heroic labor, the royalties from which eased the old age of Rhodes' widow. A good brief introduction to the man and his work is Edwin W. Gaston's *Eugene Manlove Rhodes, Cowboy Chronicler*, a pamphlet published by Steck-Vaughn in Dallas. A moving personal memoir is in Agnes Morley Cleaveland's *No Life for a Lady*. C. L. Sonnichsen's *Tularosa* is essential background reading.

With my fondness for grave pilgrimages, I set out in the fall to pay homage at the last resting place of Eugene Manlove Rhodes. I knew that the state legislature had given charge of the grave to the New Mexico State University at Las Cruces, on the campus of which stands Rhodes Hall. I also knew that the Alamogordo Chamber of Commerce could tell me how to penetrate the San Andrés range.

I had failed to reckon with higher authority, namely the U.S. Department of Army, which controls the White Sands Missile Range, an area occupying much of the *bolsón* and its guardian mountains. Here the first atomic bomb was exploded. At the Chamber of Commerce I learned that only once a year, on the first Sunday in June, does the Army permit the Chamber to conduct a four-wheel drive caravan of Rhodesians across the range to the remote gravesite.

I came in November. June was too long to wait. So I went to the Public Library and consoled myself by an open fireplace of spicy juniper logs. And I examined the Rhodes archive gathered

172

by W. H. Hutchinson and given to the library by its Friends group who also published an edition of *Pasó por Aqui*. That night I fell asleep after reading Rhodes' great *Post* success of 1912, the novel called *The Little Eohippus*, its prose so permeated with this writer's charm.

I have been chided for overstressing the value of reading a writer while in the region about which he wrote. Though it is true that a good book is universally a good book, it is also true that reading it *in situ* sometimes heightens goodness to greatness.

On the frosty clear morrow I drove north toward the shining 12000-feet peak of Sierra Blanca, passing La Luz where Anthony Adverse ended his days. They say that people come there to look for his grave and the obliging natives point one out. In Tularosa there were the poplars Rhodes detested. I was tempted to turn east past the base of the great white mountain and follow the Rio Hondo to San Patricio and Roswell on the Pecos, through a land the painter Peter Hurd has made his own.

Literature's priority was higher. At Carrizozo I turned west and threaded the *malpais*, the White Sands gleaming in the south, and then traversed a mesa of juniper forest over into rangeland falling to the Rio Grande below Socorro. From there the road wandered off into the lonely land of the Magdalena and Datil mountains and the Plains of San Agustin, setting of an early Rhodes' story, "Beyond the Desert."

Pasó por aqui? That man had indeed come this way and left his name on the land, there at "the glowing heart of the world."

READING LIST

EUGENE MANLOVE RHODES (1869-1934)

Bransford in Arcadia; or, The Little Eohippus. New York, Holt, 1914.

Once in the Saddle and *Pasó por Aquí.* Boston, Houghton Mifflin, 1927.

The Little World Waddies. El Paso, Carl Hertzog for W. H. Hutchinson, 1946.

Best Novels and Stories. Edited by Frank V. Dearing. Introduction by J. Frank Dobie. Boston, Houghton Mifflin, 1949.

The Rhodes Reader. Selected by W. H. Hutchinson. Norman, University of Oklahoma Press, 1957.

Pasó por Aquí. Alamogordo, Friends of the Alamogordo Public Library, 1963; University of Oklahoma Press, 1973. Intro. by W. H. Hutchinson, illus. by W. H. D. Koerner.

MAY DAVISON RHODES

The Hired Man on Horseback; My Story of Eugene Manlove Rhodes. Introduction by Bernard DeVoto. Boston, Houghton Mifflin, 1938.

W. H. HUTCHINSON

A Bar Cross Man; the Life and Personal Writings of Eugene Manlove Rhodes. Norman, University of Oklahoma Press, 1956.

A Bar Cross Liar; Bibliography of Eugene Manlove Rhodes. Stillwater, Oklahoma, Redlands Press, 1959.

EDWIN W. GASTON, JR.

Eugene Manlove Rhodes, Cowboy Chronicler. Austin, Steck-Vaughn, 1967.

Photograph of Eugene Manlove Rhodes, courtesy of W. H. Hutchinson.

174

Lost Pony Tracks

ROSS SANTEE

There are differing instances of the time when Southwestern writers felt that "shock of recognition" which told them they had reached their place of destiny. Such revelation came in his youth to Oliver La Farge when, as a Harvard student, he joined a summer dig in the Four Corners country. Mary Austin was middle-aged when she first saw Taos and knew her fate henceforth as a New Mexican. To the same magnetic region D. H. Lawrence's response was immediate and passionate. And when his train was delayed in the piñon forest near Laguna Pueblo, Haniel Long stepped down fatefully into what became his Promised Land.

Let Ross Santee tell of his moment of truth whereby an Iowan out of Chicago and New York became a Southwesterner:

"The country itself dwarfed everything. The little ranch house in the distance could hardly be defined against the great expanse of country and the great dome of the sky. Later on, the cowboy jogging along on his pony looked like a moving dot; if it wasn't for the dust his pony's feet kicked up, he might have been standing still. It was some place west of El Paso in New Mexico. It was the spring of 1915, and it was my first trip West."

There and then the 25-year-old artist, a fugitive from his failure to make good in New York, came to his own land and subject. In the drawings and writings of his creative work during his

177

remaining fifty years, Ross Santee immortalized the land of southern Arizona, its cowhands, horse wranglers, Apaches, and miners.

Together with Dobie and Rhodes, Santee forms the great triumvirate of rangeland writers who were also riders. In them is that blend of experience, vision, character and craft which forms creative greatness. In his drawings Santee also fixed the Southwest's hallmarks of distance and emptiness.

He was born at Thornburg, Iowa on August 16, 1888 of Quaker parents turned Methodist. The Santees were of French Huguenot stock, his mother a Pennsylvania Penrose. His destiny as a Southwesterner was not apparent during the first quarter-century of his life. The pulls on him were in the other direction, from Midwest to Middle Atlantic. One thing was apparent: he was meant to be an artist. As a child he began to draw. When his father died, his mother proved a wise parent, nourishing him on Mark Twain, Alexandre Dumas, and *Swiss Family Robinson*. His Tom Sawyerish boyhood was tempered by his mother giving him books and drawing paper which usually quieted him.

When he was ready for high school, they moved to Moline, Illinois. There the class in art bored him. "I wasn't interested in making copies of plants and flowers," he recalled. "There were too many interesting things outside. I could see the Mississippi from the room. Deep down inside I knew I wanted to draw things that lived and moved."

He did better in football although his nose was broken in scrimmage, as it was again later by a flying stirrup. He was on the way to his ultimate height of six feet three and weight of 185. When the coach took the team to Chicago to see the Carlisle Indians play the University, Ross peeled off and went to the Art Institute.

That was it. He knew what he wanted to do. Following high school he enrolled in a four-year course at the Art Institute, working his way through as a janitor, "cultivating nine acres of corridors and classrooms at the end of a broom."

His ambition was to be a well-paid newspaper cartoonist like his idol, John T. McCutcheon. This led after graduation to New York and a disillusioning year of rejection slips. His only sales were a couple of drawings to *Collier's* and *Judge* at $10 apiece. "I wasn't getting anywhere. I knew my drawings were bad. For I wasn't doing the thing I wanted to an', worst of all, I didn't know what that was."

The only good advice came from his friend Tom—also destined for fame, as Thomas Hart Benton—who told him to go to the Public Library and look at a book of the drawings of Daumier. This proved encouraging for he perceived that the French master had set down what he saw without any tricks. Until Santee had freed himself from what he had learned at school of copying the works of others, he could not be himself.

He knew that he must leave New York. Where should he go? His mother and sister were in faraway Arizona where the latter had married. He would go West. When he asked for a ticket to Globe, the ticket seller had to search out the route: New York Central to Chicago, the Southern Pacific's *Golden State Limited* to Bowie, thence by Arizona Eastern via Safford and San Carlos. Thus it was that Ross Santee came to the Southwest.

On its run to Globe, the local pulled out of Bowie in a cloud of alkali dust, rounded Mt. Graham and followed the Gila down the valley from Safford. Apaches got off and on at every stop. They fascinated Santee, and so did their land. It grew rougher as the Pinals came up ahead and he saw the peak known as the Sleeping Beauty, her classic head and flowing hair outlined against the flaming sky.

He knew it for his inevitable place. This country and its people, its ponies, wild horses, and steers, copper mines and smelters at Globe-Miami, were to be virtually all that he was ever to draw and write about, but so clearly and lovingly did he see and describe it that it is now and forevermore his land, the Gila Country of Ross Santee.

His first job in Arizona on the Bar F Bar was far from what he had ever done. He wasn't a cowpuncher. Lower than that. Lowest of low: a horse wrangler. Here is how he put it:

"For the horse wrangler's relation to a top hand is much the same as a buck private to the top sergeant or a dishwasher to the cook in any first class restaurant. At the shipping pens one spring the outfit was sitting along the top of the pens waiting to load. One of the ol' punchers was sitting on the opposite side talking to a brand inspector. I never knew what the inspector asked, but as he nodded towards me I heard the ol' cowboy say, 'Who? Him? Hell, no! He ain't nothin' but the horse wrangler.'" And then Santee added, "But I can still think of lots worse company than a bunch of saddle horses."

Because Newt Robinson, one of the owners of the Bar F Bar, had told the hands that Santee was an artist, the cowboys expected him to break out with a rash of drawings. He didn't. He had been hurt by his failure as an artist and he wanted to be alone. He had suffered a revulsion from art. And the country and the life he led overwhelmed him. One day a puncher asked pointblank, "Made ary pittures yet?" Santee shook his head. Later he overheard the waddie pass the word along. "The New Yorker ain't made no pittures yet an' furthermore he don't pack ary tools."

He was busy learning other things—roping, tying, packing, shoeing. And he was listening to the tales and lingo of the waddies. "Having long ears," he called it.

That was in 1915, the same year that Willa Cather first saw the Mesa Verde. A year passed before he began to draw again, at first with a burnt match on his chaps. He found that wrangling a remuda of a hundred head gave him both solitude and action. The hills and the horses cried out to be drawn.

Then it came fast. Each day he made at least a hundred sketches on paper, drawing with Higgins India ink and a kitchen match shaped to a point by his own teeth. Each evening before he brought the ponies in to camp, he lit a fire and burned the day's drawings.

Another year passed, and then he received a letter from a former classmate at the Art Institute, D. R. Fitzpatrick, who had made good as cartoonist for the St. Louis *Post Dispatch*. Santee replied with a sketch of the head of Martin Dodson, foreman of the Bar F Bar. Fitz asked for more. Santee sent a dozen. The newspaper's Sunday supplement gave them a full-page spread and sent him a check. Ross Santee, artist, had arrived. He was nearly 30.

The World War took a year of his life. The only fighting he did was mosquitoes in Texas. He returned to wrangling, and then between the fall and spring roundups he went back to the Art Institute, studying in night class with George Bellows. When Bellows saw the work Santee had brought with him, he declared, "Too bad more artists don't go to Arizona; maybe they'd learn to draw."

Bellows also persuaded Santee to try New York again. This time he made it, for at last he had found his own way in terse evocative drawings of things that lived and moved, of cattle, horses, and men on the open range. After eleven years of trying, he sold his first drawing to *Life*. Then *Century* bought five and in publishing them described Santee as "a cowboy from Globe, Arizona, who showed up recently in New York in sombrero and red sweater, with a portfolio under his arm."

This time he took no one's advice. When friends said his drawings would sell faster if he would add women, he refused. "They'll take them as they are or I'll head back to Arizona."

Santee's debut as an author was easy. He had never dreamed of himself as a writer nor made any kind of notes. When upon hearing one of his yarns the editor of *Boy's Life* said if Santee would write it out he would buy it. Santee was reluctant, figuring he had already enough misery. The editor insisted, and so Santee wrote it and received $25.

When the editor of *Leslie's* asked Santee if he could write, he replied that he had just sold a lousy story to a boy's magazine. The editor asked for a sample, and so that night Santee wrote another story. *Leslie's* gave him $200 for it. Whereupon Santee hightailed it back to *Boy's Life* and bought back his story for $25, took it to *Leslie's* and sold it for $200. Horse trading, he called it.

He was asked to illustrate his own stories. And so one after another the national magazines fell to his brush and pen. His first book, *Men and Horses,* appeared in 1926, followed two years later by *Cowboy.* All the while he was returning to Arizona at roundup time to wrangle for the Bar F Bar and the Cross S, both of which ran cattle on the San Carlos Apache Reservation out of Globe.

In 1926 he married Eve Farrell of Delaware whom he had met while she was working in a bookstore on New York's Eighth Avenue. It was his first book that had brought them together. From consideration for her invalid mother, they built a home near her in Arden, a suburb of Wilmington. Henceforth the Santees commuted between Delaware and Arizona.

Eve's benevolent role resembled that of Ross's mother; she typed his longhand drafts, kept the budget, and corked the bottle when it went down too fast. It was the only marriage for each, and although it bore no children, it proved ideal in every other way.

From 1936 to 1941 they lived in Phoenix while Santee served as editor of the Federal Writers Program of the W.P.A., whose major product was the state guide to Arizona. The work took him throughout Arizona, as he checked each of the itineraries on which the book was organized. He came close to the young writers and artists who contributed to the guide. When Washington officialdom excluded their names from the published book, Santee characteristically said, "Then leave mine out." They did.

Arizona was not unappreciative of Ross Santee. From the Phoenix years came one of the best friendships of his life. It was with Raymond Carlson, native son of Gila County and a Stanford graduate in Romance languages with a Phi Beta Kappa key, who had been appointed in 1937 to the editorship of *Arizona*

Highways. His transformation of that lowly house organ into the world famous monthly is one of the fabulous stories of our time.

According to Joseph Stacey, Carlson's successor, it was their Chinese laundryman who first introduced Ross Santee and Raymond Carlson. In the beginning Carlson depended on Santee's project writers for articles and on Santee for illustrations. During the next quarter century few issues of *Arizona Highways* appeared without the familiar Santee drawings of horses and men in vast landscapes, with occasional spreads of glowing watercolors. The magazine also featured stories and advance chapters from his books. With his genius for recognizing genius, Carlson saw that Ross Santee evoked the austerity of rangeland and mountainous Arizona as none other had ever done.

Looking back at his more than a dozen volumes published between 1926 and 1955 we see the opposite of the arc made by many writers' work. Instead of starting low, rising high, then falling, Santee's began on high, dipped, then rose again, so that his best work came at the beginning and at the end of his creative life. I do not mean that he ever slumped or wrote badly, but only that first and last did he achieve his finest work.

Thus his two best books, *Cowboy* (1928) and *Lost Pony Tracks* (1953) are his next to first and next to last books. His first, *Men and Horses*, is a loose group of episodes of his new life in Arizona. In it he staked out the claim he worked for thirty years, continually refining the material into different shapes.

Writers often start with themselves and proceed outward. Santee began with others and ended with himself. The land and the people of Gila County were always there. His literary ambition increased with each book as he sought better ways of presenting his vision. His second book was perhaps inspired by his boyhood reading of *Huckleberry Finn*. It is the saga of Shorty Caraway, foreman of the Cross S, who as a boy left his father's farm in eastern Texas and rode toward the rangelands of New Mexico and Arizona.

Cowboy tells of Shorty's rise from roustabout to bronc buster and horse wrangler and finally to cowhand, a story adumbrated in *Men and Horses*. Santee dedicated it to "Shorty Caraway—Top Hand." Thirteen years had passed since he had first seen the Gila country. His "long ears" had never stopped listening. What he heard and saw and felt was now assimilated and transformed.

How came Ross Santee to write that easy-riding prose? As an artist he had teachers. As a writer he must have learned from his own reading. The language of *Cowboy* is so simple as to fool those who do not appreciate the way a great writer changes life to literature without seeming to try.

Dobie was not deceived. In reviewing *Cowboy* he recognized that Santee had exalted life to the level of literature. He ranked the book at the pinnacle with Andy Adams's *The Log of a Cowboy*.

The success of his first two books established Santee as a professional writer-illustrator. He followed them with two juveniles, *The Pooch* (1931) and *Sleepy Black* (1934), the story of a rodeo horse as told by the animal; and with a spoof, *The Bar X Golf Course* (1933), about a cow country golf course 300 miles long that took 18 days to play. To this day there are readers who on coming to Arizona ask how to locate the Bar X course.

In *The Bubbling Spring* (1949) and *Hardrock and Silver Sage* (1951) Santee drew upon his own life for the stuff of two novels. Twenty years ago I gave them high marks in my bibliography of Southwest fiction. Rereading them today finds me less enthusiastic.

My preference in this middle period of Santee's career is for the nonfiction *Apache Land* (1947). It began with what Santee had learned from research for the W.P.A. project, and is a kind of anthology of Apache history, customs and ceremonials, wars and other tribulations. Santee drew upon the classic literature of the Apaches—Browne, Cremony, Bourke, Clum, Lockwood, and Comfort. He wrote with fidelity and honesty. He regretted that Geronimo, the worst Apache of all, is now the best known.

184

Any competent historian could have done as much. What Santee alone did was to write from personal familiarity with the Apaches and their land, from wrangling the San Carlos country above the Gila, on up to the White Mountain tribal domain at Fort Apache, the erstwhile base of Martha Summerhayes and her Captain Jack. The Apaches accepted Santee, calling him El Delgadito, the Slim One.

"They say it is customary to dedicate a book," he concluded in his Foreword, "so this little one is dedicated to an old Apache friend, gone these many years, who had all the virtues of his race and enough of its vices to make him lovable. To Old Jim Whitehead of blessed memory."

Santee's illustrations for *Apache Land* are his best work in the black and white medium, as deceptively simple as his prose. He drew hundreds of horses in the course of his life, no two exactly alike. He saw horses as individuals.

Santee came last to himself. In *Dog Days*, the final book of his lifetime, he returned to his turn-of-the-century boyhood in Iowa. With Tom Sawyer in mind and heart, he recalled the joys and sorrows of coming to adolescence.

The years of manhood were the subject of his penultimate book. In *Lost Pony Tracks* he remembered his making as a wrangler. It was his own story that he told, but the chief characters are others than himself. He saw those legendary cowmen, Shorty Caraway, Martin Dodson, and Ol' Ed Hill, as heroes of the range, no less noble than the knights of King Arthur. Although he wrote of cowboys and Indians, he did so without chases, shootings, and hangings. His West is free of violence for its own sake, of bloodshed aimed to serve a depraved public's lust for cruelty.

Only the violence which came from the daily conflict between rough men and their animals is present in Santee's work. The major episode of gunplay occurs in *Cowboy* when the boss lies on his bed with a snootful and picks flies off the ceiling with his .45.

Today's readers, debauched by war, violent entertainment,

and brutal sports, will not be drawn to Ross Santee. No matter. Literature has always been kept alive by a few readers. The pendulum of taste will swing again toward the quieter side. And the generations will pass.

When I think of Santee, the words that come to me are *humane, compassionate, loyal*. Never sentimental nor moralistic, he was more like Dobie than any other writer of his time.

Of all Santee's books, *Lost Pony Tracks* embodies the best of this man who looked tough and was tender. After he had modelled the portrait by Rolf Armstrong for the cover of the *Saturday Evening Post*, in which he was painted realistically with broken nose and narrowed eyes, Hollywood figured they could make Santee into a cowboy actor. They were wrong. He was too smart an *hombre* to ride that range.

Lost Pony Tracks refines the material of *Men and Horses* and *Cowboy*. Santee was in his sixties when he wrote it, at that time when a fortunate man can look back and enjoy his life in perspective. It holds Santee's mature thoughts on drawing and writing, his opinions of Charlie Russell, Gene Rhodes, Walt Coburn, Will James and Zane Grey. The Globe Rodeo is rousingly depicted. There is a fond roundup of the cowhorses, each of which he recognized as unique, and tributes to the "wild bunch," those free-running ones that thrilled him. Above all he immortalized the top hands he worked with, revered, and loved.

After the death of Eve in 1963, Ross came back to Globe for the rest of his life. He lived in Tucson for a time to study oil painting with Ted De Grazia, one of his few peers. He had long known De Grazia through his work. Meeting him for the first time, Santee said was like meeting an old friend after an absence of many years.

He was lost without Eve. On the 29th of June in 1965, while he lay ill in the General Hospital at Globe, the old black burro came to take Ross Santee on his last trip across the river. He was six weeks short of seventy-seven. Two weeks later his ashes were scattered by his friends, including Carlson, Stacey, and De

186

Grazia, on a steep slope of the Mescals twelve miles south of Globe. Red rose petals were mingled with his ashes, leading one friend to remark, "Cow chips would have been his choice." Thus Santee's last resting place was where he wanted it to be, on the hills of Gila County where he wrangled his first remuda, those rocky hills from whence came his strength and his art.

I went there last fall, coming up from Pima County across the San Pedro and the Gila and over Pinal Pass. Nothing had changed in Globe. Cowhands and Apaches sat on the pyramidal steps of the old basalt courthouse. The narrow street dropped to the smoking smelter at Miami and the turnoff of the Apache Trail to Roosevelt Dam on the Salt.

I backtracked for a look at Coolidge Dam on the Gila, built in 1930 to form San Carlos Lake. The water was low. No one was there. I recalled a story of the dedication when the unfilled lakesite was mostly grass grown and Will Rogers said to Calvin Coolidge, "If this was my lake, I'd mow it."

All around me was the land of Ross Santee, the land which he praised time and again in such words as these: ". . . the great mesas, shimmering in the sun. Beyond them the ranges rolled and pitched as far as the eye could see. I had never seen such color. But it was the country itself that did something to me."

What that country did to that man was Literature and Art, no less.

187

READING LIST

ROSS SANTEE (*1888-1965*)

Men and Horses. New York, Century, 1926.

Cowboy. New York, Cosmopolitan, 1928; New York, Hastings House, 1964. With new illus. by the author.

The Pooch. New York, Cosmopolitan, 1931.

Sleepy Black. New York, Farrar, 1933.

The Bar X Golf Course. New York, Farrar, 1933; Flagstaff, Northland Press, 1971.

Arizona, a State Guide. New York, Hastings House, 1940. New superficially revised ed., 1956.

Apache Land. New York, Scribner, 1947.

The Bubbling Spring. New York, Scribner, 1949.

Hardrock and Silver Sage. New York, Scribner, 1952.

Lost Pony Tracks. New York, Scribner, 1953.

Dog Days. New York, Scribner, 1955.

The Rummy Kid Goes Home and Other Stories of the Southwest. New York, Hastings House, 1965.

J. E. REYNOLDS, BOOKSELLER, VAN NUYS, CALIF.

"*The West of Ross Santee.*" Essays by Dentzel, Dykes, Dobie, Hutchinson, and Lauritzen, in Catalog 66, 1961.

NEAL B. HOUSTON

Ross Santee. Austin, Steck-Vaughn, 1968.

NANCY C. KIRKPATRICK

Ross Santee, Arizona Writer and Illustrator, a Bibliography. Tucson, University of Arizona Graduate Library School, 1972.

Photograph of Ross Santee by Jack Sheaffer, courtesy of the photographer.

Arizona Nights

STEWART EDWARD WHITE

The literary career of Stewart Edward White was long and prolific, beginning in 1901 with *The Westerners*, a novel of the Black
Hills, and ending in 1946, the year of his death, with *The Stars
Are Still There*, a treatise on his belief in an after-life. During
that time he wrote more than fifty books, many of them best-
sellers, including *The Blazed Trail*, *The Rules of the Game*, and
a trilogy of early California, *The Gray Dawn*, *Gold*, and *The
Rose Dawn*. As a young writer he was hailed by President Theodore Roosevelt as the forerunner of a virile new school of outdoor
Americanism.

Time deals cruelly with such miscellaneous literary remains.
Bulking the shelves ensures mere physical survival. A book truly
lives only by being read. His many books are not read now as
they were in his lifetime. The death of his wife led him to seek
communication with her and to writing several books, beginning
with *The Betty Book*, which he believed to have been dictated
by her. They will probably always have readers among those
likewise moved by grief for loved ones lost to death. The historical romances will also be turned to by escapists from the violent present. Novels of the Michigan forests and Canadian wilderness, Africa and Alaska, accounts of the Sierra Nevada, will
remain mostly unread. White wrote too much and said too little
to readers beyond his time.

Of all his work one small book bids fair to outlast the rest and be discovered anew by each generation of readers. He titled it *Arizona Nights*. It was published in 1907 with dramatic, colorful illustrations by N. C. Wyeth. Although never a best-seller and long out of print until its recent appearance as a paperback, it was hailed from the beginning as a classic of the Southwest. One reason for its persistent life is apparent in an early review; *The Bookman* for January 1908 concluded, "That Mr. White's pages do not give the impression of being overcrowded is due to the unusual clearness of his mental vision and to a terse vigorous style which, without abruptness, often compacts into a sentence the pith of a paragraph."

Arizona Nights has been taken for granted by critics and readers. No one has inquired into its origins and meaning, nor sought to determine why it stands alone among its author's books. I was no exception. When in 1955 I included it in my listing of the best novels and stories about the Southwest, I did so primarily on Dobie's word.

Later when I began to delve into Southwestern literature in search of reasons for the survival of the vital few among the thousands of books on the region, I was compelled to review White's entire work. This led to a reading of his fifty-six books, to locating his surviving manuscripts and talking to kinfolk, and even to penetrating the Monastery of the Poor Clares, a closed contemplative order of Franciscan nuns who occupy White's former home in Santa Barbara. He called it The Jumping Off Place because when he built it, after the turn of the century, it was far out on the edge of town next to the Mission.

I had a guide in the excellent doctoral dissertation on White done at USC in 1960 by Edna Rosemary Butte. She based it on a study of White's books and manuscripts, and barely in time, for many of the manuscripts she quoted from were burned in a Montecito brush fire.

Those who pigeon-hole books are thwarted by *Arizona Nights*. What is it—a novel, stories, non-fiction? It is all three.

192

Dobie's fondness for it is understandable; it resembles his *Tongues of the Monte*, his favorite of his own books, as indeed *Arizona Nights* was one of White's, the other being *The Silent Places*.

As an outdoorsman White had a reverence for the facts of life and nature. In *Arizona Nights* he sought to portray "the average life in the cattle country before the advent of the movies." At the time White wrote, Owen Wister's *The Virginian* had just begun the glamorization of the cowboy. In later years White recalled attending a trial in Arizona at which several cowboy witnesses were called. Asked their occupation they replied, "Laborer."

In this book White pointed to the directions Southwest writing was to take. In turn he was influenced in his view of the arid lands by John C. Van Dyke's *The Desert* (1901) which led many writers to an aesthetic appreciation of the region. By including folklore, tall tales, and cowboy lingo, White was closer to Gene Rhodes than to Zane Grey. His story of buried treasure in Baja California anticipated Dobie's *Coronado's Children*, and in the novelette "The Rawhide," which crowns *Arizona Nights*, he foretold Conrad Richter's *The Sea of Grass* and Willa Cather's *A Lost Lady*.

Although his setting was faithfully delineated, White's stories were invented. In "The Rawhide" he used a local rancher as a model and then involved him in an imaginative drama. And yet his characters were recognizable enough to get him into threatened legal and other trouble with their friends and relatives. In two early novels, *Conjuror's House* and *The Silent Places*, he incurred the wrath of the Hudson's Bay Company for his portrayal of their trading posts, factors, and trappers. Local indignation after publication of *The Rose Dawn*, a novel of Santa Barbara in the Boom of the Eighties, is said to have caused White to move up state to Burlingame.

White was not a personal writer. When he wrote reminiscences, they were more apt to be about his favorite dogs than people. His outlook was patrician not plebeian. The son of a millionaire lumberman, he used his pen to make a fortune of his own. That he was a skilled sailor, horseman, woodsman, backpacker and hunter, gave faithful reality to such outdoor books as *The Forest, The Mountains, The Pass,* and *The Cabin.*

Most of White's life after 1903 was spent in California, to which he came earlier as a boy when his parents wintered in Santa Barbara. Drawn by the bird sanctuary in the marshes at nearby Carpinteria, he acquired the lovely beach strand and named it Sandyland. After making Phi Beta Kappa at the University of Michigan and publishing a monograph on the birds of Mackinac Island, he began to study law at Columbia University. A literary course with Brander Matthews showed him his true destiny as a writer. Family interests in Dakota mines and Michigan forests led White to jobs therein and novels therefrom. His third novel, *The Blazed Trail* (1902) put him in orbit from which he never descended, a beginning similar to Zane Grey's a few years later.

Arizona Nights was his ninth book in six years. Thirteen years later *The Killer* was a kind of sequel. These were his only Arizona books. White's other volumes yield little information about his Arizona life. I wanted to know what had brought him there in the beginning, what were his sources, and why he did not write more about the region to which he gave such true and eloquent voice. My inquiry began with the dedication of *Arizona Nights*:

TO
CAPTAIN W. H. MCKITTRICK
OF THE J. H.
IN MEMORY OF MANY
ARIZONA NIGHTS AND DAYS

McKittrick's is a well-known name in Southern California. A town near Bakersfield is named for him. Cattle bred in Arizona were shipped to his Kern County ranch for fattening and sale to the Swift slaughterhouse in Los Angeles. He also raised prize polo ponies on the California ranch. In those early years Santa Barbara was the polo town of the West.

Although not a polo player, White was a horseman who entertained his visitors by taking them on rides to the summit of the range behind Santa Barbara. Thus it is likely that he and Captain McKittrick met socially at the livery at 227 Equestrian Street where the McKittrick ponies were stabled. In 1903 White was invited to take part in the spring and fall roundups on the J. H. Ranch near Willcox. McKittrick had acquired it in 1895. It was originally owned by Colonel Henry C. Hooker, the baronial figure who had come twenty years earlier to the Sulphur Springs Valley and developed its 350,000 acres as the Sierra Bonita, said to have been the largest ranch in all of Arizona. Named for his son Joseph, the J. H. was one of several subsidiary ranches adjoining the main spread. By an unwritten treaty with Cochise, Hooker had gained the initial protection of the Chiricahua Apaches, and later that of the U.S. Army stationed at Fort Grant on the northern edge of the ranch.

When White came to the J.H. as a successful writer at the prime age of thirty-four, he was immediately aware of its literary potential. In a journal and in letters to his fiancée in Santa Barbara (all lost in the Montecito fire), he noted words, phrases and plot ideas, and books he was reading. No tenderfoot, he rode in the roundups and shared the life of the waddies. Around the campfire on the range he heard the yarns retold in his book. His sense of direction and lay of the land gave his book topographical reality. Its next appearance might well include a map of Sulphur Springs Valley, which he renamed Soda Springs Valley.

White was also a good photographer. In the Santa Barbara Historical Society are albums of photos taken during his life, including one of masterful shots of the roundup on the Sierra Bonita. In them we see the trailing herd and the branding, even to the rising dust when the calves were thrown and tied.

Old Colonel Hooker was an inevitable literary model. His fortune was established by the crazy feat of driving a flock of turkeys over the Sierra Nevada and selling them to Nevada miners at a huge profit. The shrewd Yankee then went on to Texas and parlayed his gain into a herd of cattle, drove them to Arizona where he discovered and homesteaded the rich range of the Sulphur Springs Valley, measuring thirty by twenty-seven miles.

The playwright Augustus Thomas was the first to discover Hooker as literary material. When he believed himself written out, Thomas was encouraged by Frederic Remington to see Arizona. It was Martha's Jack Summerhayes who guided him to the Sierra Bonita. The result was the stage hit of 1898 called *Arizona* in which he cast the officers of Fort Grant and the ranchers of the Sierra Bonita as his melodramatic characters.

Years later he admitted to having taken liberties with the Colonel. "Henry C. Hooker was a quiet little man," he recalled, "under the average height of the American; and while adopting him I took the liberty of replacing him in my mind with a more robust and typical frontiersman."

Folklore followed the monarchial Colonel. In later years he commuted via Southern Pacific between the Sierra Bonita and his home on West Adams in Los Angeles. Once after boarding the *Sunset* at Willcox he said to the conductor, "I'm Hooker, just send me a bill." Whereupon the woman across the aisle said, "I'm a hooker too. Can I charge my fare?"

The manuscript of *Arizona Nights* survived the disastrous Montecito fire. It contains a note that it was being written in September 1905, the third year of White's visits to the J.H. In the last two years his bride was with him. Although a tiny 4' 11" Newport society girl, Elizabeth Calvert Grant White, called Betty, proved a tireless companion to her rugged writer-husband.

Arizona Nights is as real as *Arizona* is fake. White also took liberties with the Colonel, and this is probably why he never returned to the Sierra Bonita or the J.H. His character The Cattleman is not Hooker, but that of J. B. Parks, the foreman of the J.H. This I was told by his son Harry who as a boy of seventeen rode with White at roundup time. In the novelettes, "The Two-Gun Man" and "The Rawhide," White portrayed Hooker as Buck Johnson, with perhaps a bit of Captain McKittrick for good measure. They are not strictly portraits from life. White had creative powers. The mail order wife and the brutal revenge that was finally not consummated were White's inventions. Authentic Apache was the use of a fresh rawhide in which the tied captive was crushed to death as the hide dried and shrank in the sun. As conceived by White, the character of Buck Johnson is a sensitive and lordly figure.

Later in *The Killer* White pictured the lord of the valley, transparently named *Henry Hooper*, as a degenerate and evil person, and to confuse matters he introduced a Buck Johnson as an entirely different character. In his first book White followed Augustus Thomas in enlarging the diminutive Colonel Hooker; when he came to write *The Killer* he described him apparently from life as "not taller than my own shoulder, with a bent little figure. His bullet head had been cropped. His eyes were his formidable characteristic. I've noticed that owls have this same intent, unwinking stare—and wildcats."

White's tale is of Old Man Hooper's overthrow as "The Killer" by the brave young cowboy (White's idealized self) and the aroused posse of ranchers. Although the melodrama is a bit incredible (it was written as a serial in *Red Book* and was sold to the movies), the setting is again real and authentic, the open rangeland where White had first come as a man in love, in that time of maximum sensitivity and response.

As he did in *Arizona Nights*, White accompanied the fiction of *The Killer* with non-fiction, again making the book difficult to classify. The final 117 pages are devoted to "The Ranch," an elegiac account of the McKittrick spread in California, the prototype of the ranch settings in White's California romances, made obsolete by the automobile. Included is a flashback to the J. H. and its foreman, J.B., The Cattleman. In "The Ranch" White created a classic of rangeland Californiana.

197

Although I have no evidence that *Arizona Nights* displeased Colonel Hooker—he died in December 1907 and probably never read or even heard of it—I do know that *The Killer* angered an oldtime Arizonan. He was Dr. Joseph A. Munk, whose brother was also a Sulphur Springs Valley rancher. In *Features of an Arizona Library* (1926) Dr. Munk had this to say:

"The Sierra Bonita Ranch was established by Henry C. Hooker in 1873, and it became one of the show places in Arizona. With the generous hospitality of the pioneer, he kept open house to all travelers who chanced to come that way. The lone wayfarer was always made welcome at the Hooker Hacienda. During his life the proprietor made his ranch a rendezvous for all army officers, artists, authors, and scientists, whose duties or inclination took them into that country.

"Among those itinerants happened to be one named Edward Stewart White (sic), who wrote a book called *The Killer,* in which he slanders Mr. Hooker by innuendo in an unjustifiable manner. The writer of the book had broken bread with his host and had assuredly received every courtesy that was due any guest, yet he basely turned upon him like a cur and bit the hand that fed him.

"I knew Colonel Hooker very well and visited him often in his home, where I always found him to be the same genial, courteous gentleman. It pains me to have his name maligned and I cannot refrain from saying a good word in vindication of my old friend."

What led White to write so venomously of Colonel Hooker. Lacking evidence, I can only speculate.

Last spring I went to Sulphur Springs Valley. After the heaviest rains in many years the land was green and bright with flowers. The Valley lies a hundred miles east of Tucson over a road I had travelled many times before. This time it was with the double vision gained from reading these books of Cochise County.

There are mountain ranges on either hand—the Rincons, Santa Ritas and Whetstones, the Dragoons and Little Dragoons;

198

and finally the Dos Cabezas and Chiricahuas that wall the Valley on the east, the Winchesters and Galiuros on the northwest, and the Pinalenos or Grahams in the northeast. In the cattle town of Willcox (called Willet by White) I called on Harry Parks, now an old man in his eighties, and heard his recollections of seventy years ago.

"There was always a bit of trouble between the ranches," he recalled. "Our stock and theirs would get mixed in with each other and so we'd ride up to the Bonita to sort them out. The ranches were right together, only a dozen miles between headquarters. I was the only one the Colonel would ask in. He wouldn't ask Dad in. He liked me to eat with him. 'Send the kid in,' he'd say and I'd go in and eat at table with him while Dad and the hands ate in the bunkhouse. Don't know why he asked me in. Guess it was because I was just a kid. I rode with the hands though."

It was hard for Harry Parks to remember that far back to his boyhood on the J. H. His words came slowly, as he folded and unfolded his big gnarled hands.

"Sure, I remember Mr. White," he said in answer to my question. "He rode with the hands."

"He was a writer," I said.

"He *was* a good rider. Used to ride in the roundup. So did I, though I never drew wages."

"Did you ever read *Arizona Nights?*"

At this point Mrs. Parks spoke up. "We lent our copy and never got it back. It sure made the Hookers mad. They sued him for it."

"I never heard that before," I said.

"It's true," Mrs. Parks said. "Everybody knows that."

"Dad's in it," Harry Parks said. "He called him The Cattleman."

"Did your father die a long time ago?"

"I guess about 1920."

"Did you know Captain McKittrick?"

199

"Of course I knew him. He owned the J. H. Never spent much time here though. Dad ran the ranch. I was a kid then, but I remember Mr. White. He came every year and rode in the round-up."

After taking leave of Mr. and Mrs. Parks I headed northwest over the lonely road that lies between the Winchesters and Little Dragoons and then wanders down to the valley of the San Pedro. I traversed the land of the old J. H., now broken up, the cattle gone. On up the valley the Sierra Bonita is still a working cattle ranch, owned by a later generation of Hookers, and down to only 45,000 acres.

Before leaving the Valley I stopped on the ridge and looked back on the landscape White saw through the eyes of Buck Johnson. Grass land, brush land, flower land, and desert, still a vast chromatic landscape under the towering Arizona sky, stretching clear to the gleaming Willcox playa and the blue Chiricahuas. And I agreed with Señor Johnson, "She's the prettiest country God ever made."

Threading my way down the mesquite-lined San Pedro and then snaking up over Redington Pass to my home valley of the Santa Cruz, I let my mind play on why White had turned on Hooker in *The Killer*. If their answer to *Arizona Nights*, the book of his heart, lived and written on his honeymoon in a land he also loved deeply, and a book which he came to rank at the peak of his nearly three-score books—if their response to it was to threaten to sue him, well, by God, he'd really give them something to sue him for!

Speculation, pure speculation, with no least evidence to support it—other than my hunch that this is the way it was.

READING LIST

STEWART EDWARD WHITE (*1873-1946*)
Arizona Nights. New York, McClure, 1907; New York, Ballantine, 1973. Introduction by R. L. Grosvenor.
The Killer. New York, Doubleday, 1920.
Dog Days; Other Times, Other Dogs. New York, Doubleday, 1930.

EDNA ROSEMARY BUTTE
Stewart Edward White, His Life and Literary Career. Los Angeles, University of Southern California, 1960. Xerox copy available from University Microfilms, Ann Arbor.

CALHOUN COLLINS
The McKittrick Ranch. Bakersfield, Kern County Historical Society, Annual Publication 21, 1958.

EARLE R. FORREST
The Fabulous Sierra Bonita. Journal of Arizona History, V.6, N.3, Autumn 1965.

GERTRUDE HILL
Henry Clay Hooker, King of the Sierra Bonita. Arizoniana, The Journal of Arizona History. V.2, N.4, Winter 1961.

FRANK C. LOCKWOOD
Pioneer Portraits. Tucson, University of Arizona Press, 1968.

AUGUSTUS THOMAS
Arizona, a Drama in Four Acts. New York, Russell, 1899.
The Print of My Remembrance. New York, Scribner's, 1922.

Photograph of Stewart Edward White, courtesy of Santa Barbara Historical Society.

Riders of the Purple Sage

ZANE GREY

A wise man returneth not to the books of his boyhood. He is content to remember them (and himself) as once they were. And so it was with doubt that I opened *Riders of the Purple Sage* to the first chapter, called "Lassiter," and began to read: "A sharp clip-clop of iron-shod hoofs deadened and died away, and clouds of yellow dust drifted from under the cottonwoods out over the sage."

I need not have feared. Once again the story swept me along through gunsmoke, stampede, and heart-throb to that great climax when Lassiter rolls the balancing rock that buries the pursuing Mormons and seals him, Jane, and little Fay in the hidden valley from which there is no escape.

"Roll the stone!" the heroine cried, "Lassiter, I love you!" There is no finer moment in all of western fiction, approached only by the Virginian's "When you call me that, *smile.*"

As a boy I read Zane Grey for the story. Now as a man I reread him also for the setting and lore and overtones, and with the question, how came he to reach this highest point with what was only his second Southwestern novel? *Riders of the Purple Sage* appeared in 1912 when Zane Grey was forty. Although he lived another twenty-seven years and wrote sixty more books, never again did he attain that peak of inspiration and accomplishment.

Does not a growing skill in craftsmanship ensure a corresponding power to produce masterpieces? Has not a man at sixty more to say about life than he did at forty? He raised a family, travelled widely, and became a famed deepsea fisherman. His writings made him the foremost western writer of our time, and one of the wealthiest.

His fame was worldwide. Once in the public library of Copenhagen I talked with an old Dane enthralled by *The U.P. Trail.* "I'll never see the West," he said sadly, "but he surely makes me long to do so." In a Chicago hotel when the maid mistook me for a Scandinavian, she was led to tell me of how as a girl a reading of Zane Grey in Swedish had led her to emigrate. Although Illinois was her farthest west, she still hoped to see purple sage in the sunset. At Calcutta's Dum Dum airport sight of a man reading *Tappan's Burro* made me homesick. I found a copy on the paperback rack and read it en route to Karachi, high above a land that looked like my Southwest.

No one to my knowledge has evaluated Zane Grey's complete works and life. Such would require unlimited access to the family papers, his notebooks, diaries, and letters. Perhaps they will eventually be placed in a research library such as the Bancroft or Huntington where scholars can study them. Not that anything scandalous is being concealed. Zane Grey's life was morally exemplary. It held only a single tragedy—Success.

Early and lucrative success did to Zane Grey what it did to Jack London—raised his standard of living which led to overproduction and lowered his standard of criticism. "I used to write one novel a year," Grey once told an interviewer, "then Barton Currie of *The Ladies' Home Journal* came along and said 'It only takes you three months to write a novel, Grey. Why not double your output?' This seemed sensible, so I did. Now I write two serials a year."

For each at first he received $30,000. During the golden Twenties, by compelling magazines to bid for his work, he was paid as high as $80,000 for a single serial.

Zane Grey felt none of the revulsion that overcame Herman Melville in the century before, who upon seeing that the public wanted only South Sea romances in the idyllic vein of *Typee*, cast away his pen and wrote no more.

On the contrary Zane Grey gave the public abundant measure of what it craved. He stockpiled his publisher's backlog so that upon his death in 1939 it contained twenty unpublished manuscripts. He wrote fluently in longhand with pencil on foolscap, seated in an old Morris chair, a large writing board on his lap. He liked cats around him to help him relax.

Year after year these posthumous books have been released by Zane Grey, Inc., headed by his son Romer. I read only one of them. It was enough to convince me that in it Zane Grey had reached his literary nadir. *Boulder Dam* (1964) is a mockery of prime Grey, marked by erroneous history and bad Spanish.

A writer deserves to be judged by his best work. Zane Grey's came in a burst of creativity which lasted only five years and resulted in three books, *The Heritage of the Desert* (1910), *Riders of the Purple Sage* (1912), and its sequel, *The Rainbow Trail* (1915). They all came from the impact of a single experience upon a sensitive man whose good fortune it was to fall into the hands of a believing and able woman.

This experience was his discovery of the Southwest. He saw it first on his honeymoon in that time of supreme awareness. He and his wife arrived at the Grand Canyon on January 15, 1906. They stayed only a few days before going on to California. A year later he returned alone and went north from Flagstaff with a party of Mormons to Lee's Ferry and across the Colorado River to the North Rim of the Grand Canyon. This visit, from which his genius derived, lasted only a few weeks.

The Mormons' leader was Jim Emmett of Lee's Ferry. Grey portrayed him as August Naab in *The Heritage of the Desert*. Years later Grey acknowledged his debt to this man in these words: "I can easily see how he took powerful hold of my imagination and fixed for me an ideal which has never changed. My debt to him is incalculable. No doubt he exerted more influence over my development, creating an all-absorbing love for the Southwest, than any other westerner. I was singularly young and boyish in impressionable receptiveness. The romance of the West dominated me, though fortunately I did not wholly escape the realism."

It was during those visits of 1906 and 1907 that Zane Grey gathered the materials of landscape, lore, conflict, and romance that by the alchemy of art he transmuted into his masterpieces. That was his zenith. Although he went on to write scores of rousing stories about other parts of the West and gain millions of readers in many languages, no other place ever seized his imagination in the way the colored canyon and river country did in that time of maximum receptivity.

Forested mountains and their slopes of cedar and sage, the Painted Desert and remote canyons, and above all, the river, the sullen, roaring Colorado, were the elements that fired him. No one had ever written of those lands in this strong, romantic vein. Mormons and Indians, gunmen, cowboys, sheepherders and traders, were his characters. He involved them violently in dramatic action. As Hare, Venters, and Shefford he cast himself successively in these three novels in the role of a tenderfoot who came to manhood in the crucible of the Southwestern desert. Grey had an especial gift for portraying horses. Silvermane, Night and Black Star, Wrangle and Wildfire are unforgettable steeds.

Who was this man who imagined himself as a romantic hero? Who was the woman that fulfilled him? Zane Grey was born on January 31, 1872, in Zanesville, Ohio, a town named for his mother's people. The Zanes were a family of Revolutionary distinction. Colonel Ebenezer Zane had served on General Washington's staff and had been rewarded by the Continental Congress with ten thousand acres of land in the Ohio Valley.

The writer's father, Dr. Lewis M. Gray, was a dentist who gave his son the ludicrous name of Pearl. When the boy proved

206

to have powerful hands, his father put him in charge of extractions. Those hands also made him a remarkable pitcher. The University of Pennsylvania recruited him as a ballplayer on a dental scholarship.

Dentistry triumphed, and it was P. Zane Grey, D.D.S. (he changed the spelling of his last name) who hung out his shingle in New York.

Ever since an early boyhood attempt called "Jim of the Cave" he had wanted to write. His father thought it a waste of time. Little Pearl was also an omnivorous reader of the Harry Castlemon adventure stories. Fishing too was in his blood. As a man Sundays were spent in relaxation from dentistry deep in the countryside on the New York-Pennsylvania border, where the Lackawaxen River empties into the Delaware River.

There one fateful day in August 1900, Grey and two fishing pals flirted with three girls on shore. They landed and paired off. Dr. Grey found himself with Lina Elise Roth, the daughter of a New York doctor and a student in what became Hunter College. She was headed for Columbia University to prepare as a teacher of literature. She was seventeen, he twenty-eight. Their courtship lasted five years.

Until he met Lina (called Dolly) no one had encouraged him to write. His first stories were of fishing and hunting. Then he tried more ambitious works, leading to novels of the Ohio frontier. *Betty Zane* was his family's saga back to the Indian wars of the 18th century. When no publisher wanted it, Dolly paid to have it printed. This encouraged Zane to write two more Ohio novels, one of which, *The Spirit of the Border*, was finally accepted by a publisher.

No more encouragement was needed. He took down his shingle, closed the office, and with his meager savings took his widowed mother, sister, two brothers, and fiancée to the country where they established a colony on a five-acre tract at the confluence of the two rivers. An inheritance from her grandfather enabled Dolly and Zane to be married in 1905.

Now that he had more time, his writing improved. He began to sell his outdoor stories. Theirs was an idyllic life. "I had ample time to read and study, particularly in the winter," Grey recalled years later. "My wife and I read and studied together, while the sleet pattered on the window and the rain roared on the roof and the winter winds mourned under the eaves. Many and various were the authors who influenced me, though I leaned most to romance and poetry. Hugo, Stevenson, Poe, Kipling, became close friends and teachers. I devoured Ruskin, Hudson, Jeffries, Darwin. And I knew by heart Tennyson, Wordsworth, Matthew Arnold."

Then came an encounter as decisive as the meeting with Lina and their honeymoon in the Southwest. At the Campfire Club in New York, Grey was invited by the explorer, Alvah James, to attend a lecture by the famous plainsman, Colonel C. J. "Buffalo" Jones, who had come east for capital to carry on a hybridizing experiment with buffalo and black Galloway cattle. He hoped to produce a more desert-hardy breed called cattalo. The work was being done at a ranch on the North Rim of the Grand Canyon.

Most of Jones's audience were derisive, particularly when he told of his adventures in lassoing cougars. An enthralled Grey was sympathetic to all that Buffalo Jones said. He had a sudden vision of his future. He proposed that he return to Arizona with the plainsman and write a book about his work. Jones questioned his writing ability until Grey produced a copy of *Betty Zane*. That convinced him of Grey's competence, although he said that the younger man would have to pay his own way.

Back at Lackawaxen Zane and Dolly figured out that the trip would use all that remained of her legacy. Grey did not want to take her money and leave her at home. She insisted, sensing that this would prove to be the turning point for him as a writer. She was right. The turn he took led to a life of golden riches.

And so on March 27, 1907 Zane Grey arrived again at El Tovar. A blizzard was raging. He was lonely and miserable. In a letter to his wife he regretted ever having left her. Two weeks later, writing from Flagstaff where he was outfitting for the trip north, his feelings had risen. "I am positively quivering with joy at the prospect of the trip. I have lost my blues and I'm actually happy. I need this wild life, this freedom, and I'll come back to love you to death."

There in brief is the story of their life. Dolly Grey was its heroine. Not only did she adapt to his mercurial temperament, she was also an able critic of form and style, editing his manuscripts for structure and syntax. He had the gift of narrative. He was a born storyteller, a simplifier. Life to him was black or white, never gray. His characters were heroic figures with primitive emotions. While they lived out their melodramas, the story line never weakened.

In the novels of his prime the characters were inseparable from the setting. They merged with the landscape. "My inspiration to write," he declared, "has always come from nature. Character and action are subordinate to setting."

In addition to her belief in him and her ability to improve his writing, Dolly Grey had shrewd business sense. He had none. When the Depression reduced the huge sums he had received earlier from serialization, he was recklessly overexpended. In 1931 when he ran up costs of $300,000 in refitting a deep-sea fishing vessel, his financial ruin was at hand. She saved him with her share of previous earnings.

He was reduced at that time to writing continuity for a syndicated comic strip. Without his wife Zane Grey would never have succeeded as he did. Further proof is in what happened when because of a four months' absence in Europe, Dolly was unable to collaborate on the manuscript of *The Thundering Herd*. It was rejected by *The Ladies' Home Journal* until she returned and helped revise it. Without her literary skill and business sense Grey grew panicky.

Back at Lackawaxen in 1907 Grey wrote *The Last of the Plainsmen*, his account of Buffalo Jones as a breeder of cattalo

209

and roper of cougars. The book was illustrated from Grey's own photographs. Sales netted only $200.

This was not the ripe fruit of his Arizona adventure. That came two years later in the creation of his first Southwestern novel, written after his experiences had been refined in retrospect. *The Heritage of the Desert* was an attempt to depict the Mormons as both heroes and villains. These strong people in that great landscape were what had stirred Grey so deeply. He had seen them at their oases on the river and in their remote villages where Utah and Arizona merged. The authority of church dogma, the absolute power of men over women, and the practice of polygamy were the tenets of Mormonism that both repelled and attracted Grey.

His feelings were violently ambivalent. In a conventional sense he was outraged by the ruthlessness of male dominance. At the same time he was excited by the vision of secret villages of young "sealed wives," visited in the dark of night by husbands whose faces they never saw. These people in that setting proved to be pure gold to the writer.

The Heritage of the Desert was his first success. In the same day he sold it both as serial and as book. Until then he had received only discouragement from Harper's, the firm that was eventually to become his sole publisher. In rejecting *The Last of the Plainsmen*, their editor had bluntly said to Grey, "I do not see anything in this to convince me you can write either narrative or fiction."

Grey refused to quit, and then convinced them that they should publish his novel. Its success proved how wrong their editor had been. It sold 30,000 copies. Grey was thereby launched upon the writing of *Riders of the Purple Sage*. Did Harper's snap it up? They did not. Nor would *Munsey's*, the leading serialization magazine take it.

The reason was that, far more than *The Heritage of the Desert*, this second novel was critical of Mormon dogma and practice. The publishers feared it would offend their readers and subscribers.

Writing this masterpiece left Grey drained and exhausted. Throughout his life, and increasing as he aged, he was subject to what were called "black spells." A modern psychiatrist would describe him as a manic-depressive. To keep him from despair in the lack of a publisher's decision while they were reading the manuscript, Dolly wisely sent Zane off on a trip, this time to the Gulf of Mexico for tarpon.

Upon his return, high again in spirits, the bad news from Harper's and *Munsey's* did not break him. Instead he took his manuscript over the Harper editor's head to the vice-president of the firm, begging him to read it. It was this executive's wife who turned the tide. She stayed up reading all night, enthralled by the story.

A golden flood followed its publication. In two years' time *Riders of the Purple Sage* earned $100,000 in royalties, the equivalent of a million dollars today. It has never stopped selling. More than any other book, it has determined the universal stereotype of the West. This was Zane Grey's zenith, never again to be reached.

In the spring of 1913 he returned to the Arizona-Utah canyonlands. This time he was a known man, rich and rising famous. With John Wetherill as guide, he packed into the canyon that concealed the Rainbow Bridge. From this rugged experience came *The Rainbow Trail*, the sequel to *Riders of the Purple Sage*.

It is a lesser work. While the creative curve was downward, the sales curve soared. Although the book opens strongly, the passionate feeling is not sustained. What should be the supreme point, as the rock-rolling scene is of the previous novel, becomes in the escape down canyon, past the bridge to the river and the descent to Lee's Ferry and safety, almost mechanical plotting and description. The great wave of feeling and response had crested. There remained only a subsiding aftermath to bear the writer on.

Bear him it did, to ever higher fame and greater riches, culminating in 1925 when Grey's income was $575,000. His contract with Harper's, negotiated by Dolly and her lawyers, gave him 15 percent on the first 10,000 copies, and 20 percent thereafter. Movie leasing rights brought in another fortune. He and she divided their earnings in half.

Although they maintained homes in Lackawaxen, Altadena, and Avalon, they often went their own ways, she to Europe, he to the South Seas and Arizona. The marriage endured, however, as each proved indispensable to the other.

Fame did not rest lightly on him. Self importance came with it. Clerks in Babbitt's general store in Flagstaff once witnessed an angry Grey storming out with his retinue when he was compelled to wait his turn to be served. In 1929 he quarreled with the Arizona Game and Fish Commission when it refused to grant him a permit to hunt bear out of season. He countered by saying that he had written fifteen novels with Arizona background and had spent more than $100,000 in trips all over the state. "So in every way I have not been exactly an undesirable visitor. Now I am compelled to confess that I have given up Arizona. After twenty years of intensive and loving associations with its colored deserts, its cowboys, Indians, traders, and pioneers, I am through."

The state's press did not urge him to stay. An editorialist in the *Tucson Citizen* rose to eloquent heights in concluding, "The colored desert has never even missed the civilizations which have sought to plant themselves there. The conquistadores banged it with mailed fists and thrust at it with their spears, yet it was indifferent to their coming and their going; but Zane Grey is going to quit it, and he expects the colored desert to mourn for him. When the parent stars stalk the heavens for the lost Pleiad, wandering unmissed for aeons, the colored desert will miss Zane Grey."

I do not believe that Zane Grey returned to Arizona during

the remaining decade of his life. His cabins on the South Rim, in Oak Creek, and beneath the Mogollon Rim fell into ruin and were vandalized by souvenir hunters. Today the lodge twenty miles east of Payson has been restored by a Grey fan.

After his first love affair with the canyonlands and their prehistoric ruins, Grey was never again stirred to such feeling and masterful description. Novels laid in Texas, New Mexico, Montana, and elsewhere in Arizona, such as *The Lone Star Ranger, The Border Legion, Desert Gold, The Light of Western Stars, The Desert of Wheat, The Call of the Canyon*, and *To the Last Man*, are no more than readable romances. In *Tales of Lonely Trails* he wrote well of Rainbow Bridge, Tonto Basin, and Death Valley.

Serial publication determined the content and level of his writing. Unlike his contemporaries, Ernest Haycox, Alan Le May, and Will Levington Comfort, who succeeded in breaking free of conventional restraints and writing a last pent-up masterpiece, Grey had no such fate. His work steadily worsened.

Yet he was not without the desire to write a great work. In a family-authorized biography which equates literary greatness with sales, Frank Gruber included entries from a diary kept by Grey while writing *Wanderer of the Wasteland*, a novel of the Colorado-Mojave deserts. Embarrassing to read because of the shallow emotions it reveals, the diary is like a parody of the creative act.

"I want to write and write and write. But this week I go to the desert again, and after that to Death Valley. There I will be able to write with the fire of a living flame. This novel obsesses me. It is wonderful, beautiful, terrible. I shall lose myself in the writing."

Why do people read books such as *Wanderer of the Wasteland* that are so poor in plot, characterization, and setting? I suppose it is because popular taste is uncritical and undemanding. Given action rooted in conflict and violence and ending in virtue,

213

they ask no more. Explicit sex is not necessary. The implicit sex throughout Zane Grey is an essential part of his appeal to readers. Queen Victoria would have knighted him.

Back in the 1920's T.K. Whipple wrote a critique of Zane Grey that holds true to this day. This was his conclusion. "We turn to him not for insight into human nature and human problems nor for refinements of art, but simply for crude epic stories, as we might to an old Norse skald, maker of the sagas of the folk."

This was no mean achievement. It was enough to gain Zane Grey his unique place in American literature. His fate was to create his best work long before he was written out. Never again did he experience the creative excitement that accompanied his discovery of the magnificent borderlands, the virile people and noble animals, and those haunted vestiges of a vanished race, Betatakin and Keet Seel.

He lacked the capacity for literary growth, possessed by Willa Cather and Will Comfort, that would have enabled him to reach another peak late in his life. Age failed to mellow him. He disliked contemporary manners and morals, and in *The Day of the Beast* he devoted a novel to deploring them. The automobile he saw as a threat to American girlhood. He quarreled regularly with the tax collector. After quitting the state he declared that the beauty of Arizona was being sacrificed to commercial interests. The North Rim had become a tin can and gasoline joint, the hunting season a shambles. He was spared today's invasion of the canyonlands, the littering, the defiling.

Writing and fishing, his wife, two sons, and daughter, remained to console him. In 1937 he suffered a stroke while fishing on the Rogue River. Two years later he died. Dolly lived until 1957.

What of his books? I stopped in recently at my neighborhood public library. A nearly full set of his works occupied a long shelf. Three of the titles were out. It is not hard to guess which they were. There is no end to their reading.

READING LIST

ZANE GREY (1872-1939)
The Last of the Plainsmen. New York, Outing, 1908.
The Heritage of the Desert. New York, Harper, 1910.
Riders of the Purple Sage. New York, Harper, 1912.
The Rainbow Trail. New York, Harper, 1915.
Tales of Lonely Trails. New York, Harper, 1922.
Zane Grey, the Man and his Works: an Autobiography Sketch, Critical Appreciations, and Bibliography. New York, Harper, 1927.

T. K. WHIPPLE
Study Out the Land. Berkeley, University of California Press, 1943.

JAMES D. HART
The Popular Book. New York, Oxford, 1950.

FRANK GRUBER
Zane Grey, a Biography. New York, World, 1970.

Photograph of Zane Grey, courtesy of Harper and Row.

Laughing Boy

OLIVER LA FARGE

What are the effects on a writer when success comes early or comes late? What is the difference between a reader's view of a successful writer and that writer's view of himself?

"Success is a poison," Trollope declared, "that should be taken late in life and then only in small doses." This is a definition that applies to the life and work of Oliver La Farge.

His novel, *Laughing Boy*, achieved a meteoric success at the end of the 1920's. Written as his first book before La Farge was thirty, this love story of the young Navajos, Laughing Boy and Slim Girl, was chosen by the Literary Guild and then won the Pulitzer Prize.

Until La Farge's death thirty-four years later, *Laughing Boy* hung like the albatross around his neck. Although he wrote more books and became an ethnologist, linguist, social historian, and champion of Indian rights, he was forever known to the public as the author of that one first success.

Trollope was right. It was a kind of poison, taken in too large a dose and too early. It tasted bitter on La Farge's tongue. "I have a certain dislike for it," he wrote later, "because it has been so popular whereas my other books have done only fairly well. I grow sick of smiling fools who tell me, 'Oh, Mr. La Farge, I did so love your *Laughing Boy*, when are you going to give us another book?' Having written four other novels, a book of short stories and two non-fiction books, one can hardly avoid giving a short answer. . . . If anyone wants to seduce me into doing something for him, the most effective thing he could do would be to praise any book of mine other than that first success."

And yet, *Laughing Boy is* a classic, a book which flowered in its writer's springtime, derived from intimate knowledge of the Navajos, illuminated by love for their land and heritage, and saddened by what La Farge saw as their fate, caught between their traditional ways and the white man's progress.

Although not the first novel about Indians, it was the first to blend realism and romanticism, to lighten prose with poetry, to find beauty in bareness and temper austerity with tenderness.

Oliver La Farge was destined for success by family heritage, education, and his own achievements. At first he sought it and revelled in it. Then seeing the price, he recoiled. In the beginning he wanted to be a great writer and the triumph of his first book led him to believe that he would be one. Then came disillusionment. Twenty years after *Laughing Boy* he wrote in a contribution to the 25th anniversary report of the Harvard class of 1924 of "the slow but relentless arrival of the realization that, as one enters middle age, one may be a good writer, competent, skillful, one may have been blessed with a few inspired moments, but one will never be great. The dream one had at the beginning is still achingly real, but it will never be fulfilled."

An ancestral tradition is more burden than blessing for a member of a family with a creative nature. Too much blue blood is unhealthy. This was true of Oliver La Farge. His Rhode Island family boasted origins back to colonial times. Oliver was named for his great-great grandfather, Commodore Oliver Hazard Perry, the hero of the Battle of Lake Erie, whose brother Matthew had persuaded the Japanese in 1854 to open their ports to western trade. Oliver's grandfather, John La Farge, was an artist noted for his work in stained glass, and Oliver's father, Grant La Farge, was an architect and illustrator. An older brother Christopher became a published writer. His mother was socially authoritarian.

There was something fateful in Oliver's identification with Indians. Somewhere along the line, Indian blood had flowed into the family's veins. Because of the boy's lanky frame and dark looks and inward-turned toes, he was presciently called Indian Man by his mother.

He was expected to continue the family tradition of worldly success. He went to Groton and then to Harvard. From an early age he had a secret urge to write, and at the same time he was troubled by his family's exalted reputation. "People expect me to be artistic and literary," he complained to his mother, "and I can't draw, I can't paint, and nobody but me thinks I can write."

Write he did for Harvard publications, the serious *Advocate* of which he became President (that is, Editor) and the humorous *Lampoon*. He was elected class poet in his senior year. *Scribner's Magazine* printed an essay by him. He was no aesthete. He manned a key oar on the 150-pound varsity crew. His major at Harvard was not what might be expected: anthropology, not literature.

This came about because when he was a fifteen-year-old student at Groton his mother had sent him a clipping of a review by his idol, a family friend by the name of Theodore Roosevelt. The former president had written a review of *Men of the Old Stone Age* by Henry Fairfield Osborne. This is all that it took to turn the boy in the direction he was to follow for the rest of his life.

At first the way led not toward the Southwest, but toward France. Between Groton and Harvard, Oliver and Christopher took a European tour. As a result, Oliver expected his anthropological studies to be in the Paleolithic period of the limestone caves in the valley of the Dordogne. He did not know that Harvard's major research in anthropology had been in the American Southwest ever since the first Hemenway Expedition of the 1880's, to which Frederick Webb Hodge had been the youthful secretary. When La Farge entered Harvard in 1920, the anthropology faculty included such great names as Tozzer, Kidder, and Hooton.

Their student's seriousness of purpose was soon put to the test. Oliver was included in a field party to the Four Corners where, in the summer of 1921, investigations were continuing into the possible predecessors of the Mesa Verde people. When he proved his stamina on the end of a shovel, he was chosen again the next summer as map-maker as well as laborer, and in 1924 he had risen to head a crew of field workers.

To further strengthen the son's attachment to the Southwest, Oliver's father had been commissioned to illustrate Elsie Clews Parsons' *American Indian Life,* an anthology of articles by authorities on various tribes. Out of Grant La Farge's knowledge of the Hopi and Navajo country came encouragement for his son to continue his Southwest studies.

After the 1924 expedition and his graduation from Harvard, there occurred the decisive experience that was to lead finally to *Laughing Boy.* With two companions Oliver set out on a 175-mile pack-trip by horseback from the Four Corners across the Navajo-Hopi reservations to the Grand Canyon. En route they encountered Father Berard Haile, the authority on Navajo mythology, Lorenzo Hubbell, the greatest of the traders, and Laura Adams Armer, author of Navajo books. They lived as Navajos and were accepted by them.

One Navajo, after studying the sunburned La Farge, turned to the trader and said, "Now what the hell is that? He looks like an Indian, but he's too pink." Harzi Nez, Tall Cliff Dweller, they called him, and to his face the name he cherished, La Farchi. He proved adept at learning to speak Navajo. Verily, he had become Indian Man.

Throughout the long ride he kept hearing inwardly the music of the Navajo ceremonial chants translated by Dr. Washington Matthews which he had discovered in the Harvard Library. From them came the poetry that was to exalt *Laughing Boy's* prose above mere realism. *In Beauty it is begun.*

220

When La Farge returned to Harvard in the fall, determined to pursue graduate studies on the Navajos and Apaches, he was awarded the prestigious Hemenway Fellowship. This led to a radical diversion in the form of a well-paid job with a field expedition into Guatemala for research in Mayan archaeology and linguistics. This in turn brought an appointment with the newly founded Department of Middle-American Studies at Tulane University in New Orleans. Several expeditions were undertaken, and the Louisiana city became La Farge's home for two and a half years.

What became of his twin desires to be a writer and a student of the Navajos? The answer is *Laughing Boy*. In its writing, his two desires were fused and consummated. If the way to the creation of this novel seems circuitous, it was. If the forces that formed it seem complex, they were. Like the flower that comes from seed by the alchemy of earth, water, and sun, a work of art also dwells in embryo within the artist, destined to emerge through magical circumstances to achieve a life of its own. Thus came *Laughing Boy*.

Roughing it in the Southwest had strengthened La Farge without releasing his New England inhibitions. Such a sensual lysis occurred in the seductive French Quarter of New Orleans. There the novel was written while La Farge was on a half-time appointment at Tulane to write up his Mayan researches. Creating it came hard, as he was trying unsuccessfully to sell stories and articles. He was on his own and money was scarce. And then he was fired by Tulane for having insulted the son and daughter of one of the trustees—a result of his low boiling point and too much to drink at a masked party.

From what he estimated as an output of 120,000 words, he had sold a single story. And yet nothing more than that was needed to loose the flood against which he was fated to struggle for the rest of his life. The story called "North is Black" was based on a Navajo experience, and it appeared in *The Dial*, a literary magazine of small circulation. There it was read by Ferris Greenslet, editor of Houghton Mifflin, the Boston publishers. He sent a routine inquiry to ask if La Farge were planning a Navajo novel.

Whereupon La Farge submitted the chapters he had already written and an outline of those to follow. With Yankee caution the publishers refused to commit themselves. There was no need to. La Farge went to work and finished the book.

Laughing Boy was published in November 1929. Its choice by the Literary Guild boosted it into best-selling orbit. Then in May of 1930 it won the Pulitzer Prize, in competition with books by Sinclair Lewis, Thomas Wolfe, and Ernest Hemingway. The judges included Mary Austin and Owen Wister, two of the foremost writers on the West. How could it *not* have won?

There are reasons for its brilliant success. The author knew his subject, the Navajos and their land, and thus his book was sure and true. He had developed skill as a writer, by writing. What might have been a tract became lyrical from the love he felt for those desert people and their environment. His emotion was nostalgic. In words he wrote years later, "The book sprang from a combination of vivid memory, the sad sense of saying farewell, and the knowledge experienced in writing a thesis as part of the requirements for a master's degree."

"He believed," La Farge went on to recall of himself, "that he might never go to the American Southwest again, certainly would never again be free to soak himself in the Navajo Indians. Among them he had seen something that had moved him greatly and this was his way of recording it. As the young can do, he had made personal friendships, experienced moments of genuine contact among the Navajos, despite the barriers of language and culture, and these loopholes of insight were vastly widened by his studies."

How did success affect the young man not yet thirty years old? Both for better and worse. It brought La Farge to a lifework on behalf of the American Indians—a labor of social benefit rather than linguistic research. It brought him back to the Southwest, though not immediately. He was also assured of being able to publish everything he chose to submit. These were positive results.

On the negative side, the sudden financial success led La Farge to leave the French Quarter for New York, to marry on his social level, and to do what was expected of a La Farge—carry on the family tradition. "I was of the 4th generation of artists and they were all gentlemen," he lamented. "One was supposed to live up to them."

He came to experience the ancient conflict between the conventional and the creative, between New England and New Orleans, a closed society and the open Southwest. "I was particularly prone to aspirations toward conservative gentility which were actually alien to my make-up," La Farge wrote later in properly inflated language, "to live uptown in a presentable apartment, have friends out of the same drawer as myself, give dinners of six and eight deftly served, accompanied by the right wines, and to be asked to small, fashionable parties (white tie)— a death in life, which I eagerly embraced as soon as financial success enabled me to, and of which it took a series of disasters to cure me."

Mary Austin was not taken in. La Farge told the story on himself. When that blunt woman first met the author of the book on which she had helped confer the coveted Pulitzer, she took one look around that uptown apartment and exclaimed, "Well, I never expected to find *you* in a place like *this!*"

What were the other "disasters?" Marriage was one. Although they had two children, this was not enough to reconcile the widening differences between him and his wife. His drinking made for moodiness. The Depression robbed him of the security that would have come from his book's earnings. The genteel La Farges were not rich. To earn money to maintain his new standard of living meant that La Farge had to go on turning out romantic Indian stories for the slick paper magazines.

He sought to break the pattern by writing two novels with

settings other than the Southwest. *Sparks Fly Upward*, laid in Central America, and *Long Pennant*, an adventure story of New England privateers in southern waters, were good books, but they did not earn the money his way of life required. He realized that the kind of writer he intended to be could not be financially secure nor could flourish in a society environment. He came to know that he should not have left New Orleans.

Because of the popularity of *Laughing Boy* and his prestige as a La Farge, he was drawn into work on behalf of the Indians, first with a private organization and then on government assignment under John Collier, the Commissioner of Indian Affairs who came in with the Roosevelt New Deal. This work took him back to the Southwest, with the Hopis, the Navajos, and the Apaches. He went on to become president and eloquent spokesman of the Association on American Indian Affairs. In this capacity he worked until his death in 1963 at age sixty-one.

By his concern for Indian rights La Farge both found and lost his life. He became less of an artist and more of a man. Out of the disillusionment that ensued, particularly during the Eisenhower administration when the Indian programs were largely abandoned, he managed to write book after book. One of the most meaningful is composed of the text he contributed to a book of photographs by Helen M. Post called *As Long As the Grass Shall Grow*. In a revulsion from the romanticism of *Laughing Boy* he wrote the sombre stories of *All the Young Men* and in 1937 his next to last novel, *The Enemy Gods*, an indictment of the missionaries and government agencies that took the Navajo and Apache children away from their parents and confined them in prison-like schools. Even thus had Lummis reacted a generation earlier at Isleta.

Then the war came. Paradoxically from the destructive conflict that saw him become Chief Historian of the Air Transport Command, with a far-flung staff of two hundred fifty, La Farge derived creative strength and a new life. After serving in theaters of action the world around, he wrote the history of the Com-

224

mand called *The Eagle in the Egg*. Thus was inaugurated the Air Age in which we now live.

Yet without a happy second marriage in 1939, it is doubtful whether the challenge of the Indian work, followed by the responsibility of wartime service, would have been enough to maintain La Farge's belief in himself as a creative writer.

He met the woman who became his second wife at the Santa Fe Fiesta in 1936. They were married three years later. She was as truly of the Southwest as he was of New England. Half French and half Spanish-American, Consuelo Otille Baca came into La Farge's life at the time of his most need, as he was experiencing disillusionment and despair from the fortune that had turned him the wrong way. Her families, the Bacas and the Pendaries, were the lords of Rociada, a high valley in the Sangre de Cristos between Santa Fe and Taos. The death of her father, who had become Lieutenant Governor of New Mexico, and the collapse of the wool market in the Depression, had forced the sale of the domain and brought the Bacas to live in Santa Fe.

After their marriage and reunion after the war, Oliver and Consuelo made Santa Fe their home. In addition to his Indian work, he wrote stories, juveniles, a pictorial history of the Indians, and one more novel, *The Copper Pot*, in which he returned to the French Quarter and told of an artist who did *not* leave that creative milieu for a New York society marriage. Although good therapy for him to have written it, the novel remains undistinguished.

A better book is a group of essays toward an autobiography called *Raw Material*, written after the war on a Guggenheim Fellowship. Because of wartime restrictions on materials, the publisher gave it a wretched format. The scarcest and least known of La Farge's books, it is one of his best, an illuminating, self-searching, writer's testament.

Three peaks dominate the range of Oliver La Farge's books—*Laughing Boy*, *Raw Material*, and one which might outlive them both: *Behind the Mountains*. As much a child of Oliver and

Consuelo as their son, John Pendaries, it first appeared serially in the *New Yorker*, with which La Farge had a lucrative agreement whereby after the war that magazine had first call on his stories, sketches, and essays.

Behind the Mountains was Consuelo's story, told through her husband, of her enchanted childhood and girlhood on the Baca domain high in the Sangre de Cristos. Here in a few simple artless, artful exercises in the transmutation of one person's memories into another person's prose is the quintessence of northern New Mexico. The book has the same ambience of *Laughing Boy*, that classic of northern Arizona—romantic, lyrical, and redolent with the fragrance of piñon and juniper and sweat-stained leather, fashioned from the Southwest that La Farge had loved and lost, wooed and won again.

The last years in Santa Fe were his Indian Summer. He never wrote another novel. After his work for Indian rights there was no strength left for a major undertaking. Stories and reviews and his weekly column in the Santa Fe *New Mexican* were the most he could do. His newspaper contributions were collected posthumously by Winfield Townley Scott, another Rhode Islander who had moved to Santa Fe, in *The Man With the Calabash Pipe*. They are in turn serious and gay, angry and mellow, and always written with skill and grace.

I met Oliver La Farge only once, at a luncheon in Santa Fe. He was wearing much Indian jewelry in the Navajo manner. He was darkly handsome, and taciturn. Ignorant then of his feelings about it, I praised *Laughing Boy* which I had just re-read. He stared at me.

A year before he died La Farge wrote a new foreword to a paperback edition of *Laughing Boy*. In it he looked back in sadness at the book that had determined his life. He saw the Navajos as a "powerful community equipped with a modern government and many other improvements, treated with great respect by the Senators and Congressmen from the two states in which most of them reside. They are an unhappy people, sullen towards all others, unfriendly, harassed by drunkenness, their leaders at once arrogant and touchy. Still, here and there among them you can still find the beauty, the religion, the sense of fun, you can still attend a ceremony at which no one is drunk. In the space of thirty years, however, the wholeness has gone, the people described in *Laughing Boy*, complete to itself, is gone."

"It would have completely staggered that beginning writer," he went on in elegiac vein to say about his vanished self, "to learn that after all these years his book would still be selling. He did not expect it to sell at all. It would have staggered and gratified him enormously could he have known then, in his time of early struggle, the days of aching hope and profound self-doubt, that young readers would still be liking it thirty years later. But there is no way to reach back and tell him that, and it probably is better that he did the thing for itself, because he had to, and for no other reason. That leaves the gratification to me, his successor, who am much older and much more in need of encouragement."

In the end his devotion to the Southwest shortened his life, as he wore himself out in work for the Association he headed. Travels to reservations as distant as Alaska, legislative hearings, voluminous reports, speeches, and reviews, combined to drain his diminishing strength. His last effort was to aid the Taos Indians in their efforts to recover the Blue Lake lands in the mountains above the pueblo, taken from them in 1906 and added to the Carson National Forest. Only two months before he died, La Farge went a last time to the pueblo, so ill that he had to take an oxygen tank to aid his breathing. He did not live to see the final victory. It came on December 15, 1970, seven and a half years after La Farge's death, when President Nixon signed the Congressional bill that gave the Taoseños trust title to their sacred lands.

Lieutenant-Colonel Oliver Hazard Perry La Farge, U.S.A. F.R., lies buried under one of the small identical headstones in the National Cemetery in Santa Fe. If you would seek an epitaph for him, go to *Laughing Boy*. You will find it there in Laughing Boy's words of love for Slim Girl:

"I have been down Old Age River in the log, with sheet-lightning and rainbows and soft rain, and the gods on either side to guide me. The Eagles have put lightning snakes and sunbeams and rainbows under me; they have carried me through the hole in the sky. I have been through the little crack in the rocks with Red God and seen the homes of the Butterflies and the Mountain Sheep and the Divine Ones. I have heard the Four Singers on the Four Mountains."

In Beauty it is finished.

READING LIST

OLIVER LA FARGE (*1901-1963*)

Laughing Boy. Boston, Houghton Mifflin, 1929. Also Literary Guild. Sentry paperback, 1962, with new foreword by author.

Red Men and Pink, in *Wings*, V.3, N.11, Nov. 1929.

All the Young Men. Boston, Houghton Mifflin, 1935.

The Enemy Gods. Boston, Houghton Mifflin, 1937.

The Copper Pot. Boston, Houghton Mifflin, 1942.

Raw Material. Boston, Houghton Mifflin, 1945.

The Eagle in the Egg. Boston, Houghton Mifflin, 1949.

A Pictorial History of the American Indian. New York, Crown, 1956.

Behind the Mountains. Boston, Houghton Mifflin, 1956.

A Pause in the Desert. Boston, Houghton Mifflin, 1957.

Santa Fe, the Autobiography of a Southwestern Town. Norman, University of Oklahoma Press, 1959.

The Man With the Calabash Pipe. Edited by Winfield Townley Scott. Boston, Houghton Mifflin, 1966.

Oliver La Farge Memorial Issue. Indian Affairs, Newsletter of the Assn. on American Indian Affairs. No. 52, August 1963.

EVERETT GILLIS
Oliver La Farge. Austin, Steck-Vaughn, 1967.

DARCY MCNICKEL
Indian Man, a Life of Oliver La Farge. Bloomington, Indiana University Press, 1971.

T. M. PEARCE
Oliver La Farge. New York, Twayne, 1972.

Photograph of Oliver La Farge, courtesy of Houghton Mifflin Co.

Apache

WILL LEVINGTON COMFORT

It was Dobie who first led me to Will Levington Comfort's novel, *Apache*. In his *Guide to Life & Literature of the Southwest*, I read these words: "*Apache* remains for me the most moving and incisive piece of writing on Indians of the Southwest that I have found." I read it. As usual, Dobie was right.

Reading Comfort's sinewy story of the Apache chieftain, Mangas Coloradas (Red Sleeves) and his lost fight to hold the tribal domain, I found it hard to realize that the author was the Will Levington Comfort whose earlier books—inspirational popular novels such as *Fate Knocks at the Door* and *She Buildeth Her House*—were among my parents' favorite books. And was he the same man who had collaborated with a woman from India on a book of animal stories called *Son of Power?* If so, he was indeed a versatile writer.

The name was associated in my mind also with a philosophical study group to which Comfort issued a monthly magazine-letter called *The Glass Hive*. As a child I had gone with my mother to a meeting at the writer's home in the Mt. Washington district of Los Angeles, not far from the Southwest Museum. All I remembered about it was that I grew restless and slipped outdoors to play.

231

There was a wide gulf between these associations and *Apache*. As Librarian of UCLA at the time I first read the novel, I sought to bridge it by assembling Comfort's literary remains, so that a critical biography could be written. I learned that he had died in 1932 at age fifty-four, a year after the publication of *Apache*. His widow and two sons had also died. Only his daughter, Jane Levington Comfort (Mrs. Paul Annixter) was living. In two novels of her own, *From These Beginnings* and *Time Out for Eternity*, she had skillfully fictionized her father's life and work. Most of his papers had been lost by his son John in the course of a nomadic life. All that survived, Jane Annixter gave to the UCLA Library. Friends of Comfort added letters and reminiscences. I thought of attempting the biography, but my real interest, then as now, was in the one book, *Apache*, and I went on to other things.

Now years later, I found myself back at the unanswered question, how came this man at the end of his life to write his best book? His was the opposite of Oliver La Farge's achievement in creating his best book, at the beginning of his writing life.

In seeking the answer I did not read all of Comfort's novels, stories, essays, and letters. I only sampled the inspirational books enough to know that they are dated. We have left those times when New Thought was the fashion, that era when Annie Besant and Madame Blavatsky were household names and Uplift was the thing to do. Now our persistent sentimentality has embraced yoga, astrology, natural foods, and gurus. *Plus ça change . . .*

Among Comfort's more than twenty books, I found that only three reached the zenith on his creative arc. Derived from his deepest being, they were written almost unconsciously in the purist inspiration. The control of the professional writer was present, however, to give them form and impact.

Routledge Rides Alone, Comfort's first novel, was published in 1910. It came from experience as a newspaper correspondent in the Russo-Japanese war of 1905. In 1914 an autobiography to his 35th year was called *Midstream*. And finally *Apache* in 1931 was followed on the descending curve by a last book, *The Pilot Comes Aboard*. This was a sea story, masterfully written and yet from the surface, not the depth of his mind.

He was a Michigander born at Kalamazoo on January 17, 1878, with a dangerous heritage of Wesleyan Methodism, alcoholism, and a compulsion for self-expression through writing. He grew up in Detroit and was educated in the home and on the street. He began to write at six, to drink at sixteen. Thereafter he lived fast and hard. The stages included newspaper work in Detroit and Pittsburgh, army enlistment in the Spanish-American war ending in discharge with malaria and typhoid; a war correspondent in the Orient; a first book, *Trooper Tales*, in 1899; marriage at twenty-two to Adith Duffie-Mulholland, a union which lasted the rest of his life. It was a beginning like that of Jack London's, rich in variety and intensity.

Midstream was a shocking book in 1914. American literature was still genteel. Comfort's was the first of the confessional autobiographies in the tradition of Cellini and Rousseau. "My whole life is marked with maimed homecomings—from war and drink and dishonour," he wrote. "War and women and work—such as I am, they have made me.'" A generation later came Henry Miller and his *Tropics*.

Routledge Rides Alone blended the mysticism and melodrama which Comfort found in the Orient. It is a flamboyant, powerful narrative. In its treatment of the English in India and of the Russo-Japanese struggle, *Routledge* is anti-imperialist and anti-war. Edwin Markham declared that it should have won its author the Nobel Peace Prize. Comfort wrote it in the anguish of failure and poverty and dedicated it "To the Lady of Courage whom I married." He then went on a fifty-day drunk and landed in a sanitarium for the cure.

After serialization in the *Saturday Evening Post*, the novel was bought outright by Lippincott for $500 with no royalty payments, in the same sharp way that Harper's took advantage of Dana in acquiring *Two Years Before the Mast*.

Routledge set Comfort's star on high. He now had a reading public. He also had new temptations to add to that of drink. One was to gather disciples and the other was to grind out what publishers demanded—red-blooded action stories without literary and mystical overtones. Comfort sought in *Midstream* to reconcile these ambivalences. And he had himself to cope with— a small, great-hearted man of vitality and charm to whose outpouring of love people passionately responded.

He concluded that "The workman must either fight or conform. That is a matter of the force that drives him. If he has the endurance to take the beatings of a double-decade, gathering force all the way and faith in the human spirit, it is against nature for him to fail to be heard. His knuckle shall reach the bell, and his people respond and vibrate to the stroke."

Thus Comfort took unto himself a teaching role. Not as a messiah nor a cult leader, but simply as a charismatic man who gathered people and shared experience with them. The nucleus was his own family, grown to a daughter and two sons. He called his wife Penelope—Penel for short—because, like the wife of Ulysses, she waited at home.

They moved from Detroit to the shore of Lake Erie, where for two years a large house called Stonestudy was his teaching center. Two books came from this time, written to his own specifications. *Child and Country* (1916) and *The Hive* (1918) embodied his revulsion to the war that was engulfing the world. They bear rereading now in the light of our revulsions. He was ahead of his time. Today Comfort would be a powerful guru. In his time the response to him was largely by older people. The young men were unawakened. Now it is the other way around, and the gurus are Miller, Mailer, and Ginsberg.

In *From These Beginnings* Jane Comfort told of how her father was summoned by Mabel Dodge Luhan to her sybilline center in Taos. He went on to Southern California where the magnet was the Theosophical colony of Krotona. His family followed. Santa Monica Canyon was their first home, and then that district of Los Angeles now called Highland Park. There Comfort spent the remaining years of his life, holding Wednesday evening and Sunday afternoon study sessions in the home and issuing *Reconstruction Letters* and *The Glass Hive* to a wide list of readers.

His prolific output of the 'teens diminished as his energy went into socio-religious intercourse. Women continued to involve him while the faithful Penelope maintained the home that he also needed. He took his children into the Sierra Madre, camping in the lee of Ontario Peak. Mrs. Comfort had to stay home because her heart could not stand the altitude. Yet there was never any question of separation or divorce. "He made a mess of everything," Jane recalled, but she also acknowledged that her father held them in loving thrall.

"A sandy-haired little bunch of high-tension wires," Lee Shippey described him. In vital activity Comfort resembled his Arroyo Seco neighbor, Charles F. Lummis, while in humanitarian zeal he can be likened to that other Southern Californian, Upton Sinclair, although Comfort never advocated a politico-economic solution to society's ills.

He was a mystic. His critics regretted his having abandoned novels for moralities. One described him as a Boy Scoutmaster who had just discovered Emerson. Another declared that his work showed the necessity to write and the determination to philosophize. "This Comfort wields an easy pen," his worst critic, Mencken, began disarmingly. "He has done, indeed, some capital melodramas, and when his ardor heats him up he grows downright eloquent. But of late the whole force of his aesthetic engines has been thrown into propaganda, by the Bhagavad-Gita out of Victorian sentimentalism."

Comfort was the one literary person D. H. Lawrence sought out when he reached Los Angeles in 1923. Jane Comfort remembers Lawrence's coming to dinner and being shocked by her father's flirting with his secretary. Whereupon the prudish English writer turned his attention to Mrs. Comfort; and when his disgruntled host went off to bed, it was Lawrence and Penelope who talked far into the night.

Comfort took India as the subject matter of two books published in the 1920's, both resulting from friendship with Willimina L. Armstrong, a former medical missionary who, after a back injury, had taken to her bed in an incense-filled house in the Edendale district and there as a self-proclaimed messiah had drawn a bizarre following of believers.

Miss Armstrong was a fabulous story teller. It required Comfort to render her lush tales into lean prose and sell them to the *Saturday Evening Post* and then to Doubleday as the book, *Son of Power*. Next came an elephant novel called *Samadhi*. Comfort had adopted a style which in these Indian books brought him back from moralizing to characterization and narrative. He was approaching the creation of his masterpiece.

As the Twenties neared an end, Comfort was in an unwitting race against the enemies that were finally to defeat him as man not writer. They were alcoholism and the Depression. In 1928 Comfort reached age fifty. A year later came the stock market crash. The Comforts felt the pinch. Hard times ended his inspirational letters. Now that he had mastered his medium, would there be a worthy subject? And a market for the result? Could he stay sober during the labor of creation?

The Comfort children had since grown up. Jane was serving as her father's amanuensis while married to Paul "Steve" Annixter, a young writer who had followed the family west from Stonestudy. Tom was a painter. Like his father, John was a newspaperman and an alcoholic. His job on a Bisbee paper gave his father reason to drive over periodically to Arizona to steady him. Thus did Will Levington Comfort enter the magnetic field of *Apache*.

Arizona had been in his consciousness clear back to army days when, camped in the South awaiting transportation to Cuba, he drank with Arizona recruits among Teddy Roosevelt's Rough

Riders. Later as a war correspondent he had campaigned on Luzon with more Arizonans. One of the trooper tales in his first book had an imagined Arizona setting.

Now at last he saw it at firsthand. "For 75 miles southeast of Tucson on the El Paso highway," he described his route, "the desert grows greener and loftier, until presently it was a mile-high mesquite mesa, every leaf washed to a sparkle from the late summer rains."

En route to Bisbee he stopped over in Tombstone and visited the office of the *Epitaph*, the celebrated newspaper founded in 1880 by John P. Clum and still being published. Its back files enthralled him. "Pure horn silver," he called them. He felt, he said, "like a returned native catching up on the home news." He saw in them an article for the *Saturday Evening Post*. Editor George Horace Lorimer responded enthusiastically with an offer of double the usual rate.

Comfort made at least four trips to Bisbee to see his son, each time absorbing lore and savoring "Tombstone in enchanted sleep on its high mesquite mesa." He foresaw the Disneyizing of the town and deplored it. "Its past does not need to be restored from a showman's standpoint," he declared. "Its history is brutal, blithe, cagey, abrupt."

It was in the files of the *Epitaph* that Comfort first met the Apaches, the scourge of the territorial years. Then gradually the journalist was replaced by the novelist. Here is how he told it: "The red glistening thread of the Apache wove constantly through the gray fabric of pioneer talk, far more interesting than the attempt to put the old town back."

He envisioned a novel that would be to the Apaches what *Laughing Boy* was to the Navajos. Comfort and his publisher would not have overlooked the new audience that La Farge's success had created for books about the Southwestern Indians.

He caught fire, and as he began to read in earnest "the books tumbled over themselves"—Bartlett, Cremony, Bancroft and

more. Throughout he perceived the mighty figure of the chieftain, Mangas Coloradas, that rimrock Apache. "I stood aghast at
myself," Comfort wrote later in an essay on which he was working at the time of his death (and which was edited by UCLA
Archivist James V. Mink in "The Making of a Southwestern
Novel") "for the time I had spent fabricating stories when
stories like this already exist; have already been lived and are
already to be sung, to sing themselves, in fact, through some
workman's heart and hand."

Comfort went on from libraries in Tucson and Bisbee to field
trips in the Apache country of Arizona and New Mexico. He
was on the Tonto Rim and at Cochise's Stronghold in the Dragoons; he went up the Gila to Piños Altos and Santa Rita del
Cobre in the copper country near Silver City. This was the
heart of the Mimbreño Apaches' land ruled by Mangas. He
talked with oldtimers—forest supervisors, cattlemen, and miners—who remembered the Indian wars. Again he was experiencing the compulsion in which he had created *Routledge Rides
Alone* and *Midstream*.

Back in California his fire banked, he began to write *Apache*.
He then discovered that the greatest of Arizona collections and
the authority on the American Indians were in his own neighborhood, in the Southwest Museum and its director, Frederick
Webb Hodge. It was Dr. Hodge who confirmed the soundness
of Comfort's research and encouraged him in writing the novel,
so that after the book's publication, Comfort wrote on April 13,
1931 to Hodge,

"Dear friend, this is the first manuscript of the novel *Apache*
from which the book was printed this January by E. P. Dutton
Co., New York. I am very glad to give it to the Southwest Museum not only for the great help in writing the book but as a
neighborly gesture." And he concluded prophetically, "Too, I
am glad to report that the book is being appreciated and bids to
live well over the usual novel season."

Comfort wrote *Apache* in only eleven weeks. His daughter recalls it as the climax of his life, a joyous time of early rising and steady writing, of tennis and hiking for relaxation—and no drinking. There were weekends in the mountains during one of which he wrote to John of the completed work, "It opened to me so perfectly as a story that, catching the spirit of it, I had merely to sing through the form."

Most of Comfort's novels had been serialized in the popular magazines. The monthly *American* made a lucrative offer for *Apache*. As much as the money was needed, Comfort refused. He wanted *Apache* to appear as a whole, and without slick-paper illustrations. He wanted it to hit hard.

It did indeed. *Apache* was an immediate success with both critics and readers. Paperback reprints have continued to appear. Now with the new awareness of American Indian culture it appears destined for even more readers. The approval of Dr. Hodge and of Oliver La Farge pleased Comfort the most. In reviewing *Apache* in the New York Herald Tribune *Books*, the author of *Laughing Boy* wrote,

"Anyone who lives with a tribe for a short time can describe the simplicity, and record the physical aspect of its life and acts, but it is rare indeed for a white man to penetrate behind the alien minds, and rarer still for him, having done so, to be able to state clearly what he has found. This is the important thing the author of *Apache* has done. . . . He has created for us the real Indian, his absurdity and his greatness, in a manner that few scientists and no other writers have achieved."

Comfort was ready by temperament and training to fix the vision when it appeared. He had learned to write down and understate, to be concrete rather than abstract, and to particularize rather than generalize. It took a mystic to understand the mystical nature of Mangas Coloradas. The usurping whites regarded him only as a bloodthirsty savage and murdered him. From his own periodic degradation as an alcoholic Comfort was able to comprehend the humiliation of Mangas Coloradas. Long practice in observing and reporting prepared Comfort faithfully to present the Southwestern setting.

And there occurred a mystical transfer of identity, so that in writing the book Comfort *was* Mangas. This was borne out when I talked with Jane and Steve. In recalling their father's last day of life, November 2, 1932, Annixter said, "Bill had been drinking. He was in bad shape. That afternoon he pulled himself together and took me out on the porch. He put his arm around me and he said, 'I am Mangas. You are Cochise. We are blood brothers.' "

When he relapsed, they took him to the hospital. He died that night of heart failure from morphine injections.

They scattered his ashes on the shoulder of Ontario Peak, the mountain he loved above all others. When his Penelope followed a few years later, her ashes too were strewn there.

In *Child and Country* Comfort wrote words which perfectly describe the man he was in the creation of his masterpiece *Apache*:

"A man is at his best in those periods in which self-interest is lost to him. When the workman gives forth the best that is in him, not feeling his body, above all its passions and petty devices for ruling him, concentrated upon the task, a pure instrument of his task, and open to all inspiration regarding it—that man is safe and superb."

READING LIST

WILL LEVINGTON COMFORT (1878-1932)
Trooper Tales. New York, Street, 1899.
Routledge Rides Alone. New York, Burt, 1910.
Midstream; a Chronicle at Halfway. New York, Doran, 1914.

Son of Power. New York, Doubleday, 1920. A collaboration with Willimina L. Armstrong who took the pseudonym Zamin ki Dost.

Apache. New York, Dutton, 1931.

The Pilot Comes Aboard. New York, Dutton, 1932.

JAMES V. MINK

The Making of a Southwestern Novel. Manuscripts, V. 9, N. 3, Summer 1957.

Photograph of Will Levington Comfort, courtesy of Jane Levington Comfort and UCLA Library Special Collections.

Kino's *Historical Memoir*
Garcés' *Diary*

Always a hero worshipper, my lifelong reading has been a quest for the great ones of history and literature whose character and achievements are goals for striving and beacons for guidance. In the words of the poet, "I think continually of those who were truly great."

By your heroes are you known. If yours are The Kid, Earp, or Geronimo, then put me down, I have nothing for you. In the Southwest I have been peopling my own hall of fame, choosing heroes who ennobled the region by their selflessness, bravery, and vision.

Now I turn to an earlier time and another mode of heroism, and write of the 17th century Jesuit, Eusebio Kino, and the 18th century Franciscan, Francisco Garcés. Both left written records which, coupled with the lives they chronicle, enshrine them as classical figures of the Spanish Southwest.

Padre Garcés was the first white man to explore the lower San Joaquin Valley and the Kern River in Alta California. He reestablished Kino's Mission San Xavier del Bac and was martyred on the Colorado River below Yuma. Padre Kino came to Pimería Alta in 1687 and remained for a quarter century, establishing missions and ranches, propagating agriculture and animal husbandry, and setting records of organization, administration, and endurance which have never been matched.

Astronomer and mathematician, geographer and cartographer, it was Kino who pronounced that "California no es ysla," and proved by exploration that the land was a peninsula and not the island it was thought to be. He was led to this discovery by a quest for the blue shells, the coastal abalone prized by the Pimas and Papagos.

Kino died in 1711 at Magdalena, Sonora, in his sixty-sixth year. Only recently was his skeleton found. The renamed village of Magdalena de Kino has become a shrine for pilgrims. Perhaps the Church in its mighty, slow way will eventually canonize him and Garcés.

Kino was forty-two when he arrived in the Southwest. He was no Spaniard, although the rest of his life was spent in service of the alliance between Spain and the Church. Born Eusebio Chini near Trento in the Italian Dolomites, he was schooled in the sciences in Austria and Germany. His desire was to continue the scholarly Jesuit labors in China. He never reached the Orient. In Cádiz as an observer of the great comet of 1680/81, he drew lots with a fellow priest to determine where they would serve. Kino lost. The winner went to the Philippines and on to China; Kino went to Mexico and ultimate glory.

Today three centuries later Kino is visibly remembered by his monumental presence in equestrian statues by Don Julián Martínez in the capital cities of Hermosillo and Phoenix, a bas relief by Mahonri Young in Tucson, a statue by Ralph Hume in Nogales; and in Washington where a heroic bronze by Suzanne Silvercruys is one of Arizona's two representatives in the Hall of Fame. Italy has honored her son with a statue by Stefano Zueck in Trento which I glimpsed a decade ago on a passage through the mountain city. In 1682 Kino adopted the present form of his patronym.

If you would go beyond these metallic and lapidary representations of the man, there is an abundance of modern scholarship to inform and possibly to convert you to my belief that Kino was the noblest Southwesterner of all. Not astonishingly it begins with Bolton, titan of Southwestern historians, who came to the region by as unlikely a route as Kino.

While a young instructor in Texas via Wisconsin and Pennsylvania, Dr. Herbert Eugene Bolton experienced an illumination in which he perceived his lifework laid out before him. He equipped himself by a mastery of the Spanish language, and then for half a century he proceeded to enact his vision of discovering, translating, editing, and publishing the original documents of the Spanish Southwest. His work is a roll call of the great ones: Coronado, Escalante, Kino, Anza, Font, Palóu, and others. By his formidable energy and massive authority, Bolton bestrode the field of Southwestern history and made the Bancroft Library one of the glories of the University of California. There he trained a hundred and more historians who personify his immortality.

It was in 1907 that the inspired young Bolton discovered in the Mexican archives the manuscript of Kino's *Favores Celestiales*, an account of his lifework, and published it in 1919 as *Kino's Historical Memoir of Pimería Alta*. His next great labor was the multi-volume edition of *Anza's California Expeditions*, based equally on research in archives and field. In 1936 he published *Rim of Christendom*, a biography of Kino which remains definitive.

Bolton's work opened the gates to a flood of Kino scholarship. Professor Frank C. Lockwood of the University of Arizona came first with a readable short account of the Jesuit father called *With Padre Kino on the Trail*. In our time the Jesuit historians, Father Ernest Burrus and Father Charles Polzer, have extended Bolton's work and are engaged on a definitive edition of Kino's writings and letters.

Endearing is Kino's correspondence with a woman. His were not love letters, although the two were one in their love of God. Maria Guadalupe de Lancaster, Duchess of Aveiro, Arcos and Maqueda, was a Portuguese noblewoman descended from John

245

of Gaunt. Known as the Mother of Missions, she resided in Madrid and used her wealth to further Spanish missionary efforts throughout the world. Kino turned to her for help. His letters, writen from 1680 to 1687, were purchased in the 1920's by Henry E. Huntington when Bolton could not raise the price for the Bancroft Library. They are a prime source for the Black Robe's biography. An annotated translation of them by Father Burrus is called *Kino Writes to the Duchess.* The originals are among the lesser known jewels in that San Marino treasure house known as the Henry E. Huntington Library and Art Gallery.

As a man Kino had the human touch. During the long years on the frontier he was never harmed by the Indians. He was a kind of buffer between the Apaches and the Pimas. Unlike the Spanish civil and military establishment, unequalled in cruelty and stupidity, Kino labored for the entire well-being of the Indians. Although he sought to convert them, he also provided the means for them to live better by introducing agriculture and stock raising. For every mission he founded, he also established a ranch with cattle, horses and mules, grains and fruits.

It was Kino who led his fellow Jesuit, Father Juan Maria Salvatierra, to found the chain of missions in Baja California which flourished until the expulsion of the Jesuits in 1737 allowed the Franciscans to drain off the missions' resources to enrich their chain in Alta California.

Pimería Alta was a wide domain, bounded by river systems—Altar and Magdalena on the south, Gila on the north, San Pedro and Colorado on the east and west. Kino came to know it all, making *entradas* on horseback at least twice a year for the twenty-four years of his mission, and rarely with military escort. He was a great frontier rider, setting endurance and distance records which stand to this day.

His land is little changed. A few cities, towns, and villages. On the vast reservation of the Papago Indians known as the Papaguería, the observatories of Kitt Peak realize Kino's celestial speculations. Copper mines disturb the earth and pollute the air.

There are great cattle ranches and fields of cotton and alfalfa. Characteristic are the extremes of heat and cold under skies of blinding blue and towering clouds. Summer monsoons sweeping up from the Gulf of Mexico are bringing down the mountains. Most of Pimería Alta remains a landscape blessedly without people.

Recognition of Kino culminated in 1961 upon the 250th anniversary of his death. *Arizona Highways* devoted an entire colorful issue to Kino. In 1962 there appeared a portfolio of glowing Kino drawings by his ideal illustrator, the Arizonan Ted De Grazia, which included text by Raymond Carlson, Carl Dentzel, Ross Santee, and Thomas Hart Benton. In Tucson the Arizona Pioneers' Historical Society issued *Kino, a Commemoration,* which included an assessment by Patricia Paylore, sketches by Ted De Grazia, and a reading list by Donald Powell. Miss Paylore's conclusion is eloquent:

"For Kino was a doer, and the history of his accomplishments staggers the inquiring mind. Let those today who live lazily in the land of mañana take heed of his extraordinary energy which permitted him feats of endurance that would kill an ordinary man. But he was no ordinary man. And so his work prevails. Today we live here in Pimería Alta under the same bright sun and we sleep under the same blazing stars and we see the same mountains ringing our sights wherever we look. And we live at peace with the Pimas."

In all of Kino scholarship it has never been said better.

II

Francisco Garcés was a Spaniard from Aragon, that northernmost province at the foot of the Pyrenees whose landscape resembles Pimería Alta. He came to the Southwest in 1768, fifty-seven years after Kino's death, as a young Franciscan missionary to the tribes. In the beginning he was the resident father at Kino's Mission San Xavier del Bac, the queen of the missions, known as the White Dove of the Desert. He remained in the re-

gion until his death in 1781 at the age of forty-three. Although killed by the Yuman Indians, he was more truly a martyr to Spanish policy which lost Spain its New World empire.

Although he matched his predecessor in piety and courage, Garcés was not another Kino. He was more of a solitary who preferred to explore and convert the inhabitants where he found them by sharing their squalid way of life.

It was Juan Bautista de Anza who realized Kino's dream of an overland route to Alta California. Garcés accompanied Anza on the Spanish captain's first *entrada* as far as Mission San Gabriel. On the subsequent trek of 1775-1776 when Anza led his company of colonists, soldiers, and livestock from Tubac to Monterey, Garcés went only as far as Yuma. From there he took off on his own to penetrate the Mojave Desert, the lower San Joaquin Valley, and back via the Grand Canyon and the Hopi pueblo of Oraibi.

With a mule and a minimum of baggage he overcame every obstacle but the Hopis, who spurned his missionary approach. Garcés was a naïf. He carried his own pictorial persuasion to conversion—a painted screen on a pole, one side of which portrayed the Virgin in ecstasy, the other a sinner roasting in hellfire. Upon descending to the Havasupais at the bottom of the Grand Canyon—that tiny tribe of Blue Water People—Garcés admitted to being terrified by the narrow trail. "The New Canfranc" he called it, in a reference to the dangerous pass through the Pyrenees above his native Aragon. He reached Oraibi on the 4th of July, 1776, and was rebuffed by the Hopis. They preferred their own religion.

On the contrary, Garcés was accepted by the Yumans, although it was material rather than spiritual blessings that they craved. He took their chief, Palma, to Mexico City where Viceroy Bucareli promised grand benefits for his people—a promise never kept. A token settlement was established on the Colorado River that was neither mission nor pueblo. While spiritual responsibility was given to Fathers Garcés and Barreneche, authority over the handful of peasants from Sonora lay in the hands of the cruel soldiery.

Soldiers and colonists abused the Yumas, turning horses into their fields of maize and appropriating their rich land along the riverbanks. Garcés' warnings were ignored. The inevitable occurred. The outraged Yumans rose and clubbed to death every last Spanish man—soldiers, peasants, priests. Palma alone urged that Garcés and Barreneche be spared. In vain. They too perished under the clubs.

On Garcés word that no vengeance would be exacted for the massacre, the women and children were not killed. None was. They were eventually ransomed. When the priests' bodies were exhumed for reburial at Tubutama and later at Queretaro, they were found to be miraculously preserved, while over their common grave was growing a clump of fragrant camomile—*mucha manzanilla ollorossa*.

It is meet that in our time a mass be said each year at Mission San Gabriel for the martyrs of 1781. It is also proper that a statue of Garcés stand in the plaza on the hill of the Territorial Prison in Yuma. Unjust however is the oblivion that has descended on Garcés' loyal friend Palma, the Yuman chief. He was a good, and in some ways a great man. Anza held him in high esteem. He too deserves a memorial. The Yumans did not seek to be Christianized and colonized. Their economy, based as it was on plantings of squash and melons in the Colorado's annual overflow of silt, was destroyed by our damming of the river. They are a long suffering people.

Garcés *Diary* is one of the few major Southwestern archival discoveries not due to Bolton. It was Dr. Elliott Coues, the distinguished ornithologist, who translated and edited *On the Trail of a Spanish Pioneer, the Diary and Itinerary of Francisco Garcés in his Travels Through Sonora, Arizona, and California, 1775-1776.*

If you wonder how to pronounce Coues, you will find the answer in this passage in his Introduction: "There is another point in which I pride myself on being scrupulous even to scrupulosity, and that is, the rendering of all proper names, whether of persons or places, precisely as they occur in the Spanish. I think that translation of such terms is bad—very bad, reprehensible, and a nuisance. I should not like to figure at the hands of some Spaniard yet unborn as Elioto Vacas or Bacas, and why should I take such a liberty?"

Coues' dedication links his work with another of my heroes. It reads, "To Major John Wesley Powell . . . who first explored the cañon of the great river on the banks of which Garcés last saw the light."

Coues knew the Southwest from his having been first stationed at Fort Wingate in 1864 as a young army doctor with the Union forces. His masterful edition of Garcés' *Diary* appeared in 1900 and proved his memorial, for he died in 1899 while the work was in press, his health undermined by field work on Garcés' trail. His introduction and notes, supplemented by those of his colleague, Dr. Frederick Webb Hodge, are a model of historical scholarship, leavened, as Bolton's is not, by touches of wit and humor.

Garcés penned his *Diary* at Tubutama in 1777, after returning from his last and greatest wanderings. In its blending of hardship and faith it forms an enthralling record.

Upon leaving Anza at Yuma on December 5, 1775, Garcés halted at an Indian rancheria near what is today Pilot Knob: "I talked to them and exhibited the linen print of Maria Santisima and the lost soul. They told me that she was a nice lady, that señora; that the lost soul was very bad; that they were not such fools as not to know that up in heaven above are the good people, and down under the ground are the bad ones, the dogs, and the very ugly wild beasts; and that this they know to be a fact because the Pimas had told them so. I laid before them the proposition, whether they wished that Españoles and padres should come to live in their land and they answered 'Yes,' that they should then be well content, for then they would have meat and clothing. I gave them some tobacco and glass beads, with which they were much pleased."

Father Pedro Font, the diarist who continued with Anza to Alta California, left this profile of Garcés: "He is so fit to get along with Indians, and go about among them, that he seems just like an Indian himself. He squats cross-legged in a circle with them, or at night around the fire, for two or three hours, or even longer, all absorbed, forgetting aught else, discoursing to them with great serenity and deliberation; and though the food of the Indians is as nasty and disgusting as their dirty selves, the padre eats it with great gusto, and says that it is appetizing and very nice. In fine, God has created him, I am sure, totally on purpose to hunt up these unhappy, ignorant, and boorish people."

Dr. Coues did not care for the fussy Font, and disposed of him in this note: "What Padre Font does not say in his Diary, but doubtless thought, is, 'Faugh! What a fool that fellow Garcés is! Catch me doing anything of that sort!' There is all the difference between the Good Samaritan and the Pharisee. Font could have preached and quoted *De Imitatione Christi;* Garcés was imitating Christ."

Which emphasizes the tragedy of the martyrdom. If only Juan Bautista de Anza, greatest of all the Spanish military administrators, had been left in charge of the Yuman venture instead of being ordered as Governor of New Mexico to push back the Comanche threat, history would read differently.

Lacking a reprint of the Coues-Garcés edition, now a scarce and costly set, the interested reader should obtain as substitute one of the best of all historical novels of the Spanish Southwest and of Garcés in particular. This is *Dust on the King's Highway* by Helen C. White. Although it lacks the delicate form and style of *Death Comes for the Archbishop*, it is a work of rich texture and deep sorrow, and deserves to be better known.

Which brings me finally to an old concern of mine that our heroes should be celebrated by sculptured memorials. Not that Kino and Garcés have been slighted. On the contrary, many are their monuments. The noblest one to the latter stands beyond Pimería Alta at the farthest reach of his final *entrada*. It is the great limestone carving of Garcés by John Palo-Kangas, commissioned by the Federal Art Project, and in 1939 placed at the hub of a traffic circle in Bakersfield.

At that Depression epoch I was lounging one day for want of better to do in the stoneyard of Gordon Newell, as he and Palo-Kangas were awaiting the arrival by flatbed truck of the great monolith of Indiana limestone from which the image of Garcés was destined to emerge. I can remember the excitement of the two sculptors as they searched the stone for flaws. I must confess that in my ignorance I didn't even wonder who Garcés was.

It was during that same period that Professor Lockwood proposed that a Kino statue be erected at Mission San Xavier del Bac. His inspiration came from a statement made in 1700 by Padre Manuel Gonzalez, commenting on Kino's belief that California could be reached by an overland route: "If you accomplish this we must erect to you a rich and famous statue."

Yet even to this day there stands no memorial of Kino at San Xavier, and the area is being menaced by expanding Tucson. I envision a memorial to both Kino and Garcés which would grace the dusty plaza in front of the Dove of the Desert. Let it be a fountain, consecrated to water as well as to those holy men, for in the arid lands running water, *agua viva*, is the element sacred above all others.

READING LIST

EUSEBIO FRANCISCO KINO (*1645-1711*)

Kino's Historical Memoir of Pimería Alta. Edited by Herbert Eugene Bolton. Cleveland, Clark, 1919. 2 vols.

Kino Writes to the Duchess. Edited by Ernest J. Burrus. Rome, Jesuit Historical Institute, 1965.

HERBERT EUGENE BOLTON
Rim of Christendom; a Biography of Eusebio Francisco Kino. New York, Macmillan, 1936; Russell, 1960.

The Padre on Horseback. San Francisco, Sonora Press, 1932; Chicago, Loyola University Press, 1963.

FRANK C. LOCKWOOD
With Padre Kino on the Trail. Tucson, University of Arizona, 1934.

Kino, a Commemoration; a Short Assessment, Patricia Paylore; *Kino Sketches,* Ted De Grazia; *Bibliography,* Donald M. Powell. Tucson, Arizona Pioneers' Historical Society, 1961.

TED DE GRAZIA
Padre Kino, a Portfolio. Tucson, Arizona South, 1962.

Padre Kino; Memorable Events. Los Angeles, Southwest Museum, 1962.

Father Kino in Arizona; Fay J. Smith, John L. Kessell, Francis J. Fox; Maps by Don Bufkin. Phoenix, Arizona Historical Foundation, 1966.

CHARLES POLZER, S.J.
A Kino Guide; a Life of . . . and a Guide to his Missions and Monuments. Tucson, Southwest Mission Research Center, 1968.

Acceptance of the Statue of Eusebio Francisco Kino, presented by the State of Arizona. Washington, U.S. Government Printing Office, 1965.

PAUL M. ROCA
Paths of the Padres Through Sonora; an Illustrated History and Guide to its Spanish Churches. Tucson, Arizona Pioneers' Historical Society, 1967.

Photograph of Kino statue by Julián Martínez, courtesy of Charles Polzer, S. J.

FRANCISCO GARCÉS (*1738-1781*)
On the Trail of a Spanish Pioneer; the Diary and Itinerary. Translated and edited by Elliott Coues. New York, Harper, 1900. 2 vols.
A Record of Travels in Arizona and California, 1775-1776. Translated and Edited by John Galvin. San Francisco, Howell, 1965.

HERBERT EUGENE BOLTON
Anza's California Expeditions. Berkeley, University of California Press, 1930; New York, Russell, 1966. 5 vols.

JACK B. FORBES
Warriors of the Colorado; the Yumas of the Quechan Nation. Norman, University of Oklahoma Press, 1965.

RICHARD F. POURADE
Anza Conquers the Desert. San Diego, Union, 1971.

ARDIS WALKER
Francisco Garcés, Pioneer Padre of Kern. Kernville, Kern County Historical Society, 1946.

HELEN C. WHITE
Dust on the King's Highway. New York, Macmillan, 1947.

Photograph of Garcés statue by John Palo-Kangas, courtesy of Kern County Free Library.

J. Ross Browne

Adventures in the Apache Country

J. ROSS BROWNE

In his heyday from 1850 to 1870 J. (for John) Ross Browne was a popular writer. Scores of travel articles in *Harper's Monthly*, humorously illustrated with his own drawings, plus a dozen books and a reputation as a tireless traveller, gave him a wide renown. Then after his death in 1875 at the age of fifty-four, he was forgotten.

The knowledge that this would happen would not have troubled him. He did not regard himself as a literary genius. He wrote out of a fluent compulsion almost as easily as he breathed. And he needed money to support a large family. It was usually spent faster than he made it. His life was open-hearted and generous and lovable.

The wise writer is unconcerned about the future of his work for, as Stendhal said, a writer's books are tickets in a lottery, the drawing of which does not occur until a hundred years after his death. Although it is short of the century since Ross Browne died, I held my own drawing and found that his one Arizona book, *Adventures in the Apache Country*, published in 1869, held the winning number. Alone among his books it has attained rank as a classic of the Southwest.

How this came about and something of the life and achievements of this writer are my concern in this inquiry into the fluctuations—up, down, and then up again—of J. Ross Browne's reputation. Looking back at him and his contemporaries, we also see their books as unwitting shots at the target of literary fame. It is clear now that Browne's first book, *Etchings of a Whaling Cruise* (1846), landed between two that hit the bull's eye: *Two Years Before the Mast* in 1840 and *Moby-Dick* in 1851. Browne's book was influenced by the one and influenced the other.

Likewise Browne's later travel writings on the Near East and the Nevada silver boom showed Mark Twain the way to the fame he achieved with *The Innocents Abroad* and *Roughing It*. By his western writings in *Harper's*, Browne also helped prepare the audience for Bret Harte's triumph as story writer and versifier.

Genius is as unpredictable as fame is fickle. Dana, Melville, Twain, and Harte all had genius, which meant that they achieved and maintained fame, even to this day. What Browne had was talent, and it was not enough to give him a lasting hold on readers. His fate was to be long forgotten, except by scholars.

And then, commencing in 1929 when a Catholic priest in San Francisco, Father Francis J. Rock, took for his doctoral dissertation a biography of J. Ross Browne, a revival began. Now there have probably been more posthumous works by and about Browne than appeared in his lifetime. They culminated in 1966 with a meticulous work by David M. Goodman, originally a dissertation at the University of Arizona, on Browne's western career, followed in 1969 by the publication of his Letters and Journals. They were skilfully edited by his granddaughter-in-law, Lina Fergusson Browne, a member of the famed writing family of New Mexico.

In seeking what made Ross Browne a compulsive observer and reporter with a constant urge to travel, as well as a faithful husband and father of ten children, we open the old debate on Heredity versus Environment. He was a mercurial Celt, born near Dublin on February 11, 1821. His father was an intellectual reformer who after being freed from imprisonment for liberal writings brought his family to America when Ross was eleven. They settled in Louisville, on the banks of the Ohio River.

Robinson Crusoe was the boy's favorite book. Its reading so affected him that in 1849, when after rounding Cape Horn the sailing vessel on which he was proceeding to California as a revenue agent was becalmed near Juan Fernandez, Browne put off in a small boat with a group of fellow passengers to explore the legendary island. Out of what proved to be a dangerous adventure came his book called *Crusoe's Island*.

Boys sometimes leave home because they are badly treated. This was not true of Ross Browne. He had wise and loving parents. He was naturally a wanderer. At eighteen he shipped as a deckhand downriver to New Orleans, then tramped into Texas, an experience that recalls that of Lewis Garrard. And he was also a writer. From childhood he wrote stories and sketches, and in 1841 a satire on aviation called *The Great Steam Duck*, one of the earliest American publications on flying.

His ambition was to write travel pieces about Europe. The way there proved long and roundabout. First he shipped out of New Bedford in a whaler. Then in a trader's hut on the island of Madagascar, he came upon a copy of *Two Years Before the Mast*, which was being widely read by sailors for its exposé of the brutal conditions aboard sailing vessels. As a result he wrote his *Etchings of a Whaling Cruise*, in which he sought to do for whaling ship reform what Dana had done for the hide trade. He also wrote a fan letter to Dana which the aloof Yankee lawyer apparently never answered. While on the whaling voyage young Browne showed his versatility by writing love letters for the captain.

In the meantime Browne's parents had moved to Washington, D.C. where his father became a Congressional reporter. Ross's having learned shorthand from him gave him the asset of being able accurately to preserve the observations and impressions gained on his travels. He was also gifted as an artist, and most of

259

his works were illustrated from his own drawings rendered into woodcuts by an intermediary.

At twenty-three, Ross married eighteen-year-old Lucy Mitchell, the daughter of a Washington physician. Her family was at first understandably opposed to her choosing such a restless young man. He tried to settle down, first as a clerk in the Treasury Department and then as private secretary to Robert J. Walker, the Secretary of the Treasury. This lasted for several years, until the discovery of gold in California enabled Browne to slip his moorings and take ship for the Pacific Coast as a revenue agent for the Treasury Department.

It was the going, not the gold that lured him, as he made clear in a letter to Lucy. "Many of my literary friends," he wrote, "tell me I can make more gold with my pen than others with their pick-axes and crucibles. For your sake a competency would be desirable, but for my own I scorn the miserable lust for riches. I want no gold." His subsequent career, to the end of his life, proved that he meant it.

In addition to a fiddle and a guitar, Browne took along a supply of pencils and drawing paper. "Twenty dollars for a small sketch will be better than digging gold," he wrote to Lucy. "I have a journal, and all the implements for making a lively and entertaining book." Although Browne was to make California his base for most of his life and to know the state in every corner, he never wrote the California book. Arizona, Nevada, Europe, the Near East—all went into his books, but not his adopted state.

Because of delays in Rio, Juan Fernandez, and Callao, the voyage to California took half a year. He arrived in San Francisco to find that his appointment had lapsed. With only $5.00 in his pocket, Browne declared himself ready to take in washing. It wasn't necessary. His proverbial good fortune brought him together with Dr. William M. Gwin, a leading member of the newly elected constitutional convention, due to meet and prepare California for statehood. Gwin had known Browne in Washington and of his skill in shorthand.

And so Browne contracted to report the proceedings of the convention that met in Monterey in the fall of 1849. There is no doubt that he was correct in saying later that he was the one and only person in California capable of doing this demanding job. For agreeing to take down, transcribe and edit the confused proceedings, then see them through the press and provide copies in English and Spanish, Browne received the sum of $10,000 in gold dust to be held by the Philadelphia mint until the contract was fulfilled.

Although a large sum, it was not easy money. The convention was a rough and ready group of forty-eight delegates, most of them young men and at least one of them drunk throughout the two months, who met to determine the future of California. Their sectional quarrels are our quarrels today—over taxation and representation, between the country and the city, landholders and transients. The burning national issue of slavery and the proposed state's boundaries also agitated the delegates. The Californios, Carrillo, De la Guerra, and Vallejo, spoke only in Spanish through an interpreter. They were naturally suspicious of the Yankee invaders who had demoralized their pastoral homeland.

The published proceedings represented heroic efforts by Browne to clarify the tumultuous and chaotic discussions. The young Irish reporter's humor came through only once, when he listed the profession of one delegate as that of "Elegant Leisure."

Although the constitution they adopted was speedily printed in San Francisco at the *Alta California's* office, the proceedings took longer to prepare. Browne employed the voyage back for his editorial work, and then in Washington he saw the book through the press. His agreement also gave him further publication rights, and with the profits therefrom he finally realized his original ambition. Off he went to Europe with his growing family.

With Florence and Rome as home bases, Browne roamed through the Near East to produce in 1853 *Yusef; or the Journey*

261

of the Frangi, a Crusade in the East. This was the book that set the style and tone Mark Twain was to bring to genius sixteen years later with *The Innocents Abroad.*

In order to provide his twin need for family security and a foreign location, Browne sought to obtain a State Department appointment as chargé d'affaires in some part of the world as yet unvisited by him. He had no success. He was compelled to return to Washington and begin what became a six-year assignment back in the Treasury Department, first as Inspector of Customs Houses and then as Inspector of Indian Agencies.

It meant plenty of travel, along the Canadian and Mexican borders and then to the Far West. Browne proved to be an efficient and uncorruptible government servant, one of the best our country has ever had. He served untarnished in a time of patronage, greed, and corruption. Back again on the Pacific Coast, Browne continued to prove his courage and efficiency. His talent as a fiddler was once used as a means of getting the goodwill of a group he came to investigate.

In 1855 Browne brought his family, now grown to five, plus his favorite sister-in-law called Dart, to California where they made Oakland their home. The next four years as Indian Agency inspector revealed to Browne the deteriorating fate of the natives. His reports to Washington were truthful and humane. They have been partly reproduced and commented on by Richard H. Dillon in *J. Ross Browne, Confidential Agent in Old California,* another key work in the revival of Browne.

When Dart married a German refugee from military service, the idea was advanced that the increasing number of little Brownies would receive a better education in Germany. Whereupon Ross sent his family to Washington and prepared to sell the Oakland property and take them all to Europe again on the proceeds. Then the Nevada silver rush detoured him to Washoe for its literary possibilities.

His debunking articles, "A Peep at Washoe," in *Harper's* again prepared the way for another triumph by Mark Twain.

Roughing It was essentially the same experience brought to the level of genius. Browne's "Washoe" was reprinted in 1960 by Dr. Horace Parker's Paisano Press on Balboa Island.

He was able finally to lease the Oakland house and proceed to Germany. There for three years, while the children were being educated and Lucy held the home front, Browne roamed Europe in search of literary material. Two books came from the experience, *An American Family in Germany* and *The Land of Thor*. In the latter he covered Russia, Scandinavia, and Iceland. It includes an incident that reveals Browne's habit of traveling light.

When he came to register at the hotel in Moscow, the desk clerk raised his brows at Browne's scarcity of luggage—his customary knapsack containing toothbrush, comb, shirt, drawing paper and pencils, plug of tobacco and meerschaum pipe. Then upon Browne's writing in the register his state of origin, the clerk's manner warmed. "California!" he cried. "You're from California?" Such was the magic of the Golden Land.

Although they never reach the level of *The Innocents Abroad*, these two European books by Browne contain lively incidents and flashing insights. Such is a profile of Hans Christian Andersen, the great Danish storyteller, who warmed to learn that Browne's brood were his devoted readers.

"In Russia," Browne wrote, "there is the charm of barbarism, savagery, filth, and show; the people are loose, ferocious, daring and wild; here in Sweden the quiet, decent, home-aspect of the people, their rigid observance of the rules of etiquette, their devotion to royalty, law and order, are absolutely depressing. In the abstract many traits in their character are worthy of admiration, but as a traveller, I detest this kind of civilization. Give me a devil or a savage at all times, who outrages the rules of society and carries an advertisement of character on his back. As an artist I can make something of him, either in the way of copy or pencil sketches."

Browne was a bohemian rather than what we call a hippie. Al-

263

though unconventional, he was strongly motivated and creative. He was no passive dropout.

Need for money turned him to lecturing. In this he was tutored by his friend Bayard Taylor, one of the age's most successful writers and lecturers, who had come to California in 1849 within two weeks of Browne's arrival. "Look at the farthest parts of the audience to see that you are heard," Taylor told Browne, "and above all things *make* yourself heard by everybody. This is done by clearness of enunciation rather than loudness of voice. See that the audience smiles (at least) during the first ten minutes. Do not allow the lecture—no matter how good—to be more than an hour and a half in length."

In spite of this classic advice, Browne failed as a lecturer, primarily because he was shy before people. From his racy way of writing and the amusing drawings which illustrated it, a false image was derived of the man himself. William H. Brewer made this observation: "In the afternoon I met the celebrated traveller, J. Ross Browne. He appears a quiet fellow, not at all one to visit so many distant lands and write such genial accounts of what he saw."

By 1863 the worsening state of the Civil War made it advisable for Browne to bring his family back to California. Although raised in the South, he was a loyal Unionist. By writing for *Harper's* and the San Francisco *Evening Bulletin*, he figured on earning enough to support them all. It proved fortunate that he had only leased the Oakland home.

Browne's adventure which resulted in his Arizona classic, began with a chance encounter on a San Francisco street. There he met the eccentric Charles D. Poston, the Arizona pioneer, who had just been named Superintendent of Indian Affairs for the new territory. He was leaving that afternoon for Arizona. Would Browne accompany him?

It was not only Browne's knowledge of Indian affairs that interested Poston. The Arizonan was also desirous of engaging in mineral development, another area in which Browne had accumulated much knowledge. Add to all this, Browne was skilled in sketching natural scenery, including potential mining properties.

Browne agreed to be ready to leave by 4 o'clock that afternoon via steamer to San Pedro and thence by land to Fort Yuma. "Over to Oakland," he wrote, "a hurried explanation, a parting glance at the pleasant homestead, the garden, the wife, and the little ones—ah me! how often the same insatiable spirit of adventure has driven me blindly through the same trying ordeal! Is there no help for it in this world? Must a man when he has traveled for thirty years never more taste the sweets of content, but keep drifting uneasily along till he drifts into the final haven of rest?"

There is no doubt that Browne was driven by an irresistible force—*If I Rest I Rust* was his motto—and it was this impermanence that kept him from the heights (and the depths) of Twain and Melville, or the consistent remunerative output of Bayard Taylor and Bret Harte. In 1871 Browne's eldest son, Spencer, made his literary debut in the *Overland Monthly* with an article based on the family's residence in Peking where his father had served briefly as Minister to China.

"I belong to the family of one possessed of the Demon of Travel!" young Browne began his article. "The desire for roaming comes upon him like the drunkard's longing for liquor. In less than three days after announcing his intention, he starts off to some remote part of the globe, in quest of no one knows what; sometimes I have doubted that he himself knows. I have been flying with the rest of the flock, from one end of the world to the other, for twenty years, but to no purpose that I have yet been able to discover, except to get away from the last place."

And so it was off on a trip of four months that took him to southern Arizona. Near the end, upon learning of Lucy's illness, Browne parted with Poston who was headed north to Fort Whipple, and returned to Oakland. This cost him a complete view of Arizona. As it is, the articles which appeared in *Harper's* in

1864 and were collected in book form five years later, provide the best of all accounts of southern Arizona at the time it had become a territory.

All the circumstances conjoined to bring out the finest in Browne as writer and illustrator. The country was new to him, the weather perfect, he had no official duties, and Poston and escort were congenial, colorful companions. The danger from raiding Apaches was constant. This served to mute the jocularity that was usually too prominent in Browne's writing and lent suspense and tension to his prose.

Another factor that gave a more serious tone to this Arizona book was the uncertain progress of the war. Browne was no escapist. "When we turned-in upon our soft, grassy beds and looked up at the clear star-spangled sky above us," he wrote while camping in the lush valley of the Santa Cruz below Tubac, "there were some among us, I have no doubt, who thought that a home in such a charming wilderness would not be unpleasant, if one could be assured of such peace among men as reigned over the quiet earth. But peace like that is not for the races that inhabit this world.

"I lay for hours thinking over the unhappy condition of our country, and a profound sadness oppressed me as vision after vision of bloodshed and suffering and death passed like some funeral cortège through the silent watches of the night. Far away, friends were falling in sanguinary strife; everywhere God's beautiful earth was desecrated by the wickedness of man; even here, in this remote wilderness, we were not exempt from the atrocities of a savage foe."

Browne's illustrations for this book are the strongest he ever drew. The Apache threat quickened his pencil. Never before in sketching in Madagascar, Zanzibar, Palestine, the continent of Europe, and Iceland, had he worked with the anticipation of an arrow in his back, and a rifle across his knees as he pictured himself in the drawing entitled sardonically "The Fine Arts in Arizona." His drawings of Apaches hung and crucified by the Pimas typify the eery horror that also contributes to the book's power. He sketched the mysterious Painted Rocks in the river valley between Yuma and Gila Bend, protected today as a state monument.

After following Browne's trail from Yuma to Nogales, I can report that except for the main highways and the few urban centers, southern Arizona is unchanged from Browne's time of a century ago, the vast Papago Reservation least of all. The sacred peak of Baboquívari, sketched by him, still dominates the landscape for a hundred miles around. Mission San Xavier del Bac still dazzles the eye. Tubac and Tumacácori have been sensitively restored as state and national monuments. The high canyons of the Santa Ritas, where he sketched the silver mines, offer cool refuge in summer.

Browne would not recognize Tucson today. What he scathingly described as a wretched outpost has become a cultural community of which the University of Arizona is the heart. As for the Apaches, they have withdrawn to their mountain reservations and prospered in lumbering and stock raising.

The bond between Ross and Lucy was an elastic one. Though stretched unmercifully as he rushed about the world, it never broke. He wrote to her nearly every day that he was away, gay, teasing, lively and loving letters that were treasured by her and her son and grandson and that make up a good part of Lina Fergusson Browne's book.

Lucy also was a faithful correspondent. Her letters to him, alas, were apparently destroyed by her after his death. It was the receipt of ones from her telling of her illness, that called him home before he had completed his tour of Arizona. He writes of receiving them one night from a passing party, somewhere on the Papaguería. "Too impatient to wait for a fire, I lingered behind and read my letters by moonlight."

Before leaving Arizona, Browne "bought" a Tonto Apache girl of eight years named Lupe, whose parents had been killed by the Pimas and who had been enslaved by them. He sent her home to Lucy where she was taken into the Browne household and remained for many years as a faithful retainer.

The Arizona trip was financially profitable, as Poston paid Browne well for his reports and sketches of the southern mines. Mining and land matters occupied Browne during the remaining years of his life. In 1867 his government-sponsored *Report upon the Mineral Resources of the United States* proved an authoritative reference work even to this day. He was in England several times on behalf of American interests. Letters to Lucy were the only writing that came from these trips.

"I met Mark Twain a day or two ago," he wrote her from London in 1872, the year that *Roughing It* appeared, "He is just the same dry, quaint old Twain we knew in Washington. I believe he is writing a book over here. He made plenty of money on his other books—some of it on mine." A study has been made of parallel passages to show the extent to which Mark Twain used his friend's "A Peep at Washoe."

Still there was no bitterness in Browne. It had been his family that provided a private audience on which Mark Twain tried out his first public lecture, a debut which saw him go on to world-wide triumph.

"I see Mark Twain every day and have long talks with him," he wrote again a week later. "He looks very badly." Yet it was Browne who lived only another three years, while Twain enjoyed thirty-eight more years of life.

Browne was chagrined by Bret Harte's meteoric rise, especially as it coincided with his own decline in public favor. "It seems hard," he wrote to Lucy from New York in 1871, "that I, who really built up the reputation of *Harper's* magazine . . . should be shoved aside so cavalierly, and then gravely consulted as to my opinion of Bret Harte, and informed as to the lucrative offers they have made him."

His ministry in China was of short duration because of his uncompromising frankness in reporting the situation totally at odds with the impression given by his predecessor, Anson Burlingame. He was well liked. The American merchants in Shanghai raised $2000 to pay the return passage of Browne and his family. He refused it on ethical grounds, although he had to borrow money for the fares. A study made in 1932 by Paul H. Clyde of Browne's China policy vindicated him. "He left us a record which for accuracy of detail and forceful presentation has rarely been rivalled."

Upon his return to Oakland from China in 1870 Browne established a patriarchal domain off Chabot Road. Called by him Pagoda Hill, the house was a wondrous architectural motley, combining the styles of various countries he had visited. As a boys school it survived until 1921. Today the only vestige is a short street named Ross.

Browne's final years found him involved in various promotional schemes, all aimed at providing security for his large family. One was to organize an English syndicate to reclaim the swampy lands of the Sacramento-San Joaquin deltas. He also investigated Baja California for a land company that proposed a colony on Magdalena Bay. His report was in the negative. Lack of water and transportation made the scheme impractical.

In London he encountered his old crony Poston, grown more eccentric and a bit lecherous. The debauchery of the demimonde shocked Browne. His heart (and purse) went out to the beggarly poor on the streets.

He was always able to make ready money by describing and sketching mines for Californian capitalists. "My head aches nearly all the time," he wrote Lucy from Virginia City. "I detest this place." And in another letter from Nevada he wrote, "Good night, dearest Lucy, I must go to bed. This day I have made two reports, written four long letters, sketched two mines and finished two pictures. If I get paid for it all, it will amount to six or seven hundred dollars. I do nothing now except for pay."

A year before his death he visited the island of Santa Rosa, and in an article in the *Overland Monthly* he proposed that it be made a game refuge to preserve species in danger of extinction.

In addition to honesty in public and private life, Ross Browne had a conservationist's vision that makes him one of our time. He deplored the savage cruelty toward animals shown by the Californios and the Yankees.

He was one of those unusual writers whose main drive was for neither fame nor wealth. "It is only the excitement of the action that governs me," he wrote. "I care nothing about the result." He was also motivated by love for Lucy and their children. Characteristic of his feeling for her was a letter he wrote from Washington, where he was seeking to collect the money owed him by the government for his service in China.

"Some of the changes here within two years are very striking," he observed. "Death has been doing a heavy business and old Time is bleaching and wrinkling without pity or remorse. Think of how short a time we have, and how little it matters where we are, so that we love each other in our declining days; and walk hand in hand into the shadowy vale."

His time was shorter than he knew. Worn out by incessant activity and financial worries, he succumbed to an attack of acute appenditicis. It came after Lucy had met him with the carriage at the ferry from San Francisco and they were driving home to Pagoda Hill. He was so ill that she stopped at a friend's house and there, in spite of a doctor's attendance, he died that night. It was the 5th of December 1875. She buried him in Oakland's Mountain View Cemetery, and there she joined him twenty-three years later.

READING LIST

J. ROSS BROWNE (1821-1875)
Etchings of a Whaling Cruise. New York, Harper, 1846.
Yusef; or, the Journey of the Frangi; a Crusade in the East. New York, Harper, 1853.
Crusoe's Island; a Ramble in the Footsteps of Alexander Selkirk. New York, Harper, 1864.
An American Family in Germany. New York, Harper, 1866.
The Land of Thor. New York, Harper, 1867.
A Sketch of the Settlement and Exploration of Lower California. New York, Appleton, 1869.
Adventures in the Apache Country; a Tour Through Arizona and Sonora. New York, Harper, 1869.
———. Tucson, Arizona Silhouettes, 1950.
———. Edited by Donald M. Powell. Tucson, University of Arizona Press, 1974.

RICHARD H. DILLON
J. Ross Browne, Confidential Agent in California. Norman, University of Oklahoma Press, 1965.

DAVID M. GOODMAN
A Western Panorama, 1849-1875; the Travels, Writings, and Influence of J. Ross Browne. Glendale, Clark, 1966.

LINA FERGUSSON BROWNE, *Editor*
J. Ross Browne; His Letters, Journals, and Writings. Albuquerque, University of New Mexico Press, 1969.

Photograph of J. Ross Browne, courtesy of Lina F. Browne.

Vanished Arizona
MARTHA SUMMERHAYES

"And so, in the delicious quiet of the Autumn days of Nantucket, when the summer winds had ceased to blow and the frogs had ceased their pipings in the salt meadows, and the sea was wondering whether it should keep its summer blue or change into its winter grey, I sat down at my desk and began to write my story."

What she wrote was the story of an army wife on the Arizona frontier in the 1870's, a story that is peerless in the literature of that time and place. Not only is Martha Summerhayes' *Vanished Arizona* a primary source for that period when the Apaches had been only temporarily contained, it is also a love story unique in the literature of the Southwest. Not the kind of unreal story seen on the screen or told by Zane Grey, but nonetheless romantic in its evocation of the life led by a frontier officer's young bride.

Although written thirty years after the experience when, in the author's words, "the hardships and deprivations which we have endured, lose their bitterness when they have become only a memory," her nostalgia for what had vanished did not prevent Martha Summerhayes from describing the hazards and hardships of Arizona before rails, roads, and refrigeration.

Only youthful good health, plus a loving loyalty to her husband enabled her to survive the experience. Writing in her sixties, she was frank in confessing the narrow margin by which she succeeded. Her feelings were always ambivalent. She loathed the squalor of transient camp life until she learned how to cope with it. With a woman's longing to settle in and make a home, she was frustrated by the endless postings to which her husband was subject, and which took them in the four years of his tour of duty to camps and forts throughout Arizona, from Yuma to Ehrenberg and Mojave, from Apache high in the Mogollons to Whipple at Prescott, and to McDowell in the Salt River country. The anguish of her torn feelings is one of her book's constant themes. And yet ever and always she returned to her credo: "I had cast my lot with a soldier and where he was, was home to me."

Vanished Arizona inevitably invites comparison with *The Shirley Letters,* that other frontier book by a woman which endures as history and literature. Dame Shirley's lot was easier. The mining camp on a fork of the Feather River, deep in the Sierra Nevada, was a civilized place alongside the wretched station at Ehrenberg where Lieutenant Summerhayes was the Quartermaster in charge of supplies brought up river for transshipment to the inland posts.

Both books originated as letters to family at home; both are realistic and also romantic. Shirley never sought to make a volume of her letters once they were printed in a San Francisco periodical. Likewise, Martha took no steps toward writing a book until after her husband's retirement and they had returned to their place of birth on Nantucket and she could enjoy freedom from constant upheavals to new commands. Then, "at the urgent and ceaseless request of my children," she reread the old letters she had written to a favorite uncle who had been a whaler on the California coast in the 1820's. The other source to refresh her memory was a semiofficial diary kept by her husband.

Thus was she borne back on a flood of emotion to an Arizona

she believed to be forever vanished. Hers is a prime example of the creative process, whereby raw experience is refined and made bearable. The result is an inspired fusion of those Three L's, Life, Landscape, and Literature.

Like Dame Shirley, Martha Dunham Summerhayes came to the frontier from a genteel Massachusetts background. After a Quaker-Puritan upbringing on the island of Nantucket, she went abroad to live in a German general's family in Hanover. There she learned to read and to speak the country's language and to love its culture. She was dazzled by the Prussian army's traditions, fresh from its victory over the French. "I used to say, 'Oh, Frau Generalin, how fascinating it all is!' 'Hush, Martha,' she would say, 'life in the army is not always so brilliant as it looks; in fact, we often call it, over here, *glaenzendes Elend.*'" [Glittering misery.]

"These bitter words made a great impression on my mind, and in after years, on the American frontier, I seemed to hear them over and over again."

After returning to Nantucket, her head full of romantic German music and poetry, Martha married Lieutenant John Wyer Summerhayes. They were promptly posted to Fort Russell at Cheyenne, Wyoming Territory. She thought that her schooling had been completed with the year abroad. In reality, her education had just begun.

Summerhayes was no tenderfoot. Then thirty-eight years old, ten years his bride's senior, he had trapped beaver on the upper Missouri, gone to sea in a New Bedford whaler and served with bravery as an officer in the Civil War. He was a seasoned and model soldier, giving obedience to orders, however unreasonable they seemed, and expecting the same from those under him, including Martha.

Vanished Arizona derives interest and strength from its wealth of precise details of army life on the frontier, and also from its skillful delineation of dramatic and humorous events and its shrewd portrayal of human character. As well as a self-portrait,

Martha presents a picture of a stern yet loving husband. She resented the comedown from the pomp of the German army and his blunt acceptance of his army's Spartan ways. "Everything in me rebelled," she confessed, "but still I yielded."

Primitive though she found it, Wyoming Territory held only a hint of what was to come when the 8th Infantry was posted to Arizona Territory. John and Martha, and a detachment of soldiers under Major Worth, proceeded via San Francisco and steamer round Cape San Lucas and up the Gulf of California to Mazatlan and Guaymas, thence to Port Isabel at the mouth of the Colorado River.

There they transferred to the steamer *Cocopah* and at Fort Yuma to the stern-wheeler *Gila*, captained by the famed river pilot, Tom Mellon. Then, with the soldiers in an open barge towed behind, they started up the Colorado the two hundred miles to Camp Mojave.

The heat in August was unbearable, rising to 122° in the shade. Three of the soldiers in the barge died from it. Martha wondered how any, including herself, survived. The then unchecked river was "a mass of seething red liquid, turbulent and thick and treacherous." Eighteen days passed before they reached their destination. His skill in keeping off the constantly shifting sandbars led Captain Mellon to term it a quick trip.

When they passed Ehrenberg, across the river from today's Blythe, Martha declared "of all dreary, miserable-looking settlements that one could possibly imagine, this was the worst." She was spared the fore-knowledge that in less than a year they would be posted there.

Upon reaching Camp Mojave and preparing to trek inland to Fort Whipple near Prescott, Martha's "only feeling was to get cool and to get out of the Territory in some other way and at some cooler season." At the same time she realized that it was "a futile wish, a futile vow."

As we read deeper into *Vanished Arizona* we marvel at the way in which Martha succumbed to the spell of the land. Eastward from Mojave, the terrain rose, the air cooled, and Arizona became a different place from the broiling river bottom. First however she had to weather a sandstorm and then suffer the suicide of Major Worth's red setter. Crazed by the heat, the dog bolted for the distant mountains and death. Martha sensitively recounts this pitiful incident and its effect on their commanding officer. It recalls the similar fate of Lummis's dog on his tramp to California.

Although Martha's survival of physical hardships was due largely to her youthful stamina, it owed something also to an ability to purge herself of resentment. "Sometimes either Major Worth or Jack would come and drive along a few miles in the ambulance [as the army wagon was called] with me to cheer me up, and they allowed me to abuse the country to my heart's content. It seemed to do me much good. The desert was new to me then, and I did not see much to admire in the desolate waste lands we were travelling. I did not dream of the power of the desert, nor that I should ever long to see it again."

The rising land led to the forested mountains of Coconino County. Martha was indignant at the unromantic name given to the mountain known as Bill Williams. When she protested to her husband, he replied characteristically, "I suppose he discovered it, and I dare say he had a hard enough time before he got to it."

Today when one travels from the river-crossing below Needles toward Williams and Flagstaff or Prescott, he sees that mountain even as Martha saw it. What took her days to traverse, now takes a few hours. Her power to respond emotionally to Arizona's landscape in spite of her intellectual rejection of it, led to such passages as this:

"Our road was gradually turning southward, but for some days Bill Williams was the predominating feature of the landscape; turn whichever way we might, still this purple mountain was before us. It seemed to pervade the entire country, and took on such wonderful pink colors at sunset. Bill Williams held me

277

in thrall, until the hills and valleys in the vicinity of Fort Whipple shut him out from my sight. But he seemed to have come into my life somehow, and in spite of his name, I loved him for the companionship he had given me during those long, hot, weary and interminable days."

Vanished Arizona is the portrait of a landscape. It is also the self-portrait of a woman modified by that land. Even to this day, people do not change the essential Arizona of river, desert, and mountain; it changes them. Thus it was a hundred years ago with Martha Summerhayes. Throughout the book are instances of the way in which the frontier affected her puritan morality. Without the discipline of her husband, Martha might well have "gone native" and cast her lot with life in the Southwest.

Up in the White River country, the Summerhayes lodged overnight with the American scout, Corydon Cooley, who had two pretty and tidy Apache sisters for his house-mates. This kept Martha from sleeping. "I lay gazing into the fire which was smouldering in the corner, and finally I said in a whisper, 'Jack, which girl do you think is Cooley's wife?'

"'I don't know,' answered this cross and tired man; and then added, 'both of 'em, I guess.'

"Now this was too awful," Martha added, "but I knew he did not intend for me to ask any more questions. I had a difficult time, in those days, reconciling what I saw with what I had been taught was right."

She also confessed to being strongly attracted by certain of the Indian braves. Witnessing a Devil Dance at Camp Apache stirred her deeply. There her eyes were held by Diablo, the handsome chief of the Coyotero Apaches. A photograph of him which she included in her book tells why.

It was at Ehrenberg that she was most strongly assailed by primitive ways. In describing their Cocopah servant Charley, she dwelled on the "supple muscles of his clean-cut thighs." With her Mexican maid, Patrocina, she ventured naked into the Colorado at daybreak and let the thick red water swirl voluptuously over her body. "A clump of the low mesquite trees at the top of the bank afforded sufficient protection at that hour; we rubbed dry, slipped on a loose gown, and wended our way home." Even, she points out, as Pharaoh's daughter had bathed in the Nile.

There in Ehrenberg Martha said to her husband, "If we must live in this wretched place, let's give up civilization and live as the Mexicans do! They are the only happy beings around here." She would like to have dressed as they did. "Their necks and arms look so cool." Instead she sweltered in high-necked, long-sleeved New England dresses.

We can imagine Lieutenant Summerhayes' reply to his wife's outburst, and which led her to conclude resignedly, "We seemed never to be able to free ourselves from the fetters of civilization, and so struggled on."

Her troubles were compounded by having to care for baby Harry, born less than a year before at Camp Apache, an army doctor in attendance. Remembrance of that first summer on the river led Martha to take the baby, with Patrocina and her infant, and board the *Gila* for Yuma and thence by steamer to San Francisco until autumn cooled the river lands. She got as far as Yuma, then decided that they would turn around and go back up river to the heat and her husband.

Let her tell it: "When, after a week, the *Gila* pushed her nose up to the bank at Ehrenberg, there stood the Quartermaster. He jumped aboard, and did not seem in the least surprised to see me. 'I knew you'd come back,' said he. I laughed, of course, and we both laughed."

" 'I hadn't the courage to go on,' I replied."

This is what I mean when I call *Vanished Arizona* a love story.

The book's most harrowing passage is Martha's account of their journey from Camp Apache to Fort Whipple, en route to the supply post at Ehrenberg. There had been an Apache uprising, and they travelled with a small escort of cavalrymen. The baby was only a few months old. The climax came with their passage through a defile where an ambush was feared. Summer-hayes and the escort rode with rifles at ready, while Martha and the baby lay under a blanket on the floor of the ambulance, she with a loaded revolver to take her and the baby's life in case the men were killed.

She kept still until they came through the pass and approached the Sunset Crossing over the Little Colorado below Winslow. Then she heard her husband cry, "Get up Mattie! See the river yonder. We'll cross that tonight, and then we'll be out of their God d——d country'.'

"This was Jack's way of working off his excitement," she ex-plained. "I did not mind it. If I had been a man, I should have said just as much and perhaps more."

The river crossing proved nearly disastrous. Mules and am-bulance foundered in quicksand. All their baggage, including her books of German prose and poetry, was soaked. Then the baby's skin was burned by alkali dust and broke out in ugly blisters. There was no doctor, no nurse, no medicine chest. Coy-otes prowled the camp all night long. After that night her hair, she said, never regained its warm chestnut tinge.

When she became pregnant again, Summerhayes packed her and the baby off to Nantucket. There their daughter was born, and Martha regained her strength and equanimity. Back she came with both children to Arizona in December 1876, travel-ling by stage from San Diego to Yuma, where she was to meet her husband and proceed to his latest posting at Fort McDow-ell, up the Salt River from Phoenix.

While in New England she had acquired household furnish-ings and a new wardrobe, and these were shipped by steamer from San Francisco. At Guaymas the vessel burned to the water and everything was lost. An army wife in Yuma gave Martha an oversize gray and white percale dress, and off she went with her Jack up the Gila to Fort McDowell, "our big blue army wagon, which had been provided for my boxes and trunks, rumbling along behind us, empty save for the camp equipage."

Yet it all seemed good to her. "The old blue uniforms made my heart glad. Every sound was familiar, even the rattling of the harness with its ivory rings and the harsh sound of the heavy brakes reinforced with old leather soles."

After two years at Fort McDowell, the Summerhayes were posted to Fort Lowell at Tucson. Before they could reach there, they were overtaken by new orders to return immediately for transfer to Angel Island in San Francisco Bay. Then followed tours of duty in Nevada, Nebraska, Texas, New Mexico, and so on, year after year, as he rose slowly to the final rank of Lieutenant Colonel.

At last came retirement and they lived in Washington, New Rochelle, and finally back on Nantucket, where she wrote her book. Published in 1908 by Lippincott of Philadelphia, it was an unexpected success. Letters came from readers far and wide, including many in Arizona, soon to become a state. She included some of them in an enlarged edition, and published it herself in 1911 at Salem, just before death overtook her. It also included more photographs, including the one of that virile chief Diablo, and an account of their friendship with Frederic Remington.

In this second edition, she printed a wonderful, rambling letter from old Tom Mellon, captain of the *Gila*. He wrote from Yuma where he was seeking compensation from the government for his river boats, made useless by the newly built Laguna Dam. He concluded, "I suppose you will have a hard time wading through my scrawl but I know you will be generous and remember that I went to sea when a little over nine years of age and had my pen been half as often in my hand as a marlin spike, I would now be able to write a much clearer hand. I have a little bungalow on Coronado Beach, across the bay from San Diego, and if you ever come there, you or your husband, you are welcome; while I have a bean you can have half. I would like to see you and talk over old times. Yuma is quite a place now; no more adobes built; it is brick and concrete, cement sidewalks and flower gardens with electric light and a good water system. My home is within five minutes walk of the Pacific Ocean. I was born at Digby, Nova Scotia, and the first music I ever heard was the surf of the Bay of Fundy, and when I close my eyes forever I hope the surf of the Pacific will be the last sound that will greet my ears. I read *Vanished Arizona* last night until after midnight, and thought what we both had gone through since you first came up the Colorado with me."

Then for years *Vanished Arizona* was out of print and hard to come by; until in 1939 it was reprinted, followed by other editions in 1960, 1963, and 1970. None of these subsequent editions is entirely satisfactory. The best is that of 1960 by Arizona Silhouettes of Tucson, with historical-biographical notes by Ray Brandes.

This work, which reprints her enlarged edition, was given to me then by *Arizona Highways*, with the compelling assignment of reviewing it in the course of a field trip by automobile, in which I was to retrace, as far as possible, the routes taken by John and Martha long years before.

And so I set out in the month of December, under the threat of snow in the northern reaches. Overnight in Showlow, I encountered a field party headed back to the University of Arizona after a trip to the Navajo country. When they wondered what I was up to so far from my native heath, I said cryptically that I was on my way to Stoneman's Lake with Martha. This fooled all but one of the party who murmured to me later, as we broke up to turn in, "Good night, Jack."

Of all the places in Arizona to where the Summerhayes were posted only Camp Apache remains unchanged. The old army buildings now serve as an Indian school. I felt many unseen presences there when I walked to the edge of the ravine where Martha had witnessed the Devil Dance, thinking I might glimpse her ghost and that of Diablo.

Stoneman's Lake, described by her rapturously as Italian blue, was bone dry, Camp Mojave obliterated. At Fort Whipple, turn-of-the-century buildings now serve as a veterans hospital.

On the eastern shore of the Colorado I saw the vestiges of Ehrenberg and its cemetery that filled Martha with such horror. W.P.A. workers had raised a marker there. Down river I stood at twilight on the hill at Yuma, by the old Territorial Prison, and gazed up river, subdued by the dams which began in 1909 with Laguna and culminated with the monolith in Glen Canyon. The mesquite and arrow weed were as they have always been. And the smell of river bottom, the jagged skyline, and the stars at night were evidences of an abiding Arizona.

I left her there at Yuma, where she first met Arizona in the brutal heat of August. I have never ceased to marvel at her endurance, nor to warm to her humanity, nor to admire her literary art; and I often savor the quiet words with which she brought her classic to a close:

"Sometimes I hear the still voices of the Desert: they seem to be calling me through the echoes of the Past. I hear, in fancy, the wheels of the ambulance crunching the small broken stones of the *malpais,* or grating swiftly over the gravel of the smooth white roads of the river bottoms. I hear the rattle of the ivory rings on the harness of the six-mule team; I see the soldiers marching on ahead; I see my white tent, so inviting after a long day's journey.

"But how vain these fancies! Railroad and automobile have annihilated distance, the army life of those years is past and gone, and Arizona, as we knew it, has vanished from the face of the earth."

Jack died at Nantucket in March, 1911, Martha two months later in Schenectady, where she had gone to live with Harry and his family. She followed him to his last posting in Arlington National Cemetery. "I had cast my lot with a soldier and where he was, was home to me." There they both are buried.

READING LIST

MARTHA SUMMERHAYES (1846-1911)

Vanished Arizona; Recollections of My Army Life. Philadelphia, Lippincott, 1908.

————. Salem, Salem Press, 1911. 2d, enlarged edition.

————. Chicago, Lakeside Press, 1939. Abridged from the 1st edition by M. M. Quaife.

————. Tucson, Arizona Silhouettes, 1960. Reprints the 2d ed., with notes by Ray Brandes.

————. Philadelphia, Lippincott, 1963. Reprints the 2d ed., with introduction by W. Turrentine Jackson.

————. Glorieta, N.M., Rio Grande Press, 1970. Reprints the 2d ed., with an index by William Farrington and an irrelevant introduction by R. B. McCoy.

RAY BRANDES

Frontier Military Posts of Arizona. Globe, King, 1960.

Photograph of Martha Summerhayes, courtesy of her daughter, Mrs. Robert F. Beal, and Westways.

The Exploration of the Colorado River
JOHN WESLEY POWELL

I come now to a man and a river, neither of an ordinary kind. There is no greater western river than the Colorado. I am not referring to statistics, of length and volume and such, but rather to its impact upon the imagination and destiny of the West. Likewise there is no greater western explorer than Major John Wesley Powell, the first to lead an expedition through the mysterious canyons and hazardous rapids of a *rio bravo*—a wild river.

The expeditions of Anza and of Lewis and Clark were government missions, aimed at advancing the common weal. Major Powell was impersonally moved by scientific curiosity to venture into a vast area still marked *Unexplored* on the maps of his time. Now in our time, a century later, only the exploration of the Moon can rank with the acts of these earlier discoverers. Theirs were the greater achievements. Because of science, our moon men are near robots, with virtually all decisions made for them by remote manipulators of cunning equipment. In contrast, Powell's running of the river was an unending succession of split-second decisions by him alone. His life and those of his men were constantly at stake throughout the seven weeks it took them to come through.

It is time to reorder our hero priorities. I hope to show why Major Powell is high on my list. My motive is not familial piety.

His line and my line diverged a long while back. Let me make it clear that I am not seeking to stow away in the Major's boat.

So back to the river. I have yet to run it. Only its upper and lower reaches are familiar to me, and I have, in Haniel Long's words, peered into the colored canyon. I have fished some of the tributaries—the White and the Gunnison, down in the latter's Black Canyon, two thousand feet deep and almost narrow enough to throw a rope across. I have also seen the headwaters of the San Juan and inspected the dams at Glen, Hoover, Imperial, and Laguna for leaks. Arizona's tributaries to the Colorado have been accounted for, from the Little Colorado to the Gila. Thus I cannot write as a pedigreed river rat but only as a man who has wormed his way through books to landscape and life here and there throughout the Far West.

There are various ways to attest to my claim that the Colorado is the greatest western river in its impact upon our lives. The most obvious is the irrevocable transformation of Southern California by the generation of power and the diversion of water. If the Central Arizona Project is ever realized then that state too will suffer the grandeurs and miseries of industrial urbanization.

It took man a century to tame the Colorado. He should not fool himself that its docility is permanent. No matter how many dams are built to restrain the fall of water from snow-line to sea-level, the river will triumph in the end, filling each lake with silt, so that finally Old Man River will once again rush triumphantly to the Sea of Cortez.

So much for the river. What of the man whose prodigious feat led to the Colorado's containment? Thanks to numerous books about him, we have Major Powell's life before us like a map. There is no research left to be done. Ours is only to read and marvel at the way Destiny selects and shapes a man to work its will.

Powell's Wesleyan Methodist parents came to America from England. He was born in Mt. Morris, a village in the Genesee Valley of Western New York on March 24, 1834. They went

west with the tide to Ohio and Wisconsin and settled finally in
Illinois. Two traits in the boy foretold the man: scientific curiosity and wanderlust. It was hopeless for his father to want him
likewise to become a preacher, or more precisely, a licensed ex-
horter. A neighboring professor with his own natural history
museum was young Wes's best teacher. Also important was what
he learned from rowboat explorations of the rivers. In 1856, he
descended the Mississippi to the mouth alone in a rowboat, collecting mineral and vegetable specimens as he went. In the following year, he did the same on the Ohio from Pittsburgh to confluence with the Mississippi. His roaming boyhood was like that
of the Van Dyke brothers, Theodore and John, whose river and
lake adventures higher up the Mississippi determined their later
lives as western writers, and also like that of Lewis Garrard and
Ross Browne who followed the rivers to the Gulf and back.

Young Powell became a school teacher in Illinois, took geological collecting trips, lectured on natural history on the Lyceum
circuit, and kept quitting college because of the lack of a science
curriculum. He was marked by powerful drive, physical stamina,
intellectual curiosity, and leadership. In the Civil War, he rose
from private to Colonel, although his intermediate rank of Major
was the title that stuck. At the bloody battle of Shiloh, he lost
his right arm. Henceforth until his death he was never free from
pain which repeated operations on the stump failed to relieve.
His subsequent feats of strength, agility, and endurance are the
more remarkable for having been performed with the aid of his
left arm alone.

Back in Illinois after the war, Powell became a professor of
geology at the Illinois State Normal University. Financed by
institutions in that state he made two collecting trips to the Colorado Rockies. These were said to be the first time that a professor had taken his students on extended field trips. It was then
that he first heard the call of the river, as he explored the high
country of its headwaters and tributaries.

So rapidly has the land been settled since then, that it is now difficult to imagine that time of a vast unexplored part of our country. As I write I am surrounded by books and maps that precisely portray the western lands. Of particular interest are the three-dimensional plastic maps of the states. They reveal the magnitude of the problems Powell met in mapping that rugged terrain. He left little in the way of further heroics. Preliminary probes of outer space will make almost routine our landings on Mars and Venus. Thus we look back in admiration to that epoch when Science had not yet diminished man's stature.

By Powell's time the upper and lower stretches of the Colorado were familiar. Cárdenas discovered the Grand Canyon in 1540. Garcés descended to the Havasupais in 1776. Escalante, Ashley, Pattie, Frémont, Ives and others had crossed the river at various points. No one, however, had traversed its length. James White claimed to have run it on a raft in 1867—a claim demolished by Robert B. Stanton, the engineer who surveyed the canyons to see if a waterlevel railroad could be built. Manly of Death Valley fame and his companions gave up an attempt to float to the Gulf when their boat was smashed in a rapids.

The early trappers penetrated the upper reaches of the canyons in search of beaver. The most intriguing of that hardy breed was D. (for Denis) Julien who in 1836 carved his name on the walls at six different places. The last was in Cataract Canyon at a stretch of smooth water above a rapids and at a height which would have been possible only if he had been in a boat at the time of high water. Thereafter Monsieur Julien disappears from recorded history. It is likely that the rapids swallowed him and his craft, probably a raft of cottonwood logs.

Thus it was Terra Incognita into which Powell's ten men in four boats pushed off, May 24, 1869, on the urgent waters of Wyoming's Green River. They had no maps to guide them, no reports to consult, no help from other than themselves. It was a motley group that Powell had recruited and bound together by his overpowering will, tenacity of purpose, and fearless leadership. Included were trappers, army men, a printer, a boatman,

290

a bullwhacker, and a wandering Englishman "looking for a glorious trip." At least one of the mountain men was a fugitive from justice.

Though bold, Powell also was cautious. His meticulous preparation for the voyage recalled Anza's in organizing his heroic trek from Sonora to Alta California. Take the boats, for example. Drawing on his youthful experience with river craft, Powell designed the boats and had them built in Chicago. Watertight bulkheads fore and aft proved to be their best feature. An error of inattention by another than Powell cost them one of the boats, when it was shattered in the first rapids encountered. Powell's boat, named for his wife the *Emma Dean*, was abandoned near the end for want of crew to man it. Of the ten men, one (the disillusioned Englishman) quit early and three refused to run the final rapids which appeared (and proved to be) the worst of all. They struggled up a tributary canyon and struck out for the Mormon settlements of southern Utah, but, as Stegner observed, they miscalculated the algebra of chance and were killed by Indians who mistook them for prospectors who had raped a squaw.

Safely through the final rapids, the rest of the river known, Powell disbanded the survivors at the mouth of the Virgin River. Two floated on down to Yuma and the Gulf. Powell's primary purpose was scientific curiosity. When the uncertainties and accidents of this first expedition made the results incomplete, he organized a second voyage in 1871, with better funding and equipment.

Powell's prodigious drive carried him far beyond the Colorado. In the next two decades he became the first great government organizer and coordinator of scientific services, a pioneer of those federal achievements which have culminated in our time in NASA and all that it promises.

Though a visionary, Powell was also able to transform visions into reality. Such was the United States Geological Survey, founded by him in a consolidation of several uncoordinated surveys. To avoid any charge of empire-building, Powell made

Clarence King the first director of the Geological Survey, himself heading the also newly founded Bureau of Ethnology. Only when King's brilliant star burned out, did Powell take his place as head of the U.S.G.S. Powell was jovial and magnetic, a born leader, with remarkable perception for promising young men. He gave them the chance to demonstrate their own capacities and was thus instrumental in launching many on their own careers.

His work with the Survey led inevitably to a concern for the question of water in the West and to the publication in 1878 of his epochal *Report on the Arid Lands of the United States,* which led in turn to the founding in 1902—the year of Powell's death —of the United States Bureau of Reclamation.

The timing of this was dramatic. As Powell lay near death, the tidings were brought to him that President Theodore Roosevelt, in his message to Congress, had urged federal participation in irrigation. "It is as right for the National Government," Roosevelt declared, "to make the streams and rivers of the arid region useful by engineering works for water storage as to make useful the rivers and harbors of the humid region by engineering works of another kind."

Powell was deeply moved by the news. "These things take time," he said to his informant. "You must learn to control impatience, but always be impatient."

He was a prophet ahead of his time. Irrigation, flood control, watershed and range management, national forests and parks— the entire course of western development in the 20th century were foretold in one way or another by the short, strong, bewhiskered man.

This has carried me beyond the classic, *The Exploration of the Colorado River.* The bibliography of Powell's book is complicated, even as its writer was a complicated man, with mixed motives for all that he did. He had a scientist's curiosity and he also loved adventure, even danger. In addition he was a master politician, able to employ his knowledge and experience in virtuoso displays of public relations skill. He knew how to recognize others, to listen, to praise, even to flatter. When he appeared before congressional committees to plead for financial support, he avoided controversy, remained unruffled, and was charitable toward his harshest critics. Politicians treated him with the respect due a one-armed hero of the War and the Colorado. During the two decades of his Washington prime, 1870-90, Powell was a towering figure, certainly one of the best public servants of all time. A lighter side of his nature is revealed in the anecdote of how when he heard of a Confederate officer who had lost his left arm in battle, he wrote him to suggest henceforth they buy only one pair of gloves.

The journal kept by Powell on his river voyages was the basis of his eventual book. It was not written with publication in mind. He did not expand it until five years after the first voyage. What led him to do so was not literary ambition. Rather did he see its use in getting support for his ambition to consolidate the surveys and advance scientific knowledge of the West. One member of the second expedition had already broken into print. Powell felt the need to get his story before the public. Earlier he had written letters from the field to the *Chicago Tribune*. A new monthly magazine had been founded by *Scribner's* which featured engraved illustrations based on photographs.

Powell had superb photographs of the river taken by J. K. Hillers. When approached by *Scribner's* for a series of articles, he contracted so that the engraved illustrations would become his property. They could then be used to embellish his narrative which the Smithsonian Institution planned to issue as a government report.

This is what happened, and it was a stroke of publishing genius few authors have matched. The *Scribner's* articles gave him a wide base of interest and support and were followed in the same year of 1875 by the government publication, to which was appended solid sections of topographical and geological data on the lands drained by the Colorado.

Twenty years were to pass before Powell's river achievements would be presented to the public in book form other than a government report. In 1894 his vision of great publicly-managed irrigation works withered in the heat of opposition by vested interests and their servants in Congress. Powell fell from political favor and resigned from the Geological Survey. For the third time the stump of his arm was operated on in the Johns Hopkins hospital.

Retirement and recuperation brought the opportunity to prepare a revised and enlarged version of the 1875 report. It appeared in 1895 as *Canyons of the Colorado*, and included more text and illustrations. Today both the 1895 and the 1875 volumes are basic for the Powell and Colorado River collector, and they are correspondingly scarce and costly.

Fortunately the year 1961 brought paperback reprints of both. Their similar title, *The Exploration of the Colorado River*, is confusing, for one is a reprint of only the narrative part of the 1875 report and the other of the entire 1895 *Canyons of the Colorado* with only the title changed. For the record, so that one knows what he is buying, the 1875 reprint is a Doubleday Anchor book, and the 1895 reprint is a Dover paperback.

The 1875 takes us back the closest to what Powell saw and felt on his first epochal voyage of 1869, and even then it is not a pure version of the experience. In writing it in 1874 he took literary license and incorporated material from his second voyage, although he gave no indication that he had done so. Thus it is not a faithful narrative of the first voyage.

The Dover reprint is the most desirable, for it sandwiches the 1875 narrative between material on the wider canyonlands and also includes the original engravings that appeared in *Scribner's Monthly*. The Anchor reprint has fewer illustrations.

If only to clarify my own initial confusion I have gone to some length to establish the bibliographical basis for an appreciation of Major Powell's achievement. Let me return now to the first voyage and its leader's account of it. The primary source lies in

Powell's original journal, preserved in the archives of the Bureau of Ethnology in the Smithsonian Institution—a few long and narrow strips of brown paper, roughly bound by Powell in sole leather. This served as a key to memory when he came to undertake a more literary effort.

Rugged scientist-explorer that he was, the Major was also a man of feeling and imagination, as we can discern in the following entries. Here is his journal entry of July 23, 1869: *Difficult rapids. Three portages. Ran 5 1/2 miles. West wall of canyon vertical except 1/4 or 1/3 of height from base which has a steep talus. Camp on left bank. No. 13.*

This he expanded into an account of his men's mounting concern over the deepening canyons and towering walls. "The conclusion to which the men arrive seems to be about this: that there are great descents yet to be made, but, if they are distributed in rapids and short falls, as they have been heretofore, we will be able to overcome them. But, may be, we shall come to a fall in these cañons which we cannot pass, where the walls rise from the water's edge, so that we cannot land, and where the water is so swift that we cannot return. Such places have been found, except that the falls were not so great but that we could run them with safety. How will it be in the future! So they speculate over the serious probabilities in jesting mood, and I hear Sumner remark, 'My idea is, we had better go slow, and learn to paddle.'"

To add to their concern, their rations began to give out. Much had been lost when the one boat was demolished, and the remainder was scant, water-soaked, and mouldy. The climax came on August 28 when three of the men decided that they had had enough and that further progress would be suicidal. Powell's journal was laconic. *Boys left us. Ran rapid. Bradley boat. Made camp on left bank. Camp 44.*

In his later version these bare words were expanded into a dramatic incident in which he sought to persuade the men to continue. "We have another short talk about the morrow, and he (Howland) lies down again; but for me there is no sleep. All night long, I pace up and down a little path, on a few yards of sand beach, along by the river. Is it wise to go on? I go to the boats again, to look at our rations. I feel satisfied that we can get over the danger immediately before us; what there may be below I know not."

That was the Major's nadir of faith. Moved by the men's defection, he was tempted to call it quits and strike out with them for the Mormon settlements. If he had, they would have all been killed.

Powell's writings are not the sole authority for what happened on the first voyage. Boatman George Bradley also kept a journal —a fuller, more literary effort, actually written as the expedition went down river. Bradley was a stern and moralistic man, given to carping at the Major's frequent delays for scientific observations and his refusal to rest on the Sabbath. And yet, as Powell testified, when danger threatened, Bradley was ever cool, strong, and helpful, as once when the two of them were climbing a canyon wall and the one-armed Powell became stuck, unable to move in any direction. Whereupon Bradley, who was above, peeled off his drawers and dangled them for Powell to grasp and be hauled to safety.

Beginning in 1947 the Utah Historical Society *Quarterly*, inspired by the work of William C. Darrah, a Harvard paleobotanist who was assembling the materials on which to base his definitive *Powell of the Colorado* (1951), printed the entire documentation of journals and letters of the Powell expeditions.

In George Bradley's we learn that the three men's defection was amicable and that the expedition indeed faced grave trouble. "We have never had such a rapid before," Bradley wrote, after they had come safely through. "The cutwater rope and all flew full thirty feet in the air and the loosened boat dashed out like a war-horse eager for the fray. On I went and sooner than I can write I was in the breakers, but just as I always am, afraid while danger is approaching, but cool in the midst of it, I could steer the boat as well as if the water was smooth . . . It stands A No. 1 of the trip."

In the century since then the river has been run many a time and the literature about it continues to accumulate. These centennial years have brought numerous reappraisals of Powell and his achievements. One of the most unusual publications came in 1970 with Barry Goldwater's *Delightful Journey*, the journal of his river-run of 1940, illustrated from photographs taken by him at the time.

In his preface Goldwater expresses the ambivalence felt by many as to when public use of the environment becomes public abuse. Here is how he puts it: "I am happy that today thousands enjoy this journey where a few years previously only a handful could participate in the experience."

Then a page later he writes, "The river is certainly more accessible now to more people, and each year increasing numbers of people travel it until we are now near the saturation point. Still I must confess a nostalgia for seeing the Colorado River as it was when I first travelled it."

What would Major John Wesley Powell say about today's deafening helicopter portaging of river craft and people, of power boats screaming up stream, of water-skiers with transistor radios crisscrossing the lake that bears his name, and of the litter left by man? I have no doubt of the answer.

READING LIST

JOHN WESLEY POWELL (1834-1902)

Canyons of the Colorado. Meadville, Pa., 1895.

The Exploration of the Colorado River and Its Canyons. New York, Dover, 1961. A reprint of the foregoing.

The Exploration of the Colorado River of the West. Washington, Government Printing Office, 1875; Chicago, University of Chicago Press, 1957. Abridged by Wallace Stegner.

The Exploration of the Colorado River. Garden City, Doubleday Anchor Books, 1961.

Report on the Lands of the Arid Regions of the United States. Washington, Government Printing Office, 1879; Cambridge, Harvard University Press, 1962. Edited by Wallace Stegner.

Selected Prose. Edited by George Grossette. Boston, Godine, 1970.

FREDERICK S. DELLENBAUGH

A Canyon Voyage; the Narrative of the Second Powell Expedition. New York, Putnam, 1908; New Haven, Yale University Press, 1926.

JOHN K. HILLERS

"Photographed All the Best Scenery"; Jack Hillers' Diary of the Powell Expeditions, 1871-75. Edited by Don D. Fowler. Salt Lake City, University of Utah Press, 1972.

ROBERT B. STANTON

Colorado River Controversies. New York, Dodd, 1932.

UTAH HISTORICAL SOCIETY QUARTERLY

Vol. 7, nos. 1-3, 1939 and Vol. 15, 1947 are devoted to the various diaries, documents, maps and photographs relating to the Powell explorations, 1869-72.

The Exploration of the Colorado River

WILLIAM C. DARRAH
Powell of the Colorado. Princeton, Princeton University Press, 1951.

WALLACE STEGNER
Beyond the Hundredth Meridian; John Wesley Powell and the Second Opening of the West. Introduction by Bernard De Voto. Boston, Houghton Mifflin, 1954.

COLIN FLETCHER
The Man Who Walked Through Time. New York, Knopf, 1967.

ROBERT WALLACE
The Grand Canyon. New York, Time-Life, 1972.

Photograph of Major Powell by De Lancey Gill, courtesy of University of Arizona Library.

At Occidental College
Los Angeles, Cal.
Mar. 22, 1911   Chas. F. Lummis   Theodore Roosevelt   Photo by Bob Whitley
                                                                            Evening Express

Ranch Life and the Hunting Trail
THEODORE ROOSEVELT

Those knowledgeable in western lore will ask why I include Roosevelt's book among Southwest classics when it is a book of the High Plains, the Short Grass Country, the Badlands, admittedly a classic but one whose setting is other than Southwest.

Roosevelt never wrote a book about the heartland and its adjacent lands. All that is classically Southwestern by him are a few essays on the region around the Grand Canyon.

Why then include this outlander? My answer is because of Theodore Roosevelt's influence on the West. More than any other person, he led the federal government to develop and preserve our natural resources. He is the patron saint of all the West. Far West, Southwest, Northwest—all owe him reverence.

During his presidency, 1901-08, the dream of Major John Wesley Powell came true when Roosevelt led Congress to pass and then signed the bill establishing the Bureau of Reclamation. Dams and waterworks began to appear all over the western map. Under the conservationist, Gifford Pinchot, the U. S. Forest Service was established in the Department of Agriculture. National forests, parks, monuments, game and bird reservations proliferated. Mesa Verde became a national park, Inscription Rock the El Morro National Monument. Roosevelt Dam on the Salt River made possible the agricultural and urban development of the Valley of the Sun whose capital is Phoenix.

Throughout the West we find evidence of Theodore Roosevelt's influence, not necessarily on the scale of a national park or monument. I once stopped to stretch my legs on a lonely strand of the Oregon coast near Cape Meares. A light rain was falling and I could see in the mist an offshore rock covered with seabirds. A posted sign on the beach told that it was Three Arch Rock Bird Reservation, established on October 14, 1907, one of the first of the many such wildfowl preserves created by Executive Order of President Theodore Roosevelt.

His influence on the arts was also strong. By choosing the young Frederic Remington to illustrate his *Ranch Life and the Hunting Trail* and by the example he set for his friend Owen Wister of an aristocratic easterner coping with crude westerners, Roosevelt dressed the national stage for the success of *The Virginian,* that prototype of cowboy novels.

Not since Lincoln and not again until Kennedy has America known a president with such power to evoke a mystical response from the people. May I offer a child's testimony? I was born in Washington during the presidency of Theodore Roosevelt. We moved to California when I was four years old. There remain two memories of the capital, one of being awakened and held by my mother at the bedroom window to see Halley's Comet, the other of standing on our terrace above Park Road and waving to the president as he went by on his Sunday morning horseback ride in Rock Creek Park. He waved back and left the abiding memory of a great man.

What led him west? How came this sickly intellectual eventually to be the exponent of the Strenuous Life, the Big Stick, and the Square Deal? The answer goes back to his origins. A passion for hunting led to his becoming the greatest sportsman of his time. He justified controlled game-killing as compatible with conservation. Without such control, wildlife would be hunted to extinction. After graduation from Harvard in 1880, he went to live in New York with his wife and mother. Politics and history interested him. Declaring that he intended to join the "gov-

302

erning class," he ran for and was elected to the New York State Assembly. He later became Police Commissioner. He proved incorruptible.

Then in 1883 that passion for hunting, and a need to strengthen a weak body, led him west on a buffalo hunt in the Badlands of North Dakota. He felt at home there and bought two cattle ranches on the Little Missouri.

A year later he lost his wife, Alice Lee, the day after she gave birth to the girl destined to live on into our time as Alice Roosevelt Longworth. By one of those strange blows of fate, his mother died three hours later. A deep melancholy ensued. Back to the Badlands he went and for the next two years he found surcease in ranching, hunting, reading and writing. He built his body into a dynamo that never ceased to hum until it stopped in his 61st year. It was his enormous energy that most impressed his contemporaries. Henry Adams expressed it thus: "He showed the singular primitive quality that belongs to ultimate matter—the quality that medieval theology assigned to God—he was pure act."

William Allen White said the same thing differently: "He ruled not because he was brave and wise and kind, though he was all three, but because his courage, his wisdom, and his heart were hitched to a dynamo, which gave him a sort of imperial authority."

Roosevelt's toothy visage became the cartoonist's delight, as much as his kinsman's cigarette holder. "Occasionally he used the loose underlip as a shutter," White wrote, "to uncover a double row of glittering teeth that were his pride. He knew that his display of teeth was effective as a gesture of humor or rage. When he was excited he worked his jaw muscles with an animal ferocity."

So many-faceted was Theodore Roosevelt and so harmoniously were the facets joined, that it is hard to write about one without involving them all. Although as a hunter he filled his home on Long Island—and later the White House—with mounted trophies, he had a reverence for wildlife. He was a learned watcher and recorder of birds. Once during his presidency he alarmed a cabinet meeting by exclaiming, "Gentlemen, I must tell you what has just happened!" He then proceeded to describe two species of birdlife never before observed in Washington.

The therapeutic ranching years were also the time of Roosevelt's best writing on the West. His first book was *Hunting Trips of a Ranchman*. In the memorial edition prefaced by George Bird Grinnell, the famous naturalist remarked on the freshness and enthusiasm of the book which he had reviewed upon its first appearance in 1885. He compared its qualities to those of earlier writers on the West, such as Parkman, Garrard, and Ruxton. According to Grinnell, it was he who persuaded Roosevelt of the importance of conservation if there were to be game for future sportsmen. This led Roosevelt to found the Boone and Crockett Club, dedicated to exploration, sportsmanship in hunting, and the preservation of wild species.

Essays which first appeared in *Century* during 1888 were collected in book form as *Ranch Life and the Hunting Trail*. The long winters in the Badlands gave Roosevelt ample opportunity to read and write. If he had been ranching in the Southwest, where he could have been outdoors the year around, he might not have written at all.

Completion of the transcontinental railroad in 1869 accelerated the westward movement. *Century* reflected this. Richard Watson Gilder, its genteel and perceptive editor, was ever ready to print authentic western material. The art of steel-engraved illustration was at its height. When Roosevelt first saw Remington's work in *Outing*, he recognized the ideal illustrator of his work.

And so it was that the magazine essays and the book were embellished by Frederic Remington. As Owen Wister was to do later in *The Virginian*, Remington took the western commonplaces—cowboys, Indians, miners, and badmen—and by blend-

304

ing the real and the romantic he created a stereotype of lasting influence. Roosevelt's gusto, Wister's sentiment, and Remington's art merged in the popular view of the West that abides to this day. Television has spread it worldwide.

Of the twelve essays in *Ranch Life and the Hunting Trail*, eight are on ranching, four on hunting. They are Roosevelt at his best as a writer before he became immersed in the making and moulding of history. Loss of wife and mother and the austerity of the Badlands lent sombreness to his writing, a quality accentuated by Remington's stark art. Never again did Roosevelt write as simply and forcefully. His later work, Van Wyck Brooks said, was written "with his foot on the loud pedal, and the charm of his books on the Old West had vanished with it."

Ranch Life and the Hunting Trail is sought after by Roosevelt and Remington collectors so that it has become scarce and costly. In 1968 the Northland Press in Flagstaff took six of the original *Century* essays, with the Remington illustrations, and reproduced them in facsimile. Their *Ranch Life in the Far West* is an inexpensive way to acquire the best of the two men's collaboration.

Although Roosevelt's outfit of buckskin suit and his spectacles made him first appear as an easy mark for the suspicious Badlanders, he toughened up and proved himself as a natural leader. That first experience and Roosevelt's later returns as president are told by Herman Hagedorn in *Roosevelt in the Badlands*. The setting of those crucial years on the Little Missouri is preserved in the Theodore Roosevelt National Memorial Park along the North Dakota-Montana border. It is a memorial he would have loved above all.

In 1901 the assassination of President William McKinley elevated his vice president to the highest office. Word spread to the Badlands that "the cowboy bunch can come in to the White House whenever they want to." Come they did. Now and then there was some difficulty in getting by the guards. It took one cowboy two days to make it. Roosevelt was indignant. "The next time they don't let you in, Sylvane," he declared, "you must shoot through the windows."

When in 1903 as president he returned to the Badlands for the last time, he stood on the rear platform of his private car and said to John Burroughs who was beside him, "I know all this country like a book. I have ridden over it and hunted in it and tramped over it in all seasons and weather, and it looks like home to me." Although Roosevelt's intellect was eastern, his heart belonged to the West.

Charles F. Lummis came from Los Angeles in answer to the president's summons to discuss the plight of the Mission Indians. Roosevelt named him a special commissioner and helped him found the Sequoyah League. Don Carlos created a stir when he appeared at the White House in his customary garb of green corduroy suit, red sash, bandana headband, Indian jewelry, and sandals. In answer to critics, Lummis replied, "I don't change my face for anyone; why should I change my clothes?," which though not good logic was good Lummis.

Never has the White House seen as many various Americans as it did during Roosevelt's tenure. Cowboys and poets, sculptors and reformers, streamed in and out. He had St. Gaudens redesign the coinage. His reaction to *The Jungle* led to the cleanup of the stockyards and packinghouses whose muck had been raked by Upton Sinclair. After being called to Washington, the novelist was ready to stay, forcing the president to say to a friend, "Tell him to go home and let me run the country."

Roosevelt became world renowned. Lord Morley declared that the two most extraordinary works of nature in America were Niagara Falls and the man in the White House. He received the Nobel Peace Prize for his arbitration of the Russo-Japanese War. The crowned heads of Europe deferred to him. His widely publicized African safari led the English upon his arrival in London to post the stone lions at the base of Nelson's Column in Trafalgar Square with a sign reading THESE LIONS ARE NOT TO BE SHOT.

It was after his presidency that Roosevelt came best to know Arizona, although he had visited the Grand Canyon once in 1903. He continued to seek Lummis's counsel on irrigation, archaeological remains, Indian welfare, and the meaning of Spanish words used in writing *The Winning of the West*. He subscribed to *Land of Sunshine* which became *Out West*, and allowed Lummis to quote him on the masthead. When Roosevelt first came to Arizona, Lummis wanted to show him the pueblos of Isleta and Ácoma. Instead the president invited Lummis to meet him at the Grand Canyon and visit on the train en route to Los Angeles. It was Roosevelt's first trip to California. As a politician he whistle-stopped the state from Barstow to Dunsmuir. It was in the speech he made at Ventura that he said, "When I come here to California, I am not in the West. I am west of the West." He went into Yosemite with John Muir.

His name is linked with Arizona in the dam which bears his name. Built on the Salt River above Phoenix to provide flood control and irrigation water, Roosevelt Dam was a result of the Reclamation Act of 1903. An engineering marvel of the time, made of stone quarried at the site and bonded with cement manufactured there, the Roosevelt was the highest masonry dam ever constructed. It can be reached today by paved road over the Apache Trail from Globe or up canyon from Apache Junction over the West's dustiest road.

Six years were required to build the dam at the astronomical cost of ten million dollars. Roosevelt dedicated it on March 18, 1911. Great things will take place in the Salt River Valley, he foretold, because of this project. Reclamation work in the West and the Panama Canal were the proudest achievements of his administration. He went on to say, "I do not know if it is of any consequence to a man whether he has a monument; I know it is of mighty little consequence whether he has a statue after he is dead. If there could be any monument which would appeal to any man, surely it is this. You could not have done anything which would have pleased and touched me more than to name

307

this great dam, this great reservoir site, after me, and I thank you from my heart for having done so."

The Reclamation Act also created the first dam on the Colorado River. A short distance upstream from Yuma, Laguna Dam was an Indian weir-type, brush-filled, earth barrier which diverted water by the All American Canal to the Imperial Valley. It was made obsolete by Imperial Dam, a modern structure a few miles farther upriver.

Roosevelt returned to Arizona in the summer of 1913 for a cougar hunt on the North Rim of the Grand Canyon, followed by a journey through the Navajo and Hopi reservations. These experiences led to several essays in his best vein. "Across the Navajo Desert" culminates in a visit to the Rainbow Natural Bridge. Guided by John Wetherill from his trading post at Kayenta, they rode across the Painted Desert, past Navajo Mountain, to the great arch which had been "discovered" by Wetherill four years before, though long known to the Indians. Only ten other parties of whites, including Zane Grey three months earlier, had made the difficult ride.

Roosevelt lived each experience as naturalist, conservationist, and historian, fields in which he was eminent. Had he not served the year before as head of the American Historical Association and delivered a moving presidential address entitled "History as Literature"? Since Jefferson, no president of the United States was as culturally accomplished as Theodore Roosevelt, and none since has had such wide interests and attainments and intellectual curiosity.

After paying tribute to the American explorers, Frémont and Carson, Roosevelt went on to say that the achievements three centuries earlier of the Spanish soldiers and priests was an even greater triumph "during Spain's brief sunburst of glory." He praised those hardy ones who "first broke through the portals of the thirst-guarded, Indian-haunted desert."

His descriptions of the Rainbow Bridge—seen while floating on his back in the cool water beneath, and later by campfire, and again while waking in the night to gaze up at the great bow in the moonlight—are eloquent. They are even more moving today because of the proximity of people who litter and destroy, and the threat of rising water in the reaches of Lake Powell.

Roosevelt's final Arizona essay described the Hopi Snake Dance, after which Lorenzo Hubbell took the ex-president to his trading post at Ganado and on to the railroad at Gallup. A memorable account of this camping trip was published in 1968. In *Theodore Roosevelt, the Man as I Knew Him*, Nicholas Roosevelt wrote one of the best of the many memoirs of his cousin. It was this younger Roosevelt, then employed by the Indian Service, who arranged the unpublicized trip in correspondence with Hubbell. At the end of the reptile ceremony at Walpi, Nicholas observed in his diary that in thanking the Hopis for their courtesy, Colonel Roosevelt asked what he might do more tangibly to show his appreciation. "Send us shells," the Hopis said, pointing to their bracelets. "Tell them I shall send them a sack full," he promised, and then added, characteristically, "Two sacks full."

These descriptions of Arizona are in the volume *A Book Lover's Holiday in the Open*, the last of Roosevelt's many books. Included is an essay on books to take on camping trips. It reveals his varied tastes. He was a constant and voracious reader, with a photographic memory, adapting his diet to need and mood and aware of the value of contrast.

"To me Owen Wister is the writer I wish when I am hungry with the memories of lonely mountains, of vast sunny plains with seas of wind-rippled grass, of upspringing wild creatures, and lithe, sun-tanned men who ride with utter ease on ungroomed, half-tamed horses. But when I lived much in cow camps, I often carried a volume of Swinburne, as a kind of antiseptic to alkali dust, tepid, muddy water, frying-pan bread, sow-belly bacon, and the too-infrequent washing of sweat-drenched clothing."

In addition to Owen Wister's, Roosevelt also enjoyed the western books of John Burroughs and John Muir, Stewart Edward White and Bret Harte. We know from family evidence that he was a rocking-chair reader and that, as his interest rose, he rocked faster. We no longer hear his favorite expletive, *Bully!*

I have left to the last the most dramatic event of Roosevelt's life, the one that propelled him into the governorship of New York, the vice presidency, and finally into the White House. This was the Spanish-American War of 1898 and the recruitment of the mounted volunteers organized by Roosevelt as the Rough Riders. Public imagination was electrified by Roosevelt's theatrical daring and undisguised lust for conquest and glory.

What enabled him to succeed was his western heritage of the 1880's. He was rough and ready when he heard the call to drive the Spaniards from Cuba. Time has spared him the irony of Castro's driving the Yankees from the island. The Rough Riders came from the Southwest's four territories of Indian, Oklahoma, Arizona, and New Mexico. It was the latter who supplied the most, including Hispanos with the characteristic names of Luna, Capron, and Armijo. From Arizona came Bucky O'Neill, frontier sheriff and mayor, who endeared himself to his Colonel as a poetry-quoting philosopher and who was killed in Roosevelt's presence at Santiago. Today in Prescott there stands in front of the Yavapai County Courthouse a Remingtonesque statue of the mounted Bucky by Solon Borglum.

After "Bull Moose" Roosevelt fatally split the Republicans and lost the election of 1912 to Woodrow Wilson, his fortune faded. The World War roused his patriotism. He was blinded to reality when he sought again to enlist mounted volunteers for service overseas. President Wilson prevented what would have been a fiasco. The old Rough Rider's spirit and body failed, and he died in 1919.

Although his home on Oyster Bay enshrines his guns, trophies, and other memorabilia, it is in the West, all the way from the Little Missouri to the Salt and the Colorado, that Theodore Roosevelt's more indelible memory remains. It is a memory as lasting as the land itself, for it is formed of forests and rivers, of dams, green fields and fruitful orchards, of game preserves and bird sanctuaries, and those places of immemorial meaning and beauty, Mesa Verde and El Morro.

READING LIST

THEODORE ROOSEVELT (*1858-1919*)

Hunting Trips of a Ranchman. New York, Putnam, 1885.

Ranch Life and the Hunting Trail. New York, Century, 1888.

Ranch Life in the Far West. Flagstaff, Northland Press, 1968.

The Winning of the West. New York, Putnam, 1900. 6 vols.

A Book-Lover's Holidays in the Open. New York, Scribner, 1920. Includes three prime Arizona essays.

Theodore Roosevelt's America; Selections from the Writings. Edited by F. A. Wiley. New York, Doubleday Anchor paperback, 1962.

The Rough Riders. New York, Scribner, 1899. Signet Classics paperback, with an Afterword by Lawrence Clark Powell, 1961.

History as Literature and Other Essays. New York, Kennikat, 1967.

JOHN BURROUGHS

Camping and Tramping With Roosevelt. Boston, Houghton Mifflin, 1907.

WILLIAM C. DEMING

Roosevelt in the Bunkhouse. Laramie, Laramie Printing Co., 1927.

HERMAN HAGEDORN

Roosevelt in the Badlands. Boston, Houghton Mifflin, 1921.

311

LINCOLN A. LANG

Ranching with Roosevelt. Philadelphia, Lippincott, 1921.

OWEN WISTER

Roosevelt, the Story of a Friendship, 1880-1919. New York, Macmillan, 1930.

G. EDWARD WHITE

The Eastern Establishment and the Western Experience; the West of Frederick Remington, Theodore Roosevelt, and Owen Wister. New Haven, Yale University Press, 1968.

NICHOLAS ROOSEVELT

Theodore Roosevelt, the Man as I Knew Him. New York, Dodd, 1967.

Photograph of President Theodore Roosevelt and Charles F. Lummis, courtesy of Southwest Museum, Los Angeles.

The Desert

JOHN C. VAN DYKE

All Southwestern book trails lead to *The Desert* by John C. Van Dyke, published in 1901. Many writers on the Southwest have acknowledged their debt to it for having given them a clearer vision of the arid lands. I knew the book first as a boy, although I did not read it until I became a man. Only the back was familiar to me from staring at the gold lettering and saguaro vignette on the spine. I used to take my forced nap on a couch in front of the bookcase which held *The Desert* and other books belonging to my father and mother. They included works by H. G. Wells, W. J. Locke, Will Levington Comfort, Edward Carpenter, Whitman, Tagore, and Nietzsche. I read the backs of them all.

The years passed, and then in 1951 Franklin Walker's *A Literary History of Southern California* described John C. Van Dyke as the first to exalt the desert as a place of beauty. "The desert has gone a-begging for a word of praise these many years," he quoted from Van Dyke's Preface. "It never had a sacred poet; it has in me only a lover."

Walker went on to cite the illustrious lineage of desert writers sired by Van Dyke, including Mary Austin, A. J. Burdick, George Wharton James, Idah Meacham Strobridge, J. Smeaton Chase, Stewart Edward White, and Zane Grey. Others continued to follow, such as Edwin Corle and Joseph Wood Krutch, all cited ultimately by E. I. Edwards, the desert's bibliographer.

Professor Walker did what literary historians should do for their readers: led me to more reading. Then it was that I remembered *The Desert* in its terra cotta binding. My parents' books were dispersed and my own did not include a copy of the Van Dyke. It soon did, however, for *The Desert* is not a scarce book. It went through many printings between 1901 and 1918 when an edition appeared with J. Smeaton Chase's photographs and was expanded in 1930 also to include "Desert Notes" by Dix Van Dyke, the author's nephew.

It was in the early 1950's that I talked about *The Desert* with Edwin Corle, at the time I was writing an Introduction to a new edition of *Fig Tree John*, his novel of the Coachella Valley.

"We desert writers," Corle said, "are forever in the debt of John Van Dyke. He saw it first and said it best. What I have never understood though is how an eastern art professor, a tenderfoot dude, could come out here and break a trail the rest of us have been following ever since."

I couldn't answer Corle nor was the answer in Walker's book. Clues were there, however; and now, twenty years later, I have followed those leads. Alas, Edwin Corle is no longer living to share what I have discovered about John Van Dyke and how he was able to write knowingly about a land to which he first came as a stranger.

We live in a time of concern for destruction of the desert fabric. The books of Joseph Wood Krutch contain the most eloquent statement of this concern. Is ours the first generation thus to be aroused? Indeed it is not. Van Dyke's voice gave warning years ago. As a conservationist he took an extreme stand, opposed to *all* desert development.

"The deserts should never be reclaimed," he declared. "They are the breathing spaces of the West and should be preserved forever." He believed that the irrigation of the Imperial Valley being undertaken at the turn of the century when he was writing would change the climate of Southern California by an excess of

316

humidity. He contrasted the murky air of the Old World with that of the pre-urban Southwest. What impurities there were then in the latter came from natural causes—wind and dust— and produced the coloration he adored. In our time accelerated urbanization and industrialization have poisoned the air and made Southern California an unhealthy place to live.

A book's power of survival depends upon its appeal to later generations. *The Desert* is newly harmonious with our concern for preservation of the environment. Van Dyke called a sorry roll of destruction by wanton mining and foresting, in Pennsylvania, Minnesota, the Dakotas, Montana, Arizona, California, and Alaska. So-called practical men, he wrote, have "stripped the land of its robes of beauty, and what have they given in its place? Weeds, wire fences, oil-derricks, board shanties and board towns." He foresaw that the Southwestern desert would be harder to subdue, and that in the end it would do to us what the Sahara did to the Romans—overwhelm us. His vision of an earth without man preceded that of Robinson Jeffers. They perceived that all civilizations end in disease and death.

Van Dyke wrote knowingly of the geology, the vegetation and flora, the fauna and the weather; and above all of color dominating form. He referred to the effort of the French Impressionists, especially Corot and Monet, to escape the tyranny of form and "to suggest everything by tones of color, shades of light, and drifts of air. How they would have revelled in the dream landscapes of the Southwestern desert!"

Van Dyke found the power of healing that lies in desert solitude. He wrote as a naturalist, a romantic, and a prophet. He can be read today across a wide spectrum of interest. I had this brought home to me recently when in a single day I heard tributes to *The Desert* by two Arizonans who from differing viewpoints share a love of the region. Dr. William G. McGinnies, the ecologist and director emeritus of the University of Arizona's Arid Lands Studies, cited Van Dyke's accuracy in describing desert life, while Joseph Stacey, editor of *Arizona Highways*, said that

317

he regarded Van Dyke as the most inspirational of all desert writers.

How did I begin my quest for John C. Van Dyke? In the card catalog of the nearest library I found his full name and dates of birth and death: *John Charles Van Dyke, 1856-1932.* Then in *Who's Who in America* for 1932 the outline of his career: Occupation, university professor. Born in New Brunswick, New Jersey; educated privately and at Columbia; studied art in Europe many years. Unmarried. Admitted to bar, 1877. Librarian, Sage Library since 1878; professor of history of art, Rutgers University since 1889. Lecturer Columbia, Harvard, Princeton. Numerous memberships and honors. And a list of his works, from *Books and How to Use Them* (1883) to *In the West Indies* (1932), representing a half century of creativity which yielded more than forty books.

At that point I admit to having paused to consider the state of my eyesight. Of the forty, I had read only the one. Reading them all might still not tell me who he really was and what had led him from art gallery to desert. Or how it happened that his last three books, which came at the end of his life, were on such widely separated areas as Java, Egypt, and the West Indies.

Curiosity motivated me to keep searching. I sought for his literary archives at the places of his professional appointments—Rutgers University and the Sage Library of the New Brunswick Theological Seminary. They proved meager. I wrote to Princeton and the Library of Congress.

Information came back in the form of letters, Xeroxes, and microfilms, all the while I kept reading my way through his voluminous publications assembled from several sources. His books classified as art appreciation and gallery guides, essays on nature and environment, and books of travel. They also included a work on New York City, illustrated by Joseph Pennell.

Throughout this multiplicity of print the man remained shadowy. A curtain of academic reserve hung between him and the reader. Then as he neared sixty, he began to raise it a bit. In 1915

318

appeared *The Raritan, Notes on a River and a Family*. From the Library of Congress I obtained a Xerox of this privately printed rarity. In its Preface Van Dyke declared, "These notes have very slight historical or even genealogical interest. They mean nothing to the stranger."

I did not take that to apply to me, for as I continued to read his books, I felt no longer a stranger to John Van Dyke, and the bonds between us kept strengthening. From *The Raritan* I learned more than he had listed in *Who's Who*—that he was a cousin of the poet-essayist, Henry Van Dyke (1852-1933); and more pertinent to my quest, that he was a younger brother of Theodore S. Van Dyke (1842-1923) who had come to Southern California in the 1870's, written several books on the region and, after a newspaper career in San Diego and Los Angeles, had ranched on the Mojave Desert near Barstow and served until his death as Justice of the Peace in Daggett. There appeared to be the magnet that drew John Van Dyke to the Southwestern desert.

I learned also that their father was a distinguished New Jersey legislator and jurist who, at the age of 60, left public life and went with his wife and five sons to take up large-scale farming in Minnesota, on the Mississippi across from the mouth of the Chippewa.

As a lad of twelve, John took with a will to the wilderness, to forest, prairie, river and lake. The father's dream of an agrarian dynasty faded when all five boys spurned farming for professional careers—the law, medicine and education. When their parents died, the sons left the land.

John developed as both an indoorsman and an outdoorsman in a fusion, he declared, of his Dutch-English-Scotch-Irish blood. In *The Raritan* he wrote of himself, "The years of study have been interrupted by much travel on both hemispheres, by many returns to the sea, the mountains, the prairies, and the desert. Nature has proved the most lasting love of all and though the Younger has not yet broken away from civilization and gone back to the soil, he keeps threatening to do so and eventually it

319

may come to pass. For with each succeeding spring the honk of the wild goose keeps calling to the northern waterways and brings back memories of early Minnesota days, and the note of the sand-hill crane unfolds the Montana uplands in their pristine glory when they were known only to the buffalo and the Sioux Indians. The spell of the wild grows with the years and becomes more insistent. What after all are the tales of books and art compared with nature—nature before the page has been smeared by the hand of man!"

There were the forces that had made John Van Dyke—a love of learning, a love of the land. Writing was the way he succeeded in unifying them, as his educated mind came to bear upon nature. The gift of style illuminated his prose. He had the perspective of a learned and sophisticated man, never merely a local observer. He became one of the most civilized of all writers on the South-west, a forerunner of Dobie and Krutch, a successor of Lummis.

His writings on art are still being read by art students. They contain passages of flashing insight, such as this: "The pictures in a gallery are at best only the reminders of high aspiration and noble ideals. Unlike Shakespeare's pages they cannot be eternally revised, reproduced, and kept alive. They are fading slowly into ashes; and what they have to say to us, with all their beautiful way of saying it, is becoming less legible year by year."

More slowly did I savor his books on nature which form a series beginning in 1898 with *Nature for Its Own Sake*, followed by *The Desert, The Opal Sea, The Mountain, The Grand Canyon of the Colorado, The Open Spaces*, and finally in 1926 by *The Meadows*. In this last book he returned to his natal river valley and wrote of the natural life and round of seasons along the Raritan. All are learned in content and graceful in expression. They are also attractive in format, bearing marginal captions in italic type.

In writing of art and nature in a manner both realistic and aesthetic, Van Dyke was a disciple of Ruskin, the greatest art critic of the 19th century. He was also a Ruskinite in his turning against the materialistic trend in society. In 1908 this produced a crow among swans when Van Dyke wrote *The Money God: Chapters of Heresy and Dissent Concerning Business Methods and Mercenary Ideals in American Life.*

This was highbrow muckraking, not aimed at such philanthropists as Rockefeller and Carnegie. Wearing his librarian's hat, Van Dyke rejoiced in the Carnegie benefactions which provided more than 4000 public library buildings in North America and Great Britain. Van Dyke became friends with Carnegie and fished with him in Scotland for trout and salmon. After the Laird of Skibo's death his widow commissioned Van Dyke to edit her husband's unfinished memoirs. Thus the published *Autobiography* of Andrew Carnegie bears an introduction by John C. Van Dyke.

Throughout a half century his publisher was Charles Scribner's Sons. In their archives at Princeton University I found over two hundred letters between author and publisher, written during that span of time. They came to me in the form of a roll of microfilm. In a darkened room I scanned the film on a lighted reader, learning more about a tireless, genial and generous man of letters who was ever motivated by a desire to write better. His correspondents were Scribner's senior editors, W. C. Brownell and later Maxwell E. Perkins. In 1893 when his *Art for Art's Sake* was in press, he wrote to Brownell, "It is the first time that anything of mine has been under critical fire and like the man kicked by the mule, it may be that I'm not as handsome as formerly but 'I know a darned sight more.'"

Thirty years later he was writing to the same editor about the manuscript that was to be published as *The Open Spaces*, "I am very glad that you think well of the new book. My own feeling about it was that it was perhaps more human than anything I had yet put forth."

Van Dyke was right. In *The Open Spaces* he again raised the curtain between him and the reader. The book is a kind of autobiography of the outdoor man in essay-chapters with such titles as Sleeping Out, Riding the Open, Riding the Ranges, The Cowboy, Desert Days, Trailing in Moccasins, and similar subjects.

He was then sixty-six years old, and although he revealed more of himself than ever before, it is through a veil of nostalgia that we gaze with him on a vanished past. "Alas! for the changes brought in by civilization!" he wrote in the Preface-Dedication. "The prairie has been ribbed by the plough, the forest has fallen before the axe, the waterways have become turbid with commerce, even the deserts have been invaded, and the borderland has slowly slipped back to the inaccessible barrens of the north or the bare ranges of the south. Yet the whilom schoolboy still sees that wilderness of his youth—sees it as clearly as he hears the long-ago honk of the gray leader calling from the blue sky of spring. The love and the lure of the wild have remained with him, and now, after many years, he is writing for you some happenings of those early days—living over again in memory the wonder of his lost youth."

His was a rich life on levels both physical and intellectual, in settings of Midwest, Northwest, Far West, and Southwest, a vigorous life of canoeing, riverboating, fishing, hunting, cowpunching, backpacking, and desert trailing.

Here lay the answer Edwin Corle had asked for. Now I knew how it was that an academic man from back east had been able to write with such authority about a land so different from his native Raritan. It was clear that the word *tenderfoot* did not apply to him.

John Van Dyke first came to Southern California in the summer of 1897, seeking relief from respiratory illness, and drawn there by the presence of his brother, Theodore, fourteen years his senior, who was already established as an authority on the ecology of the region. He too had come for his health, recovered, and remained for the rest of his life. His books, *Southern California, The Still-Hunter,* and *Flirtation Camp,* were celebrations of the pastoral land he had loved in the 1870's and which was disappearing under the impact of railroad-spawned immigration

322

and subdivision. The mad boom of the '80's had been Theodore's target in the satirical *Millionaires of a Day.*

"I was already ill," John wrote in *The Open Spaces*, "and I went into the open of the desert to get well. Many of my days in there were ill days. But I kept busy making notes and studying vegetation and animals. I had determined to write a book about the desert, and it was necessary that I should know my subject.

"The book was written during that first summer at odd intervals when I lay with my back against a rock or propped up in the sand. That was a summer of strange wanderings. The memory of them comes back to me now mingled with half-obliterated impressions of white light, lilac air, heliotrope mountains, and blue sky. I cannot well remember the exact route of the Odyssey, for I kept no records of my movements. I was not travelling by map. I was wandering for health and desert information."

His companions were a horse and a large fox terrier named Cappy to whom he talked continually, so that they came to understand his language. Although he was finally to leave the horse at a ranch near Hermosillo, Cappy went all the way with Van Dyke and eventually back together to New Jersey. Water supply was the constant problem, especially for the animals. Although Van Dyke toughened, his health remained precarious as malaria replaced asthma as a chronic ailment.

Van Dyke went first from Hemet through the Pass of San Gorgonio down the Coachella Valley into the Salton basin (eight years before the Colorado breakthrough that formed the Sea) to Yuma. Lower down river he made a reed raft to ferry his supplies across, not trusting them to the back of his horse, then swam back and rode the horse over to the Arizona side.

A long dry trek brought him to Casa Grande from where he followed the Santa Cruz upstream to Tucson. There he rested and gained information on geology and botany from University of Arizona professors Blake and Forbes. On he travelled into Sonora, past Baboquívari and Arivaca down toward Tiburon Island. As he ranged much farther than his two successors,

Wharton James and Smeaton Chase, his *The Desert* goes beyond their Mojave and Colorado desert books to include the Sonora. Van Dyke was at home in Mexico. In the chapter "Desert Days" in *The Open Spaces* appear tributes to the hospitality of Sonoran ranchers and Yaquis. He spent two winters in Guaymas and one far south in Oaxaca.

We can only marvel at the courage and adaptability of this creative man in facing the desert before it was subdued by the automobile, electricity, and air conditioning. During one six-week period he encountered no other living soul. He shocked the old-timers by not wearing the customary mining costume of flannel shirt, heavy pants, boots, and felt hat. Instead he dressed in the Mexican-Indian way of thin cotton shirt and pants, straw hat, and moccasins.

He carried a rifle and pistol for shooting small game, a shovel, hatchet, blankets, tin pan and cups for cooking, a gallon of water, and several shot-sacks of dehydrated food. In those days before such food could be bought, he made his own by powdering parched corn and beans, coffee, chocolate, and dried venison. His whole outfit weighed less than fifty pounds.

He thought his provisioning was meager until later he met John Muir at Theodore's Silver Valley Ranch and learned that he trod the Sierra Nevada with only tea, dry bread, and no blanket. "But Muir was Scotch and tough as a bit of heather," Van Dyke explained, "with all the beauty of character and fine colortone belonging to that shrub."

When Van Dyke did encounter prospectors or Indians, he could not persuade them that he was in the desert only for his health and for beauty's sake. Going on foot and leading his horse, as Smeaton Chase was wont to do, he perceived details of desert life he would otherwise have missed; and thus his book is microscopic as well as cosmic in its vision.

As for the automobile, here is how he viewed it in 1922: ". . . these wonderful places are now being desecrated, if not destroyed, by the automobilist—the same genius that has invaded the Yosemite and made that beautiful spot almost a byword and a cursing. No landscape can stand up against the tramp automobile that dispenses old newspapers, empty cans and bottles, with fire and destruction in its wake. The crew of that craft burn the timber and grasses, muddy up the streams and kill the trout, tear up the flowers, and paint their names on the face-walls of the mountains. They are worse than the plagues of Egypt because their destruction is mere wantonness." If his shade wanders the West today, it is not a happy one.

After spending the winter of 1900-1901 again in Guaymas and bringing *The Desert* nearly to completion, Van Dyke started north. His Preface-Dedication was dated February 1901 at La Noria Verde, a ranchería thirty miles beyond Hermosillo (where he had been wont to leave his horse) watered by a *noria*, a mule-drawn, bucketed water-wheel. Back in Arizona he explored the Santa Ritas, tarried not in Tucson but pushed on through New Mexico to El Paso and south again to Del Rio on the border of Chihuahua. It was from there that he posted his manuscript by registered mail to Scribner's, confident that they would publish it as the second in the series begun three years earlier with *Nature for its Own Sake.*

"It is a whole lot better than the swash which today is being turned out as 'literature,'" he wrote to his editor, W. C. Brownell, "and it will sell too, but not up in the hundreds of thousands. It is not so bad as that. My audience is only a few thousand, thank God."

A week later he wrote again to Brownell, though less euphorically. "I wish you would read the galley proofs and give me the benefit of your suggestions. I haven't lost any idiocies since I have been out here, and I surely must have picked up a lot of mannerisms. I am relying upon you to keep me from making too big an ass of myself."

He went on to say that he would be back in New Jersey before long and hoped that the climate there would not force him to emigrate again. He wanted to read proof at home in New Brunswick, since "proof reading in Mexico with the *Police Gazette* for reference library is unsatisfactory."

Duly published in September, *The Desert* was reprinted year after year. The appearance in 1918 of the illustrated edition gave it renewed life. The story of how it came to include Smeaton Chase's photographs is also told in the Scribner archives. It was Chase who wrote to the publisher from El Monte, California, on April 20, 1915, offering (because of "the well known pecuniary disabilities of authors as a class") a selection of his desert photographs to illustrate "Dr Van Dyke's classic work." His price was $100. He was on an extended horseback journey on the Colorado Desert, he said, preparing a book of travel and description to succeed his *California Coast Trails* and *Yosemite Trails*, and would be taking enough photographs so that duplication need not occur.

The result was that Chase and Van Dyke met two years later at the Century Club in New York and selected the photographs that were to illustrate *The Desert* in 1918 and *California Desert Trails* in 1919. Common to several of the photos in both books is Chase's horse Kaweah (named in honor of Clarence King) which he sometimes posed in order to show the relative sizes of desert objects. That Van Dyke never intended *The Desert* as a guidebook accounts for its not having contained a map.

Reprints of *The Desert* culminated in 1930, two years before Van Dyke's death, with the edition bearing twenty pages of "Desert Notes" by Theodore's son, Dixon called Dix, who had inherited the Mojave ranch and lived thereon until his death in 1954. These notes were meant to clarify and supplement his uncle's text, particularly in the developments that had occurred in the three decades since the first edition, notably the breakthrough and containment of the Colorado River, the reclamation of the Imperial Valley, and the proposed dam in Boulder Canyon.

Van Dyke's text was never altered. What he wrote with such brilliance about the desert's coloration had not changed—and will not change as long as the sun continues to rise and set and the wind to blow. The book ends on high, with the distant view from San Jacinto, westward over the coastal plain to the Pacific and eastward to "the faint forms of the Arizona mountains melting and mingling with the sky; and in between . . . the long pink rifts of the desert valleys and the lilac tracery of the desert ranges."

Color, always color, intoxicated him and fired his prose to rainbow hues. If a modern reader should find Van Dyke's book excessive in its chromatic exuberance, it would surely not be when reading it at sunrise or sunset on the desert.

Conceived in passion, written with precision, and created in the wilderness "with my back against a rock or propped up in the sand," *The Desert* is the enduring work of one who truly saw it first and said it best.

READING LIST

JOHN C. VAN DYKE (1856-1932).

Nature for Its Own Sake; First Studies in Natural Appearances. New York, Scribner, 1898.

The Desert; Further Studies in Natural Appearances. New York, Scribner, 1901.

————. Scribner, 1918. Illustrated from Photographs by J. Smeaton Chase.

————. Scribner, 1930. Chase photographs and Notes by Dix Van Dyke.

The Opal Sea; Continued Studies in Impressions and Appearances. New York, Scribner, 1906.

The Mountain; Renewed Studies in Impressions and Appearances. New York, Scribner, 1916.

The Raritan; Notes on a River and a Family. New Brunswick, Privately Printed, 1916.

The Grand Canyon of the Colorado; Recurrent Studies in Impressions and Appearances. New York, Scribner, 1920.

The Open Spaces; Incidents of Nights and Days under the Blue Skies. New York, Scribner, 1922.

The Meadows; Familiar Studies of the Commonplace. New York, Scribner, 1926.

Photograph of John C. Van Dyke, courtesy of Charles Scribner's Sons.

The Desert Year

JOSEPH WOOD KRUTCH

Now that the life of Joseph Wood Krutch has ended, we can view it and his work as a whole. We can look on the map of his peregrinations and discern a logic in his progress from birth at Knoxville, Tennessee in 1893 to death at Tucson, Arizona in 1970.

For his was no aimless wandering through a life in the course of which he left nearly two dozen books as milestones and monuments. Each of his moves came naturally from the one before. His life was a river-like flow, rising periodically to surmount dams that would have back-watered a man of less creative momentum.

Krutch's was a calm and ordered life. Good fortune was his. One joyful marriage. Rewarding intellectual employment. Wide recognition as a writer. And a creative well that never ran dry and that yielded books to the end of his life. It was a life of major moves and of perennial renewal.

Southerner, New Yorker, New Englander, Southwesterner— what a protean man he was! His autobiography was called *More Lives Than One*. It is the Southwestern life which occupied his last twenty years that concerns me here, a life he began at fifty-seven, an age when many lives are drawing to a close.

During the 1950's and 1960's when he resided in Tucson,

Krutch's books established him as the conscience-voice of the arid lands. He became the foremost ecological spokesman of our time, a writer of quiet eloquence whose books could serve as holy writ for today's idealists. I recall what the *New York Times* said after his death: "The current wave of concern for the environment, the contempt for materialism voiced by so many youthful Americans, and now perhaps their growing rejection of nihilism as well—these should turn a generation unfamiliar with Joseph Wood Krutch to a reading of his books with delight to themselves and profit to the world."

As Dobie was to Texas so was Krutch to Arizona, a not entirely unhonored prophet, although both were ahead of their time.

Part of genius is the writer's ability to read the road signs that lead in the right direction, and to take the way to the promised land where his unwritten books await him. Joseph Wood Krutch had this gift. Throughout his life he never took the wrong turn, never found himself with sterile associates. Colleagues, friends, wife, all were the right ones to ensure the fulfillment of his gifts. It was not that he chose them deliberately. His choices were instinctive ones, determined by fate, fortune, destiny, or whatever we call the power that governs a man's life.

These fruitful turns and encounters may be seen as manifestations of divine will or as illuminations by which the truth was revealed. The first one happened in Knoxville near the end of Krutch's undergraduate years at the University of Tennessee. With a flair for mathematics, he was headed for graduate study in that field at the University of Chicago. A chance reading in the *Literary Digest* of George Bernard Shaw's witticisms led Krutch to read a Shaw play for the first time. He found *Man and Superman* in his neighborhood library.

That was his moment of truth. Literature replaced mathematics. Columbia was chosen over Chicago. Joseph Wood Krutch was launched on the stream that led to his becoming the drama editor of *The Nation* and Brander Matthews Professor of Dramatic Literature in Columbia University, two prestigious and powerful positions of literary authority. The move to New York brought lifelong friendship with Mark Van Doren, his Columbia colleague also destined for literary fame.

Manhattan also meant Krutch's meeting the woman of his life. She was Marcelle Leguia, a French Basque from the northern side of the Pyrenees. Krutch's recognition of her was as instantly perceptive as his discovery of Shaw. As a young Columbia instructor he was dining with his landlady's daughter in a Greenwich Village restaurant . . . but let him tell it:

"Shortly after we had finished dinner, three young ladies entered alone. One was quite commonplace, the two others very pretty, obviously sisters, and somehow or other just faintly exotic. Before they had advanced more than a few steps into the room I said with a sincerity at which myself was astonished, 'That's the girl for me.' 'Which one?' asked the landlady's daughter, and when I pointed to the slightly older of the two sisters she went on: 'I don't know her but (indicating the uninteresting member of the trio) I do know that one.' 'Call them all over,' I said."

Marcelle wasn't as certain as Joe was. It took him time and effort to woo and to win her. They were radically different in appearance. She was short, dark, and Latinesque; he was tall, blonde, and Nordic.

What was it that she did for him? What you would expect a practical Frenchwoman to do. She brought him down to earth. By inducing him who had become a Manhattan intellectual—a bit of a "city slicker" she likes to recall—to spend part of each year at a village in the Berkshire foothills of Connecticut, Marcelle Krutch turned her husband toward his career as a writer of essays in natural history. And it was she who first showed him the Southwest, the region that was to prove his ultimate home and the source of his most influential work.

Without her, Krutch might have remained an academician, a dramatic critic, and a literary biographer. As a result of country living, books on Edgar Allan Poe and Samuel Johnson, a critical work called *The Modern Temper* (which voiced Existentialism long before Sartre), were followed by a psychological study of Thoreau, the greatest of the New England naturalist-philosophers. It was Thoreau who rose to the zenith in Krutch's pantheon and succeeded Shaw as the dominant influence of his subsequent work.

Toward the end of the 1940's occurred another of the Krutch illuminations. "One winter night," he recalled, "shortly after I had finished *Thoreau,* I was reading a 'nature essay' which pleased me greatly and it suddenly occurred to me for the first time to wonder if I could do something of the sort. I cast about for a subject and decided on the most conventional of all, namely Spring."

Within thirty days and in utmost creative urgency, Krutch wrote a book of a dozen essays which Mark Van Doren happily titled *The Twelve Seasons.* Along with *Thoreau* this was the harvest of the rural life into which his wife had initiated him. "For Marcelle," the dedication lovingly read, "who will be found between the lines." Time and again his books were dedicated to her.

The book's swift creation was the product of skilled craftsmanship. Twenty years of discipline as a dramatic critic had taught Krutch how to make words say what he meant. *The Twelve Seasons* is a book of spiderweb strength and beauty, the work of a poet, the work of a naturalist.

Twenty years earlier during a summer in Paris when Krutch had written the 30,000-word second half of *The Modern Temper* in the record time of thirty days, he had shored his future with the purchase of a microscope. That early scientific bent which had promised to make him a mathematician had never been completely suppressed. As Krutch matured he developed a kind of triple vision: the power to perceive the wide landscape as well as the minute details, plus the ability to relate both large and small meanings in a unified philosophy of life. The interest, vitality, and meaning of Krutch's nature essays, first seen in *The*

Twelve Seasons, came from this three-dimensional view of life.

Reading the book upon publication twenty years ago one would have concluded that its author was an immoveable New Englander. Who on earth could have predicted that a little more than a decade later in another book of essays, *The Desert Year,* its author might with equal certainty have been termed an immoveable Southwesterner?

One would have failed to reckon with Marcelle. Just as she planted his feet in Connecticut earth, so did she bring him to the dry and wrinkled land of the arid Southwest. It was to prove the last move of all, and a long way from Pyrenees, Great Smokies, and Berkshires.

In the summer of 1937 Marcelle was led by a friend's glowing account to see New Mexico. She and her sister set out by automobile. At the end of the Columbia summer session, Krutch followed by train. Marcelle met the Santa Fe at Lamy. Then it was that occurred the final illumination, as New Englander was transformed into Southwesterner. Again let him tell it:

"No sooner were we speeding along the roller-coaster road that leads to Albuquerque than I felt a sudden lifting of the heart. It seemed almost as though I had lived there in some happier previous existence and was coming back home."

Each succeeding summer until the war interfered and then summers thereafter, the Krutches came back to the Southwest. They drove thousands of miles throughout the heartland of New Mexico-Arizona. Long a sufferer from asthmatic colds, Krutch found the desert air good for what ailed him. And his scientific curiosity was aroused by the unfamiliar flora and fauna. These were the twin forces of the new magnetic field into which he had been drawn by his wife.

In 1950-51 they spent a sabbatical leave of sixteen months near Tucson in a house on the *bajada* of the Santa Catalinas. During that time he wrote *The Desert Year,* a book which came from the success of *The Twelve Seasons.* Before leaving New York, Krutch was asked by his publisher to write a book on the experiences of a newcomer to the Southwest, in Krutch's words, "whose innocence and ignorance might give a special tone to his discovery of the desert and its life."

Only two weeks after they had settled in Tucson he began to write the new book. Again the years of dramatic criticism, during which he had trained himself to say quickly and meaningfully what he saw, had prepared him to deal promptly with the sun-drenched Arizona landscape. It was not all new to him. Those earlier summers in the Southwest had prepared him for a longer look during the sabbatical year.

Upon Krutch's return to Columbia he shocked his friends by announcing that after another year he and Marcelle were moving to Arizona for good. His colleagues were incredulous in the way that New Yorkers are prone to regard their little island world as The World.

In the spring of 1952 the Krutches returned to Tucson with all their worldly goods and built a home in the desert east of the city, facing the Santa Catalina mountains ten miles away. He found the library of the University of Arizona an indispensable resource for his writing. Today it houses the manuscripts of his Southwestern books.

Three years after *The Desert Year* came *The Voice of the Desert*. It represents a widening and deepening of the knowledge which marked his book of discovery. Although there is some repetition in the second book, there is also new experience and material. If he had lived longer, Krutch might have combined them in a single book.

Why are they on my short shelf of Southwest classics? Because they are learned and wise and written with ease and grace in beautiful prose. The longer he lived and the more he wrote, the more insistently did Krutch ask the ultimate question: what is Life and its meaning? By Life he meant all living things, not man alone. It is this moral questioning that elevates his books above the category of ordinary travel literature.

The Desert Year is the record of a wise man's response to a new environment. *The Voice of the Desert* is a later account after settling in. Better than any books known to me, they embody the facts and the feeling of desert living, the unusual nature of its seasons, plants, and animals. Likewise they express a moral philosophy of life as evolved by Krutch after he had gone, in a religious sense, into retreat.

Though he expressed himself in graceful prose, Krutch was essentially an austere writer. After Shaw his masters were Samuel Johnson (for common sense) and Thoreau (for independent thinking). That early predilection for mathematics had conditioned him against sentimental romanticism. His religion was pantheism. All of life interested him, the life of the protozoa, the life of the mammal called man. Like Robinson Jeffers he abhorred cruelty and wanton killing. When man destroys a work of man, he is called a vandal, Krutch wrote; when man destroys a work of God, he is called a sportsman. Hemingway was not one of his idols. His reverence for life is the theme of *The Great Chain of Life,* essays in natural history written after Krutch's move to Arizona. This book was illustrated by Paul Landacre, the masterful Los Angeles wood-engraver.

It was inevitable that Krutch became our foremost spokesman for Conservation. He was an anachronistic figure in Arizona. He was honored as its most distinguished writer and intellectual, nationally respected for his books and philosophy and familiar to TV audiences from the desert documentaries he narrated for NBC.

At the same time he was out of step with progress as espoused by the politicians and developers. While Tucson's civic leaders were pressing to expand the Old Pueblo as a military-industrial center, Krutch marched to the beat of another drummer. He remained withal a gentle critic. When in addressing the Rotary Club he suggested that Tucson would do better to shrink than to grow, his auditors concluded that the good doctor was talking with tongue in cheek.

He was never more serious. Growth of the city had lapped up

to and beyond the Krutch home on East Grant Road. When they had built it in the early 1950's, there was not a light between them and the mountains, while to the south in winter Canopus, never visible in New England, rose above the horizon. By 1970 that bright star could hardly be seen for the city's lights. This tract-housing, black-topping, and power-poling of what had been beautiful earth was identical with that in a thousand other cities, while over Pima County stretched a brown veil of vehicular pollution.

More serious than the loss of his solitude was the disruption of the desert fabric by rampaging vehicles. The balance of nature, the ecology (literally the *housekeeping*) of the land was being destroyed by the proliferation of urbanism.

In *Grand Canyon* Krutch wrote an authoritative natural history and guidebook. In its final chapter called "What Men? What Needs?" he voiced the concern of thoughtful people in saying, "Increasingly men tend to think of the terrestrial globe as *their* earth. They never doubt their right to deal with it as they think fit—and what they think fit usually involves the destruction of what nature has thought fit during many millions of years." There in few words in the text and tenor of Conservation.

A writer's books open doors for him. It was a reading of *The Desert Year* that led Kenneth Bechtel, the scholarly San Francisco industrialist-conservationist, to ask Krutch to speak to a meeting in Phoenix. The wealthy philanthropist had his own plane, a swift and commodious Lockheed Lodestar. In it he and the Krutches took off on a series of Southwestern surveys. They were often accompanied by William Woodin and Lewis Walker, directors of Tucson's Arizona-Sonora Desert Museum of which Krutch was a valued trustee.

It was Bernard De Voto who recommended that students of western history and geography take to the air. By seeing landscape from on high, a vision was gained that could be had in no other way. Krutch's comprehension of the region was extended by these sweeping flights.

"Now what would you like to see?" Bechtel asked, after they had covered the American Southwest.

Without hesitation Krutch replied, "Baja California."

More journeys were taken, by plane, yacht, jeep, and truck. From them came two books by Krutch which rounded out his writings. They are the crown of his work on the arid lands.

The first of these, *The Forgotten Peninsula*, is the richest and the second, *Baja California, the Geography of Hope*, is the most beautiful, the latter because of the Sierra Club format, with color photographs by Elliot Porter and text drawn from Krutch's earlier writings on natural history.

The former is the most varied of his desert books for the reason that, although it embodies as much natural history as the earlier works, it also embraces more human history and lore. The Arizona books minimize people. This first Baja book includes sketches of Mexicans encountered in village and on ranch, as well as the missionary, mining, and whaling history of the long land.

It is understandable why the Arizona books concentrated on natural rather than on human history. When Krutch came to write them, he was in a revulsion from life in the eastern ant-hill. He needed a decade of desert living to restore his soul.

In order fully to appreciate Joseph Wood Krutch we must go back to his books on Johnson and Thoreau, especially the latter, and then re-read *Walden*. Johnson's common sense, which he shared, was perhaps what kept Krutch from ever becoming a radical conservationist. At his most damning, his voice always remained low and even, which is why the Rotarians missed his message.

That maverick Yankee Thoreau was never far from his side. It could have been Krutch who wrote these words of Thoreau:

"I have sworn no oath. I have no designs on society or nature or God. I did not come into the world chiefly to make it better but to live in it, be it good or bad."

Among his friends Krutch was gay and witty. In public he appeared dignified, slightly withdrawn. He was a diffident speaker. He preferred to speak to an unseen audience. Once upon sharing a platform with him, I felt guilty of being histrionic.

The Voice of the Desert ends with a chapter on "The Mystique of the Desert." Therein Krutch recalls what a powerful generative force the desert has been in giving the Hebrews Religion and the Arabs Astronomy. Could it not give us a new concept of life?—one founded not on exploitation nor sports, but on reverence and love, on feeling for every least living thing, plant and animal. That, Krutch said, could prove our salvation from a fate which is fast leading to the destruction of our environment and then, inexorably, of ourselves.

I called on Marcelle Krutch to learn something of his ways of working. "He was long disciplined," she said. "Every morning at his typewriter he wrote at least a thousand words a day. I was his audience. Toward noon he would come to me and ask, 'Do you want to hear what I've written?' He kept this up until the month of his last illness."

I spoke of those writers—Robinson Jeffers, Raymond Chandler, and Aldous Huxley—who survived their wives on whom they had been creatively dependent. "It was fortunate for Dr. Krutch," I remarked, "that he went first."

She smiled ruefully. "For him, yes, but not for me." Then she said, "I'm finally reconciled to losing him. It came suddenly. One morning I woke up and knew that it was all right."

I stood at the window, looking toward the mountains. The Krutchs' five acres are still a sanctuary in the enveloping city. I counted five cardinals like fire flashes. Mrs. Krutch filled our teacups and spoke again. "After the second cancer operation he knew he was dying. I never let him know that I knew. 'It's not so bad,' he said, 'although with people's new awareness of their environment, I'd like to live a while longer. I could be useful.'"

It was his wish that there be no funeral. In the fall of the year his former colleagues at Columbia held a memorial service in the university chapel. Mark Van Doren was the speaker.

Joseph Wood Krutch's books will continue to speak for him and for all who sense what he is saying but who lack the skill to speak so that they are heard. They are his abiding usefulness—books which are the man himself, learned and visionary, earnest, decent, and eloquent.

READING LIST

JOSEPH WOOD KRUTCH (1893-1970).

The Modern Temper. New York, Harcourt, 1929.

Samuel Johnson. New York, Holt, 1944.

Henry David Thoreau. New York, Sloane, 1948.

The Twelve Seasons. New York, Sloane, 1949.

The Desert Year. New York, Sloane, 1952.

The Voice of the Desert. New York, Sloane, 1955.

The Grand Canyon; Today and All its Yesterdays. New York, Sloane, 1958.

The Forgotten Peninsula; a Naturalist in Baja California. New York, Sloane, 1961.

More Lives Than One. New York, Sloane, 1962.

Baja California and the Geography of Hope. San Francisco, Sierra Club, 1967.

A Krutch Omnibus; Forty Years of Social and Literary Criticism. New York, Morrow, 1970.

Photograph of Marcelle and Joseph Wood Krutch by Alfred Eisenstaedt, courtesy of Marcelle L. Krutch.

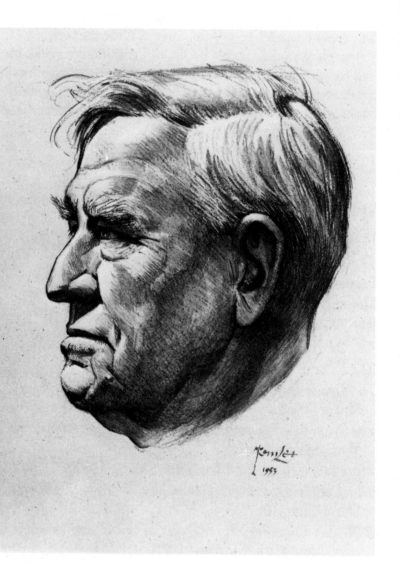

Coronado's Children

J. FRANK DOBIE

If Mary Austin's *The Land of Journeys' Ending* is the book I hold to be the epitome of creative Southwestern literature, then is J. Frank Dobie the laureate of Southwestern writers. In breadth of interests, intellect, sympathy, and perspective, he is the greatest soul the Southwest has sired. His score of books about the region represent the life and literature, the legends, lore, and natural history of the land. They are for me the most nourishing of all works about a land which reaches from the deep heart of Texas and the red earth of Oklahoma to the river and desert of the Colorado and the mountains that isolate Southern California, and which runs from northern Mexico to the Sangre de Cristo.

Although Dobie sprang from Texan earth and remained rooted in it as an earthy man of the soil, he also inherited a birthright mind that he never stopped cultivating. Up to his peaceful death in 1964 at the mellow age of seventy-six, he kept growing in intellect and sympathy. He was no Texan braggart. The affinity he felt for his own land was deeper than slogans. Dobie ended by universalizing the Lone Star state. He surpassed its provincial limitations to become an American writer for all people, places, and times. Earthy in his desires and also intellectual in discernment and scope, he added to those qualities a compassionate understanding of life. He ripened into a man of harmonious body,

343

mind, and spirit. Such men are rare, such writers even more so.

My perspective on Dobie widens as I age and his death recedes in time. I have come to rank him with Yeats, the Irish laureate, in what each did to give his locale wider meaning. They reached heavenly heights paradoxically by looking earthward and listening to the tales of their rural countrymen. The ruined towers of Yeats's Ireland have their Dobiean counterparts in the derelict haciendas of the Texan's borderlands.

I find it hard to write coolly of the writer so dearly did I love the man, so influential was he in providing me with standards by which I came to measure all Southwestern writing. With Jeffers who gave me continent's end, Dobie was the other writer whose realm became mine, first through reading and then by friendship. Not only did they orient me in a literary sense, as men they proffered ideals of character and conduct by which it was possible more fully and usefully to live.

Such a bonus is seldom given by writers. There is often a gulf between what the writer seems and what the man is. A classic instance of this dichotomy is Robert Frost whose poetry personified the homely New England virtues, and yet whose own life was discordant and fraught with jealousy of his peers.

Frank Dobie was no saint. In the biography upon which he is now engaged, Lon Tinkle, a fellow Texan, will for the first time draw the man in the round. Dobie waited too long to write his autobiography. By the time he had the desire to do so, his strength had waned. A miscellany of his essays was collected by his widow as *Something of Myself*.

From it we learn of how he was born of educated parents on a ranch in the Brush Country south of San Antonio and went on to a career as teacher, writer, public spokesman and conscience-voice. The universities of Texas, Columbia, Oklahoma, and Cambridge knew him variously as student and professor. His life and work grew slowly into greatness.

I have chosen *Coronado's Children* as the book to peg this final chapter to not because it is his best book—my favorite is

The Mustangs, his was *Tongues of the Monte*—but rather because it is the one that made him into the legendary figure he became, the one that first brought him national recognition. It is an enthralling book about buried treasure and lost mines of the Southwest. In its subject and form he found what was needed to coalesce his gifts and his purpose. If it were he who made the book, the opposite was also true. By its success he gained authority and confidence in himself and his subject matter.

It was in 1540 that Francisco Vasquez de Coronado rode into the Southwest from Mexico in search of the Golden Cities of Cibola. Rumors of their treasure had lured him and his men. They were disillusioned. The fabled cities proved to be only the mud pueblos of the Zuñis. Nevertheless his *entrada* led to the colonization of Nueva España and the development of its mines. Bullion from them was rumored to have been buried hither and yon. The hunt for such treasure has gone on for centuries. The Children of Coronado, Dobie fancifully termed those who seek and never find those lost riches.

Tales of the treasure seekers were fashioned by Dobie into his book. The result was a new kind of folk history. "I look for two things in folklore," Dobie wrote, "for flavor and for a revelation of the folk who nourished the lore." And in another place, "Folklore, I'd say, is history embellished by the imagination of a thousand minds." Today readers of *Coronado's Children* can use the book as a guide to follow Frank Dobie, not in search of buried treasure and lost mines, but rather to share the storied landscapes that his prose enlivened. It is an ever-renewing, fecundating book, a landmark work in Southwestern literature.

Dobie's collecting was carried out more in the field than in the library. Although a questing mind led him to university training and pursuits, his free spirit was often oppressed by academic specialization. After service in France in World War I as an officer in the field artillery (horse-drawn, to be sure), he quit an appointment in the university at Austin to return to his ranching origins. He took up the management of his uncle Jim Dobie's

345

spread between the Rio Nueces and the Rio Grande, deep in his natal Brush Country.

It was not Frank Dobie's fate to be a rancher, and yet this return to the land, rather than via the academic road, proved to be *the* way to his calling as a creative writer. By a figurative sojourn in the wilderness, he discovered what the Lord intended him to be: a communicator, both a talker and a listener. He recognized that a compulsion to communicate was in his blood. Communicate what? Knowledge and wisdom learned from living close to his native earth and communing with its inhabitants.

To be able to hear, one must listen. Dobie was a great listener. This faculty never left him. Even in the last decade of his life when he was increasingly famous and sought after, he remained a sensitive listener. Not to gossip nor idle talk. Certainly not to the radio. He wanted to hear stories by those who lived close to the land, or to talk about writers' problems of finding form for their material. Or, as he used to say, to the sweet sounds of silence.

He was bluntly honest. He despised cruelty, sham, and pretentiousness. In Southern California, to which he came late in life to lecture and to research in the Huntington Library, he scorned the way of terming anything larger than a town lot a ranch. Paved roads and parking lots displeased him. Always his thoughts went back to his own land. "Human tracks and human blood will not wash out of a soil," he once wrote, "although cement may hide them. The region between the Nueces and the Rio Grande is not cemented over; it will always be a land with a past."

Dobie's ability to listen and to remember what he heard were major factors in making him the writer he became. Chance also played a part, as it always does. During his teaching years in Oklahoma, Dobie owned a copy of Mark Twain's bawdy *1601*, a fanciful sketch which purported to document the earthy way Queen Elizabeth and her courtiers held conversation. When the editor of the *Country Gentleman*, the Curtis Publishing Company's widely read weekly, came to town and heard by chance that Professor Dobie had a copy of the rare Twain item, he sought to borrow it. On meeting Dobie he learned of the Texan's firsthand knowledge of cowboy lore and his desire to write about it. This led to Dobie's becoming a contributor to the Philadelphia weekly. His articles on Southwestern lore brought him a good income. Thus did he achieve independence and a measure of security. He was no longer tied to an academic career.

Coronado's Children came out of such preliminary writing and the year Dobie spent in managing his uncle's ranch. It was not his first book. *Legends of Texas,* a compilation edited for the Texas Folklore Society, and *A Vaquero of the Brush Country,* his reworking of a rancher's life story, preceded it. Neither was wholly his own. They were exercises in finding his true voice and style.

A vaquero storyteller named Santos Cortez opened the door through which Dobie walked into his own. Lon Tinkle explains this as an epiphany or revelatory experience. Let Dobie recall it:

"During the year I spent on Los Olmos ranch, while Santos talked . . . while the coyotes sang their songs, and the sandhill cranes honked their lonely music, I seemed to be seeing a great painting of something I'd known all my life. I seemed to be listening to a great epic of something that had been commonplace in my youth but now took on new meanings."

After that the way was clear and Dobie followed it to the end of his days. When he went on to collect legends of buried treasure and lost mines, he found them on the increase. Added to those of the early Spaniards, Mexicans, and Texans, were later ones created by the California gold and the Nevada silver rushes. The resulting book gained its wide readership because the yarns were permeated with the mesquite flavor of the land Dobie knew and loved. Reading them is both a hungering and a satisfying experience.

Although competent to pursue orthodox library research, Dobie preferred open-air investigations. After thanking librarians and archivists for their aid, he went on with pen in cheek lyrically to declare "Who preside over the genial branches of the Grasshoppers' Library in the sunshine of the Pecos, beside the elms and oaks of Waller Creek, down the mesquite flats of the Nueces River, up the canyons of the Rio Grande, under the blue haze of the Guadalupes, deep in the soft Wichitas, over the hills of the San Saba, and in many another happily remembered place where I have pursued 'scholarly enquiries,' I cannot name. I wish I could, for in the wide-spreading Grasshoppers' Library I have learned the most valuable things I know."

First published at Dallas in 1930, *Coronado's Children* was chosen a year later as a Literary Guild selection. This recognition led to a lifelong publishing affiliation with Little, Brown of Boston, and to a Guggenheim Fellowship. The latter enabled Dobie to take sabbatical leave from the university, with which his relationship had become tenuous. Promotion had been withheld when he scorned taking a Ph.D., which he called transferring the bones of scholarship from one graveyard to another. He also met departmental skepticism of a course he proposed on the Life and Literature of the Southwest. When his colleagues questioned that there was any literature, Dobie countered that there was plenty of life and he'd teach it.

He did both. The course proved legendary. He kept expanding its syllabus until its final publication as *Guide to Life and Literature of Southwest*, then and now the best of all books of its kind.

Generosity was a hallmark of Dobie's character. The final edition of his *Guide* bore these words: "Not copyright in 1942. Again not copyright in 1952. Anybody is welcome to help himself to any of it in any way." Has any other book ever borne such a notice?

Dobie helped any whose talent was promising. Tom Lea, the El Paso painter and novelist, became his most renowned protégé. Vitality was the quality he prized above all. That and perspective. His own perspective came from a solid grounding in Anglo-

American literature. In 1945 he was called to Cambridge University to fill the recently created chair in American History. When he protested his ignorance of such, at least in an academic sense, his sponsor replied that Dobie's assignment would be as elementary as teaching a hound to suck eggs. What Cambridge wanted was an explainer of America who had American mud between his toes and grass burs in his heels.

Thus assured, Dobie proved an enormous success, although the students were prone to steal his Stetsons. At the end of the year the university conferred on him an honorary Master of Arts, the citation for which read *De bobus longicornibus quod ille non cognovit, inutile est aliis cognoscere,* which is to say, What he doesn't know about longhorns isn't worth knowing. *A Texan in England* is Dobie's remembrance of that golden year. It proved a more creative experience than his service in the World War.

I have gotten ahead of myself. Let me return to the earlier period and see what came out of the Guggenheim grant. Again it was the vaquero Santos Cortez who determined the way Dobie went. Many of the Mexican's stories were of things other than buried treasure. They determined Dobie to spend a wander-year in Mexico, loafing, listening, and living close to the earth. By horseback and muleback, with pack outfit and *mozo* (combination guide and servant) he travelled through the mountainous Mexican states beyond the Rio Grande, lingering at ranches and mining camps, enjoying, he said, the freest times of his life.

The work that came out of this experience, called *Tongues of the Monte,* is correspondingly the freest, most creative of his books, a work that other great wanderer Robert Louis Stevenson would have loved. "Anybody who reads the present book," Dobie wrote in the preface, "will make a mistake if he takes everything literally. The characters are inventions, patched up from realities. The main one, Inocencio, my old *mozo* and friend, had a prototype, but he combines several *mozos* in himself and arrogates to himself a great deal of wisdom common to the Mexican *gente.* I invented a slight string of experiences on which to thread tales and people. I tried to weave the life of the Mexican earth into a pattern. It is truer, I think, than a literal chronicle of what I saw, whom I heard, and where I rode or slept would have been.''

Dobie was a creative and recreative writer, certainly an exotic bird among the sober academicians. Incidentally, the paisano (roadrunner) was his totem bird. It was not that he was untruthful. His credo was rather that of the immemorial fabulist, the teller of tales by firelight. "A lie," he once declared, "for the purpose of entertaining was as righteous as a lie for deceiving, cheating, covering up meanness was vile."

Rare is the storyteller who writes with equal effectiveness, the writer who can enthrall listeners with the spoken word. "Pancho" Dobie was such a man and writer. His face was an encyclopedia of human emotions, his grin capable of emitting heat. I once suggested to the White House, where Dobie was *persona grata*, that his visage be placed on a piece of our national coinage, thus causing people with money to feel doubly good.

Tongues of the Monte is a deeply moving book, deriving power from understatement. The chapter called "Tiger Claws" offers a glimpse into the writer's depths, yielding more than a hint of the richness that marked Dobie's emotional relationships. Or does it? I like to think that it is one of the rare instances in his writing when he drew the veil, although if he had been questioned, I believe he would have declared that chapter to be one of sheer invention. No matter. Its effect does not depend upon whether or not it is autobiographical.

Do we regret that Dobie did not create more such romantic stories, or transmute more of his experience into novels? It is true that he once thought of himself as a playwright, a novelist. Whatever form it took, that which he wrote was creative writing. It is power governed by form that raises writing to the creative level. Dobie was a powerful man and writer and in a literary sense he was a formal man. He had no patience with slovenly, formless writing.

350

After the Mexican book came a sequel to *Coronado's Children*. He called it *Apache Gold and Yaqui Silver*. Whereas the earlier book focused on Texas, its successor ranged over New Mexico, Arizona, and Sonora. Tom Lea's illustrations catch the eerie quality of treasure hunting under the threat of scalping knives. In search of Yaqui legends, Dobie found the Mexicans of Sonora to be among the greatest of tale-tellers. "In the summertime they shift their positions with the crawling shade and talk. In the wintertime they squat in the sunshine and talk. The nights were made for talking, they say. Their women do all the work."

This was followed by books of nearly equal excellence on *The Longhorns*, *The Voice of the Coyote*, *Rattlesnakes*, *The Mustangs*, *Cow People*, and finally the posthumous *Something of Myself*. Time and again in his books Dobie paid tribute to his wife Bertha, who had been a fellow student at Southwestern University in Georgetown, Texas, back in the early 1900's. A copy of his book, *Cow People*, reached him on the morning of his death, on September 18, 1964, a week before his 76th birthday. In the preface to it are these words: "The person to whom I owe the most is a critic of style and a thinker named Bertha McKee Dobie. She has overlooked every line and influenced me to exercise the never sufficiently accomplished art of omission."

She was the perfect mate—charming hostess and gardener in their home on Austin's Waller Creek, literary critic, a woman of strong character, taste and judgment. Hers was a loose rein that held him. Goethe said that in order to fulfill himself a man of genius should marry a woman of character. Such was the union of the Dobies.

On a return to Texas I came at a time when the oaks and elms opposite the Dobie home were being bulldozed to make room for an expanding campus. "I am glad he didn't live to see it," Bertha Dobie grieved, then flared, "If he were alive, he wouldn't have let it happen." No one has replaced him as a warrior spokesman for all that is decent and good.

351

We dined in a club high above Austin. It was just past Mrs. Dobie's 80th birthday. She was easily the most beautiful woman in the room, her unadorned grace infinitely more attractive than the slick chic of the younger matrons.

We recalled that time of drought and dying trees in the 1950's when Dobie begged me to make rain medicine. I did so. What I could never do for droughty Southern California worked for Texas. Soon after my incantations I received a telegram from Dobie, addressed to Elijah the Rainmaker, imploring me to cease and desist. Three and a half inches had fallen in twenty-four hours and was still coming down.

On campus the next morning I visited the Dobie Memorial Room, lovingly cared for by Willie Belle Coker, the writer's longtime secretary. It houses his peerless collection of range and ranching books of all times and places, as well as his own works in many editions and translations. Remingtons and Boreins and Tom Lea's rugged portrait of Dobie hang on the walls. From the house of his birth in Live Oak County came the fireplace mantel on which is carved, "Thou shalt be in league with the stones of the field and the beasts of the field shalt be at peace with you"— words which epitomize Dobie's life and work.

I pored through his sources for *Coronado's Children*—notes, outlines, and manuscript drafts. They revealed the background of his apparently free and easy results. He was a meticulous craftsman. I read a few of the thousands of letters that came to him after the book was published, many asking for a grubstake in return for which they would go halves. No letter went unanswered. Time and again Dobie replied that he cared naught for buried treasure and lost mines, only for tales about them.

His cherished library friend was Maud Durlin Sullivan, librarian of the El Paso Public Library, whose Southwestern collections served him well. On December 30, 1931 she wrote to Dobie, "*Coronado's Children* still has a long waiting list in this library. There is no end to the steady interest in such a book, and

352

it will always have the enduring quality of the real literature of the world."

I also liked the letter from Stanley Stubbs, curator of the Laboratory of Anthropology Museum in Santa Fe, who wrote, "One day a Mexican man and his wife came to the desk for information. They wanted to borrow our maps that showed the locations of buried treasure. The man was quite indignant when I told him we had none. He said public museums should have them for poor people to borrow so they could find the money and not be poor anymore."

When my eyes tired I went outdoors and wandered about the campus, filled with memories of the man. I recalled that he once wrote, "When I like a man my nature goes out to him and warms him." The warmth of him has never left me.

Dobie was not always an honored prophet on that campus, although they came eventually to hail him as the noblest Texan since the Alamo. His was a Jeffersonian, Lincolnesque Americanism. It and his salty candor made him unacceptable to the politicians who sought to dominate the university. Yet his loyalty to Texas and its university endured.

Today, in addition to the Dobie Room, a priceless resource for research in Southwestern culture, Dobie's beloved ranch called Paisano, a hideaway in the hill country west of Austin, is a retreat for writers and artists, administered by the university and the Texas Institute of Letters.

As I walked about the campus, observing the students, I thought that the Dobie Room could also serve as a retreat for disaffected young people. There they would find that everything they seek, in a mistaken belief that it can be attained without reference to the past, was dealt with by Dobie in his time and manner. He was never more relevant than he is now, a determined foe of the despoilers of natural resources and a scorner of demagoguery and cheapness. By his courage and genius he raised the level of culture and made it easier for those who follow.

After reading Dobie—better yet, while reading him—one travels in the Southwest with new awareness of the land, its history and peoples, its configurations and biology. This seems to me the supreme gift a Southwestern writer can make to a reader. Moving is the tribute paid by a young Texan, Warren Roberts, director of the Humanities Research Center which houses the Dobie Memorial Room. Born and raised in the Dobie country at Menard, between the Llano and San Saba rivers, he wrote,

"No child should grow up in Texas without a sense of the reach of history, the kind of history Frank Dobie wrote; and to-day as I open the pages of *Coronado's Children* to the story of the lost San Saba mine I can still recall the excitement and wonder which I felt that day long ago when the book first came into my hands. The hills ever after were peopled with bearded conquistadores, priest and Indian, and every track through the persimmon flats was a Spanish road marked by the wheels of wagons loaded with bullion for Mexico."

To hear the voice of J. Frank Dobie in this strident time one must stop talking and demanding and listen to this great Texan, this eloquent Southwestern spokesman, one must be willing quietly to read him. Then will he find his books as I have found them, a radiant nourishing source of light and of life.

READING LIST

J. FRANK DOBIE (1888-1964).

A Vaquero of the Brush Country; Partly from the Reminiscences of John Young. Dallas, Southwest Press, 1929; Boston, Little, Brown, 1959. Preface by Lawrence Clark Powell.

Coronado's Children; Tales of Lost Mines and Buried Treasures of the Southwest. Dallas, Southwest Press, 1930; New York, Literary Guild, 1930.

Tongues of the Monte. Garden City, Doubleday, 1935. Also as *The Mexico I Like.* Dallas, Southern Methodist University Press, 1942.

Apache Gold and Yaqui Silver. Ill. by Tom Lea. Boston, Little, Brown, 1939.

The Longhorns. Ill. by Tom Lea. Boston, Little, Brown, 1941.

A Texan in England. Boston, Little, Brown, 1945.

The Voice of the Coyote. Boston, Little, Brown, 1949.

The Mustangs. Boston, Little, Brown, 1952.

Guide to Life and Literature of the Southwest. Dallas, Southern Methodist University Press, 1952.

Some Part of Myself. Boston, Little, Brown, 1967.

FRANCIS E. ABERNETHY
J. Frank Dobie. Austin, Steck-Vaughn, 1967.

RONNIE DUGGER
Three Men in Texas: Bedichek, Webb, and Dobie. Austin, University of Texas Press, 1967.

LON TINKLE
J. Frank Dobie; the Makings of an Ample Mind. Austin, Encino Press, 1968.

MARY LOUISE MC VICKER
The Writings of J. Frank Dobie; a Bibliography. Lawton, Oklahoma, Museum of the Great Plains, 1968.

Photograph of J. Frank Dobie drawn by Tom Lea, courtesy of the artist and Humanities Research Center, University of Texas.

AFTERWORD

Word after what? What comes after man, in the name of progress, has mastered his environment? In the years since Van Dyke made his way across the Mojave, Colorado, and Sonora deserts, dependent only upon himself for survival, and wrote his prose-poem to a wilderness that could have destroyed him, the desert no longer threatens man. His cleverness has conquered it.

Has it really? And for how long? *Le monde passe, la figure de ce monde passe.* No part of the world that does not change and pass away. Even the mountain, the granite mountain, falls at last to the wind and the rain. Have the sophisticates of Phoenix and Tucson, of Albuquerque and El Paso discovered a secret unknown to the primitives of Mesa Verde and the Salt River Valley, those simple ones who went away?

If comforting is not our need, we can go to the poet for an answer. Robinson Jeffers foretold what follows after man has gathered the world into a few megalopoli: splinters of glass in the rubbish dumps, a concrete dam far off in the mountain, a colony on the morning star. A bleak prospect.

What of these writers brought together in this book, can they reconcile us to fate and make our life more bearable, we who live in an age of violence and imminent holocaust? By reading them can we escape to their world of color and configuration? Yes, I say, all twenty-seven chapters yes! We are indeed transported

356

by Lawrence and La Farge, by Cather and Comfort and their fellow romantics into their Southwest where life and landscape are wedded in literature. If this be escapism then let it be.

If their vision of life seems unreal, there is realer (though still magical) stuff in Doctor Gregg and Father Garcés, in Father Kino and Major Powell. And if our final need is moral, then are there moralists among them, writers who in celebrating life also predict disaster if man persists in regarding the earth as his alone.

This is why the book ends as it does with a progression of moralists, with Roosevelt and Van Dyke, Krutch and Dobie. Answers are in them, both in who they were and what they wrote. Each in his way insists that we acknowledge the interdependence of nature and safeguard the sacred chain of life; and further, that we cherish our life-giving environment lest its destruction destroy us, its destroyers. They warn us that by uncontrolled urbanization, mineralization and lust for power and energy, by wastage of water and squandering of resources do we slide toward disaster.

We need not wonder at what Theodore Roosevelt would say in our time when he saw the Grand Canyon menaced by dams above and below. "Leave it as it is," were his words, "it cannot be improved upon." Long ago Van Dyke foresaw the automobile as destructive to the desert fabric. *Respect all life* was the credo by which Krutch lived and wrote. *Tolerance* and *perspective* were the watchwords of Dobie.

From reading these writers on the Southwest our own perception and enjoyment of life is widened and deepened. They lead us to love and to cherish life more.

Bajada of the
Santa Catalinas
At the flowering
of the palo verde

ACKNOWLEDGEMENTS

Much of this book was written, I say again, under the sheltering roof of the University of Arizona to which I came first in 1971 as professor in residence. This change of life is owed to the urging of President Richard A. Harvill, now Emeritus, and to the continuing support of his successor, John P. Schaefer, as well as to the University of Arizona Foundation and its president, Leicester H. Sherrill, and its executive director, Samuel C. McMillan. My colleagues, F. Robert Paulsen, dean of the College of Education, and Donald C. Dickinson, director of the Graduate Library School, have been good and easy to work with. In a seminar in the School I have shared my work each year with vital students to our mutual benefit. Inspiration has come from friendship with Laurence M. Gould and Emil Haury, equally distinguished as professors respectively of geology and anthropology.

Help has been cordially given by many members of the University Library staff, particularly W. David Laird, University Librarian, Donald M. Powell, Arizona authority, Phyllis Ball, archivist, Mary Blakeley, map room, Robert Poland, acquisitions, Cecil Wellborn, circulation, John McKay, inter-library borrowing, Judith Graham, library science, the late John Thayer, bookman, and the entire Reference and Special Collections staffs formerly under Lutie Higley.

Also at the University, William G. McGinnies, director emer-

ACKNOWLEDGEMENTS

itus of the Office of Arid Lands Studies in the College of Earth Sciences, and Bernard L. Fontana, ethnologist of the Arizona State Museum, aided me. Vice-President Marvin "Swede" Johnson guided me to the J. H. Ranch in his natal Cochise County.

Dorothy McNamee of Tucson's Overland Bookshop stayed me with volumes and comforted me with pamphlets, while at the Arizona Historical Society, Librarian Margaret J. Sparks and Editor C. L. Sonnichsen were ever helpful. The staff of the Tucson Public Library never failed to aid me.

In Gila County during a meeting at the Miami Memorial Library with Librarian Emily Cheves and the library's commissioners, I gained a deeper appreciation of Ross Santee and his work.

At the University of New Mexico in Albuquerque, University Librarian David Otis Kelley and Librarian Martin Ruoss of the Coronado Room facilitated my work with the papers of Erna Fergusson and Ross Calvin, as did Professor Emeritus T. M. Pearce my research on Oliver La Farge and Mary Austin. Claire Morrill of the Taos Book Shop provided details of Mabel Dodge Luhan's life there. Peggy Pond Church of Santa Fe saved me from error about Mary Austin's New Mexico years. In Las Vegas Diana and Joe Stein of La Galeria de los Artesanos were gracious hosts as I came their way, and with William S. Wallace, former librarian of New Mexico Highlands University, I have been having good talk about Southwest literature since the day we met back in the 1950's. June Harwell of the Alamogordo Public Library provided me with Rhodes material and the warmth of a juniper fire.

At the University of Texas help came from Chancellor Harry H. Ransom, F. Warren Roberts, director of the Humanities Research Center and Mary Hirth, the Center's librarian, while Willie Belle Coker, curator of the Dobie Room, helped me survey its riches.

I am also indebted for essential assistance to John C. Finzi, Library of Congress, William S. Dix, Princeton University Li-

359

brary, D. L. Engelhardt, New Brunswick Theological Seminary Library, Donald Gallup and Archibald Hanna, Beinecke Library, Yale University, and Frederick H. Wagman, University of Michigan Library.

In California many persons answered my calls for aid. At UCLA's Department of Special Collections Wilbur J. Smith, James V. Mink, F. Brooke Whiting III, Saundra Taylor and their colleagues, made my work fruitful and joyful. At the Southwest Museum help came from Director Carl S. Dentzel and Librarian Ruth M. Christensen, while at the Henry E. Huntington Library nourishment was received in reading room and cafeteria, my genial hosts being James Thorpe, Ray Allen Billington, Carey S. Bliss, and Edwin H. Carpenter, Jr.

Librarian Tyrus G. Harmsen of Occidental College and his staff gave this alumnus unlimited support. Roy Kidman and Helen Azdherian of the University of Southern California Library opened its resources to me, as did Robert Hart of the Santa Barbara Public Library, Catherine S. Chadwick of the Ventura County Library, and Edwin J. Hughes of the Oxnard Public Library. The Bancroft Library drew me by its rich source material on the West, and there James D. Hart, director, John Barr Tompkins, head of public services, and James Kantor, university archivist, welcomed me as a shareholder in that great enterprise. Booksellers Jake Zeitlin, Rosalie and Jack Reynolds, and Dawson frères did more than sell me books.

Many persons not connected with libraries helped my work. These include Lina Fergusson Browne and Francis Fergusson who allowed me access to the papers of their sister Erna and brother Harvey, as did Mrs. Browne to the papers of her grandfather-in-law, J. Ross Browne. From Bertha McKee Dobie came deeper insight into her husband's genius. Jane Levington Comfort Annixter and her husband Paul illuminated her father's nature, while Marcelle Leguia Krutch, the prime agent in her husband's move to the Southwest, gave me of her time and memories of Joseph Wood Krutch. Anton V. Long, devoted son of Alice

ACKNOWLEDGEMENTS

and Haniel Long, allowed full access to his father's papers preserved at UCLA. Quail Hawkins recalled her long friendship
with Harvey Fergusson. My work on Stewart Edward White
was aided by his sister-in-law, Mrs. Harwood White, and her
son Richard, and by Mr. & Mrs. Harry Parks and Mrs. Hazel
Johnson of Willcox, Cochise County. W. H. Hutchinson guided
me along the trail of Eugene Manlove Rhodes, and Dudley C.
Gordon gave without stint of his unrivalled knowledge of Charles
F. Lummis. From Joseph Stacey, editor of *Arizona Highways*,
and executor of Ross Santee, I learned more about the laureate
of Gila County. E. I. Edwards of Yucca Valley was my informant
on all matters relating to the California deserts. Harry C. James
of Lolomi Lodge in the San Jacintos shared his knowledge of the
Hopis. During stays in Tucson Alfred A. Knopf talked with me
about his publishing of many Southwest writers. Long friendship with Paul Horgan has enriched my life and work.

There are those no longer living who helped in the beginning.
Lastingly grateful is my memory of Henry R. Wagner, Freder-
ick Webb Hodge, Robert Ernest Cowan, J. Gregg Layne, Phil
Townsend Hanna, J. Frank Dobie, Haniel Long, Erna Fergus-
son, Harvey Fergusson, Frieda Lawrence, Consuelo La Farge,
Frank McNitt, Dwight L. Clarke, and W. W. Robinson.

The selective reading lists indicate my debt to other writers
on the Southwest. I have drawn on the bibliographies and anthologies of J. Frank Dobie, C. L. Sonnichsen, Mary Tucker, Lyle
Saunders, Jack D. Rittenhouse, Donald M. Powell, Mabel Major and T. M. Pearce, as well as on my own earlier works, notably
Heart of the Southwest, *A Southwestern Century*, *Books West
Southwest*, *The Southwest of the Bookman*, and *Southwestern
Book Trails*. I have always sought to locate and use primary material—manuscripts, journals, letters—which would illuminate
the authors' intentions and methods.

Great is my debt to *Westways*, the magazine of the Automobile Club of Southern California for which I have been writing
since 1934 and in whose pages these chapters first appeared and

with whose permission they are reprinted here in rearranged sequence and revised form. Its former editors, Larry L. Meyer and Davis Dutton, and its present associate editor, Frances Ring and her staff, are this book's godparents. *Westways'* vigilant readers have cheered and chastised me in about equal proportions.

Stenographic help was freely given by Ellen Cole and her staff of UCLA's Central Stenographic Bureau, and by Margaret McGillivray, Helen Sigmund and their colleagues in the President's office at the University of Arizona, while in the Graduate Library School on that campus Marcia Forsberg and Jennifer Gelder kept me on schedule and in coffee.

My friend and colleague, Patricia Paylore, assistant director and bibliographer of the Office of Arid Lands Studies, brought to a critical reading of the manuscript a long familiarity with the landscape and literature of her native Southwest.

The presence of Fay, companion this nearly half-century, enriches all that I do. I hope that something of her is apparent throughout this and all my books, gracing their prose as she does my life.

L.C.P.

INDEX

PREPARED BY ANNA MARIE AND EVERETT GORDON HAGER

Huml
PS
277
P63

WYO

Salt Lake City

COLORAD

UTAH

RIZONA

Canyon de C

Painted
Desert

NEVADA

Death Valley

GR

OF THE COLOR

Coconino
Plateau

Mojave
Desert

SALT RIVER

Phoenix ✳

CALIFORNIA

Salton Sea

RIVER

GILA

Yuma

San Xavier del Bac

Tucson

Baboquivari

Cochise
Strongh

Nogales

S O N O R A

*Heart of
the Southwest*